From Dunkirk to D-Day

From Dunkirk to D-Day

Jeff Steel and Linda Adlam Nash

Pen & Sword
MILITARY

First published in Australia by Big Sky Publishing Pty Ltd in 2022
www.bigskypublishing.com.au

First published in Great Britain in 2024 by
Pen & Sword Military
An imprint of Pen & Sword Books Limited
Yorkshire – Philadelphia

Copyright © Jeff Steel and Linda Adlam Nash 2024

ISBN 978 1 39903 566 8

The right of Jeff Steel and Linda Adlam Nash to be identified as Authors of this Work has been asserted by them in accordance with the Copyright, Designs and Patents Act 1988.

A CIP catalogue record for this book is available from the British Library

All rights reserved. No part of this book may be reproduced or transmitted in any form or by any means, electronic or mechanical including photocopying, recording or by any information storage and retrieval system, without permission from the Publisher in writing.

Typeset by Mac Style
Printed in the UK by CPI Group (UK) Ltd, Croydon, CR0 4YY.

Pen & Sword Books Limited incorporates the imprints of After the Battle, Atlas, Archaeology, Aviation, Discovery, Family History, Fiction, History, Maritime, Military, Military Classics, Politics, Select, Transport, True Crime, Air World, Frontline Publishing, Leo Cooper, Remember When, Seaforth Publishing, The Praetorian Press, Wharncliffe Local History, Wharncliffe Transport, Wharncliffe True Crime and White Owl.

For a complete list of Pen & Sword titles please contact

PEN & SWORD BOOKS LIMITED
47 Church Street, Barnsley, South Yorkshire, S70 2AS, England
E-mail: enquiries@pen-and-sword.co.uk
Website: www.pen-and-sword.co.uk
or
PEN AND SWORD BOOKS
1950 Lawrence Rd, Havertown, PA 19083, USA
E-mail: uspen-and-sword@casematepublishers.com
Website: www.penandswordbooks.com

Contents

Preface vii

Chapter 1   Bill Goes to the Flicks   1

Chapter 2   'This Country is at War with Germany'   4

Chapter 3   Bill Wins his Military Medal   9

Chapter 4   The Road to Ledringhem   18

Chapter 5   The Road to Dunkirk   29

Chapter 6   The Road to Buckingham Palace   45

Chapter 7   With the Commandos at Weymouth   53

Chapter 8   Of Cromwell and Cavalry   60

Chapter 9   The Road to the Isles   67

Chapter 10   Lofoten, Here We Come! Operation Claymore   75

Chapter 11   Bill Sets Foot on Enemy Territory   82

Chapter 12   Bill's Raid is Reported to the Führer   93

Chapter 13   What Adolf Hitler and Bill Adlam Did Not Know   95

Chapter 14   Operation Pilgrim – Bill Goes to Africa   99

Chapter 15   Under Starters Orders   106

Chapter 16   Dieppe – Operation Cauldron   113

Chapter 17   Adolf Hitler's View of the Dieppe Raid   128

Chapter 18   Apotheosis and Beyond!   130

Chapter 19	The Road to Achnacarry	136
Chapter 20	The Dark Mile, the Death Slide and the Opposed Landing	145
Chapter 21	The Achnacarry High Period	160
Chapter 22	The Road to D-Day	171
Chapter 23	Embarkation for D-Day	185
Chapter 24	A Trip across the Channel – Operation Neptune	192
Chapter 25	Adolf Hitler Responds to the Normandy Invasion	197
Chapter 26	D Day: Bill Adlam Wades Ashore	198
Chapter 27	The Road to Bayeux	205
Chapter 28	Bayeux	215
Chapter 29	The Road to Tilly – Operation Perch	221
Chapter 30	The Road to Caen – Operations Bluecoat and Charnwood	229
Chapter 31	The Road to La Mailleraye and Endgame	238

Epilogue   250
Acknowledgements   251
Select Bibliography   253
About the Authors   255

Preface

My family knew there was a story. It was just that my father Bill never spoke about it. He had mentioned that he enjoyed training with Lord Lovat. He had mentioned seasickness. He had mentioned that he always had his toothbrush with him even on the frontline when bullets flew around him. This was to encourage me to brush my teeth. He was proud of the award of a Military Medal. The story of its award and Bill's other experiences remained cloaked in silence.

A sudden illumination of a light bulb would lead him to dive into a corner, head in hands. Whatever the story was, it remained out of sight to us, unexpressed and (as far as we knew) largely unvisited.

At least, it did until some 30 years after Bill's death in 1980. I had begun to wonder what dramatic events; battlefield trauma and impossible acts of bravery lay behind that opaque curtain. Bill clearly did not want to tell the story about his wartime experiences to me, my half-sister Poppy or my mother, Moreen.

During the 1950s, Bill fell on hard financial times and had sold the Military Medal to a collector. My mother said that he immediately regretted it and never stopped regretting it. Once gone, the medal disappeared out of sight until much later.

From the droplets of evidence that seeped out, a story clearly existed but what was it?

'Do you think you could find out what my dad did in the war?' I asked Jeff Steel.

'Yes, I could give it a go.'

My orders were, 'Bring him back to life for me.' The result of that chance conversation is this history: the dramatic story of Bill Adlam in World War II.

Linda Adlam Nash

Linda had given me the brief, 'Bring him back to life'. But where to start? Linda obtained Bill's service record from the United Kingdom Ministry of Defence. That told us what units he had been in. We had started the journey. But what then?

Then we started having some luck. Bill's military postings, the Gloucestershire Regiment, No 4 Commando and the Commando Training School, were all well documented. From newspaper cuttings from before World War II, I could track Bill as a keen, indeed, vocational soldier. From books on the regiment, I could track him across northern France before Dunkirk. I even discovered that Bill's adventures had been celebrated in two boys' comics in the 1970s, when he was still alive. *He never knew!* From newsreels and other film material I could even view events at which he had been present.

From two books by a former commando, Jimmy Dunning, I could track Bill in the commandos. I contacted Jimmy Dunning just before he died. He remembered Bill and gave me valuable information.

We were on a roll! And I as I looked for more information on Bill's units the roll kept going until I had tracked him for almost every day of World War II!

At the end of two years, I was able to say to Linda, 'I found the facts, all of them; I have added dialogue to bring him back to life for you.'

This is that dramatic story. The story did not end with the writing of this book. There was the matter of the missing Military Medal. That worried Linda. Was it humanly possible that after seven decades we would find it?

Jeff Steel

We Didn't Know the Story

We didn't know the story,
Or what was locked inside:
The heartbreak, toil and glory,
The friends that he'd watched die.

We didn't know the terror,
The daily dance with death,
With every moment likely
To bring his final breath.

He'd only mentioned fragments,
Like shards of broken glass,
From a shattered stained-glass window,
From an unforgotten past.

His Military Medal sold to put,
Food on the family's plate.
But Dunkirk, Dieppe and D-Day's beach
He never would relate.

What was it that was locked inside?
However harsh or sad,
Daughters need to know these things,
They need to know their dad.

Linda Adlam Nash

Chapter 1

Bill Goes to the Flicks

Thursday, 23 March 1939, Gloucester, England

He looked at the cinema screen, and his flesh crawled. In his stomach. he felt fear, loathing and revulsion.

The newsreel that night at the Picturedrome Cinema in Gloucester showed what people in Britain had been dreading for a week. Adolf Hitler's Germany had occupied Czechoslovakia, dissolved it and incorporated it into its own territory. As was normal in those days, people read the news in newspapers and then saw it on the cinema newsreels a week later. There was television, but it was only in London and Bill had certainly never seen it.

The newsreel showed Hradcany Castle above the River Vltava in Prague. He saw the German soldiers speeding on motorcycles through the snowy roads of rural Czechoslovakia. More German soldiers were filmed on bicycles, carrying rifles, smiling and laughing for the cameras. The effect was almost comic, except that this was not a joke. Then the German soldiers arrived with field artillery followed by transport after transport, carrying what Winston Churchill would call 'the hideous apparatus of aggression'. High on the hill in the background, the silhouette of St Vitus' Cathedral was visible, a huge black shape through the snowstorm. Prague Streets were already festooned with large Nazi flags, and they were being blown by the freezing, pitiless wind.

The newsreel showed Hitler arrive in his huge custom-built six-wheel Mercedes Benz car. Hitler looked out of a high window, Lord of all he surveyed. That raised a question for people in the United Kingdom. Does Hitler fancy his chances of peering down on St James' Park in London from a top window in Buckingham Palace with The Mall festooned with Swastika flags? Most people in Britain thought that that was exactly what Hitler had in mind. They were frightened to the soles of their boots.

We do not know what film Bill Adlam saw that night, but we can be certain of his thoughts on the short walk back to his typically English small terrace house at 18 Carmarthen Street.

Bill – and the rest of the world – had seen Hitler's forces occupy the Rheinland in contravention of various treaties. He had seen Adolf Hitler merge Germany and Austria, also in contravention of international treaties. He had seen the newsreel footage of Hitler's sinister Olympic Games in 1936. These were perverted into a propaganda show for the rising might of Hitler's Third Reich. The newspapers now carried reports of new laws in Germany, which took all the money and property off the Jews and then threw them out of the country. There were reports of some kind of camps where opponents of the regime were sent. Some came out battered, some did not come out.

Three inevitable questions arose. Where would it end? What could Britain do about it? Would there be another war with Germany?

Bill was frightened of Hitler and Nazi Germany. Everyone in Gloucester was frightened of Hitler. Everyone in England was frightened of Hitler as was everyone across Europe, including some of his own master race. Everyone in the world was frightened of Hitler and if people in China, New Zealand or Brazil thought that they were immune to his malign influence then the full weight of subsequent history was going to demonstrate that they were quite deluded.

In answer to the question 'what could Britain do about it?' the answer was 'little if anything'. It was true that the British Empire was powerful militarily, but the majority of its power was on the sea. Bill would have been aware of a sharp increase in the number of Gloster Gladiator fighter planes parading through the streets on the massive Queen Mary transporters. These were biplanes, if put up against the new German Messerschmitt 109s, they would only last for a minute or two. After some months, the Gladiator biplanes were to give way to Hawker Hurricanes, lots of them.

The British Army was a fraction of the size of the vast and brilliantly led German Army. In recent meetings with Hitler, the British Prime Minister, Neville Chamberlain had been outmanoeuvred, out negotiated and outplayed by the brilliant but evil dictator of Germany.

'Would there be another war with Germany?' The question nagged like toothache. Most people thought, 'Yes, it is now inevitable.' The world teetered nervously on the precipice.

Bill had joined the Territorial Army in 1935. This was a reserve army made up primarily of civilians. He was a lad of a robust disposition and had achievements as a cross-country runner. At age 17, already a part-time soldier, Bill was to take part in a cup-winning team for rifle shooting. This was later to serve him well. Bill was a machinist by trade but a soldier by inclination, indeed by vocation. In the territorials, he was attached to the 5th Battalion of the Gloucestershire Regiment. He discovered that he had what it took to be a soldier and approximately once each year, he was given a promotion. That was no mean token of his talents and character.

On 23 March 1939, Bill had had the good news from his commanding officer that he had been promoted from corporal to sergeant. Bill would certainly have heard about Gloucestrians, who would have been role models in his military vocation. Daniel Burges of the Gloucestershire Regiment had a Victoria Cross from World War I. Harry Hook of the South Wales Borderers had come from Gloucester and had fought at Rorke's Drift in South Africa in 1879. Bill's rapid promotion in the Territorial Army marked him as a man with great military potential. His role models were displayed before him, those medals in a glass case. He knew of the heroes. He wanted the same.

Either Hitler's Germany was going to be blasted into dust, ruined cities, and smouldering ruins or that same sorry fate awaited the civilised world. No other outcome was available. There would be no quarter asked or given. This was going to be a Darwinian struggle in which the fittest would survive and the less fit would perish. This was going to be a fight without rules to the death. Could the civilised world meet the challenge? Could Bill meet the challenge himself? He could only hope that he would not let the country, his mates and his family down.

Chapter 2

'This Country is at War with Germany'

Friday, 25 August 1939, Gloucester, England

From around the corner in Westgate Street, they could hear the soldiers already. They could hear the thumping of the huge, regimental bass drum. They heard the clatter of 800 pairs of hobnailed boots. They heard the band playing the regimental song 'Where be that blackbird be?'.

The regimental flag was on its way from the barracks. It was to be placed into Gloucester Cathedral, for the duration of hostilities. In the procession, there were several hundred soldiers led by a colonel on horseback. It was now understood, with crystal transparency from the inner sanctums of Downing Street to the most rural pub in nethermost Gloucestershire, that hostilities against Germany were not to be avoided. The thought processes of those in the crowd were clear. 'What sort of world will we have when all of this is over?' 'Which of these soldiers will not come back?' 'Who do I know that will die?'

Something else was placed at Gloucester Cathedral for the duration of hostilities, the Coronation Throne from Westminster Abbey. It was all so relentless. Everywhere you looked, every small fact that you learned, behind every corner of existence, there was something, which said 'war is just around the corner'.

The huge primrose-coloured regimental flag, fluttered and flapped along the street, borne by a colour guard of six.

A junior officer carried the flag with a magnificent sense of military occasion, gravitas, and ceremony. Behind him marched the colour sergeant, with no less authority, certainty, and magnificent military self-confidence. Behind the colour sergeant marched the colour guard, with their red sashes, rifles and fixed bayonets and great pomp and ceremony. Bill had been selected for this party, which was a substantial accolade for a man who had been a sergeant for less than six months. Bill Adlam was developing already as a soldier's soldier.

On that sunny day, as he escorted the yellow flag with pride and panache into the Gothic mysteries of Gloucester Cathedral, he would have been amazed, even shocked, had he known what lay in store for him. He would receive the Military Medal. He would meet King George VI in Buckingham Palace. He would be within a hand's shake of Winston Churchill. He would fight alongside some of the best soldiers that Britain ever produced. He would fight against the 12th Waffen SS and Panzer Lehr, two of the most effective and formidable units in military history. On two occasions, he would be a hedgerow or two away from one of the third Reich's most infamous war criminals and on each occasion, narrowly avoid being massacred. He would take part in a raid of extraordinary significance in Norway whose importance he would never know. He would take part in another raid which became the template on which later special forces operations were based.

After the war, he would never talk about those years of the roaring furnace when killing Germans was not only good, it was a sacrament. After the hostilities, the crimson sash was still in his possession. He had a commando's green beret. He had the swagger stick of a British officer. Otherwise, the only tangible souvenirs of his time in the Army were to be shards of shrapnel in his legs and a hole on the left side of his chest where a major muscle had been surgically removed. There was also the intangible souvenir which would have him diving for cover if someone turned a light on unexpectedly.

Bill's heart would have burst with pride representing the 5th Battalion in this breathtaking high Gothic setting. His spirit could not but have been overawed at the sense of history which weighed upon him and on all those who carried a rifle as he did now.

Friday, 1 September 1939, Gloucester, England

A foreman came onto the shop floor.

'Listen, everyone!'

He stopped. He looked worried.

'Have I got everyone's attention? It's just come over on the radio that Germany has invaded Poland this morning. That bastard Hitler is not going to stop until he's taken over the whole bloody world.'

'Christ!'

'Oh, bugger!'

'Are we at war?'

'It doesn't sound like we're at war yet, but the radio report said that the Foreign Office would be summoning the German ambassador later today and giving him a letter.'

'That'll terrify old Hitler, that will!'

It became clear why children were now being evacuated by the hundred thousand out of main stations in large cities. Another radio report announced that the stock exchange was closed, and that civil aircraft were prohibited from flying over Britain on pain of being shot down. A general mobilisation was announced. All army, air force and naval reservists were to be called to the colours. That included Bill Adlam.

It transpired that a new War Agriculture Executive Committee had been formed for Gloucestershire, as for all other English counties. The executive committee may have been brand new, but its powers were unmistakable. There were shocked voices in the streets. The Bishop of Gloucester had simply been booted out onto the street, albeit in a civilised, apologetic British way. His mansion was commandeered with immediate effect to be used as administrative offices to organise and co-ordinate local agriculture. From 1943, the 16-year-old Moreen, who was to become Bill's second wife, was to work in this building.

Bill would have been in a sombre mood as he returned home on the bus. As expected, a letter awaited him on the mantlepiece. It was buff-coloured and bore the words 'On His Majesty's Service'. He was to present himself without delay to the local barracks on Monday morning. He was now a full-time soldier. He would have to walk around to the foreman's house to let him know what happened. He wondered if he would be able to resume his job after hostilities had finished. Well, if he was still alive.

This was the point at which the world seemed to accelerate until it was speeding along like an express train.

Sunday, 3 September 1939, Gloucester, England

People who heard it would never forget it.

> I am speaking to you from the Cabinet Room at 10 Downing Street.
> This morning the British Ambassador in Berlin handed the German Government a final note stating that, unless we hear from them by 11 o'clock that they were prepared at once to withdraw their troops from

Poland, a state of war would exist between us. I have to tell you now that no such undertaking has been received, and that consequently this country is at war with Germany.

In the Adlam household, as in millions of households the length of the United Kingdom, families looked at each other with dread in their eyes, wondering who of their family had been condemned to death by these few words uttered in Downing Street in smoky Central London.

After the initial shock, they continued to listen to Mr Chamberlain's address:

When I have finished speaking, certain detailed announcements will be made on behalf of the government. Give these your closest attention. The government have made plans under which it will be possible to carry on work of the nation in the days of stress and strain that may be ahead...

Now may God bless you all. May He defend the right. For it is evil things that we shall be fighting against – brute force, bad faith, injustice, oppression, and persecution – and against them I am certain that right will prevail.

Bill had two daughters, the lights of his life, Gladys (known as Poppy), and Pamela Pauline (known as Pauline). That was where the news hit hardest. If Britain lost the war, then he had to face the prospect of his two daughters, then aged four and two, being brought up in a Nazi state. What sort of subservience did that mean for them? What sort of demeaning life would they lead? Just what level of humiliation and degradation did the all-conquering Nazis offer with their 1000-Year Reich? There was so much about the Nazis that made his flesh crawl but nothing as much as this. His call-up letter would put a rifle, bayonet and grenade into his hand to defend them. That felt good! It felt good even if it meant that he would not pull through it himself.

Within the hour, Bill heard on the radio that Australia, India, and New Zealand had also declared war on Germany. This was when Bill Adlam, and everyone else in Britain, began to learn more about the emergency powers. The first and most obvious was that it became illegal overnight to show any light from a house. Most people purchased heavy black material to comply with the blackout. If the slightest chink of light showed, then a large unpleasant man would appear on the doorstep. He wore a black uniform and a helmet with the letters ARP on it. These were the Air Raid Precautions wardens. If you continued to show a light, which could be of use to enemy aircraft, then a prosecution would follow, and they would jail you.

Bill and everyone in the country were issued with two key items of equipment. Firstly, there was the identity card, which had to be carried at all times and which had to be shown on demand to any policeman or member of the armed forces. Secondly, there was the gasmask. It was expected that Germany would attack the civilian population with poison gas. Bill Adlam had to consider the possibility that his two daughters could be gassed to death by Nazis. This was not going to be a war of ideology or argument. It was to be personal.

All civilians were then issued with ration books. The *Daily Express* newspaper ran a campaign to ward off rationing but without any success. Butter, cheese and cream disappeared out of the shops. Food rationing was on the way.

Allowances were laid down and the population had better abide by them 'or else…'

- Meat – between one shilling (5p) and two shillings (10p) a head a week
- Bacon – four ounces (113 gm) to eight ounces (227 gm) a week
- Tea – two ounces (57 gm) to four ounces (113 gm) a week
- Cheese – one ounces (28 gm) to eight ounces (227 gm) a week
- Sugar – eight ounces (227 gm) a week.

The government and railway companies then collaborated to make available small patches of land called allotments. Civilians could rent these for growing extra vegetables. Meat became very scarce and as a result, the government encouraged the keeping of rabbits as a food source.

Railway station names were removed. If Germany invaded, these were thought to be of too much help to the invaders. It was better if they did not quite know where they were.

Back in Gloucester, Bill Adlam took his smartly pressed army uniform out of the wardrobe and removed the mothballs. He looked at the sergeant's stripes and hoped he would keep them in the real Army. He put on his khaki uniform. It felt right. It felt good. He wondered when he would ever wear *civvies* [civilian clothes] again.

It would not be for six years.

Chapter 3

Bill Wins his Military Medal

It was a very strange time. After the flurry of activity in the first week of 1939, the country had gone from a peacetime footing to a wartime footing. Day after day, nothing happened. The mood was uneasy. Every man, woman, boy and girl was on edge. Nerves were frayed. For day after day and week after week, nothing happened.

Bill, now mobilised into the 5th Battalion of the Gloucestershire Regiment, was in training at Plymouth and Lyme Regis in Dorset. On 14 January 1940, he made his first trip overseas. He was sent to the border between France and Germany in the Saarland. This was a curious area. At different periods of history, it had belonged to both France and Germany. Some five years previously, it had chosen to be part of Germany.

Most of Bill's time was spent patrolling the Maginot Line. This was a line of fortifications on the border between the two countries. It was too strong for the Germans to perform a frontal attack. The Germans knew it and the French knew they knew. Northern France was now a vast armed camp. The British Army numbered some 150,000 and the French even more. Such a large force was much too big to be beaten by any German army, so the current wisdom went. The mood was unworried, controlled and the British and French Armies were confident in their own invincibility. At least, they were for the moment.

Bill Adlam's B company patrolled in the vicinity of Grindorff. This is a small village near where Luxemburg, France and Germany all meet. Small though it was, the village was of some significance, right at the end of the Maginot Line. If the Germans were going to attack from the east, then they would have to come through here. German patrols were frequent and there was a constant dribble of low-level skirmishes. They were not large, pitched battles but soldiers were still being killed in them. A few prisoners were being taken on each side. It still fell short of what they had all expected in a shooting war. It was clear to all that this would change. The smouldering questions were 'when?' and 'how?'

Sunday, 3 March 1940, Grindorff, North-eastern France

On this day, the skirmish came where Bill would win his Military Medal. Grindorff was close enough to the German border that the local church tower afforded a panoramic view into Hitler's empire. If Bill climbed the tower, he would find that the 'lair of the Nazi beast' (as the British tabloids styled it) looked surprisingly civilised. The neat, sleepy, traditional farms were very similar to those in Lorraine, which is the province in which Grindorff is situated. More to the point, they were similar to those in Gloucestershire. It all looked so somnolent and peaceful. In the distance, he would have seen the 'dragons' teeth'. This was a barrier formed of three parallel lines of concrete pyramids, so designed that tanks or other motorised transport could not cross them. They were a cheap but extremely effective way of preventing Germany from being attacked by the French and British.

Lieutenant Shephard of B company led a late evening patrol away from the Gloucesters' main positions. The mission was to enter no man's land between the British and German lines and to listen for and report any enemy troop movements. The men did not wear helmets but woollen cap comforters. Their faces were blacked out so as to be less visible to the enemy. The men were heavily armed and carried hand grenades. They quietly achieved a position on the barbed wire which marked the start of the German fortifications.

Suddenly, they heard an outbreak of gunfire behind them. The Germans were mounting an attack onto the Gloucesters' main positions. Lieutenant Shephard told the patrol to lie low and not give their position away. The likelihood was that if they were seen, then they would then be attacked by a much larger German force and annihilated. As they lay low, they could see the silhouettes of German troops moving up to the barbed wire. Sniper fire started coming in their direction. They had been spotted.

The enemy troops now formed a continuous line on the skyline against the setting sun. Shephard's patrol lay low in a hollow, but its position was becoming perilous. Enemy fire was building up and it was all in their direction.

Bill Adlam was back in the main position firing his rifle at the gathering German troops, who were massing for a concerted attack. The company's Bren gunner, Private Bayliss, was crucially positioned on a parapet and in front of the platoon headquarters. A German soldier had infiltrated close enough to wound the Bren gunner with a rapid-fire Schmeisser machine gun and also to throw a 'potato-masher' grenade, which had wounded him severely. As Bayliss was carried away wounded, the Bren gun slid away from the Gloucesters and down the parapet. It was their only light machine gun. Its operation was vital if the German armed patrol was to be beaten off.

A group of Germans had cut the barbed wire and were working their way through it. Without the Gloucesters and their Bren gun, there was little to hold the German forces back. Bill ran down the parapet in full view of the enemy. The bullets whizzed and ricocheted around him. *Fffffft! Fffffft! Thunk!* Any one of these bullets could have killed him outright in an instant. He flattened himself on the ground and brought the Bren gun to bear.

'Cover Sergeant Adlam!' shouted a voice from somewhere. The noise of rifle fire was deafening. He could not hear the German guns at all or the bullets whizzing around him. He could still see the angry yellow-red spurts as the Germans fired at him. He moved the Bren to his left and began to spray bullets from left to right, wriggling backwards back up the parapet. Then he sprayed from right to left. Grey silhouettes dropped. The noise from the Gloucesters' rifles was still so loud that he could not hear his own weapon fire. He made it to the top of the parapet and dived down behind it. The Germans had pulled back. It was clear to the officer in command and the men that they would regroup and attack from a different direction.

'Cease fire!'

'Well done, sarge!' 'Flippin' brilliant!' 'Well done, Adlam!' 'Great stuff, sarge.'

'How many did I get?'

'Dunno, sarge, it was raining hot lead out there.'

'Are any of the bastards still moving?'

'Hilfe! Hilfe!' [Help! Help!]

'You two, those two Germans lying down to your right, can you see them?'

'Yes, sir!'

'Right, well shoot them.'

'Sir! Got him! Got the bastard… and that one… I think I got both of them, sir.'

'Can anyone see Lieutenant Shephard's patrol?'

'They're still down in that hollow, sir.'

'Give them covering fire and try and let them get back. Adlam are you OK?'

'They missed me, sir. Horrible bloody shooting!'

In the lull which followed, Lieutenant Shephard led his men through darkness of the evening back to Grindorff. The trick now was to get back through the British lines without being raked with friendly fire on the expectation that they were German. As they neared the British lines, Shephard gave the password, 'Blackbird coming back wounded'. This was a reference to 'Where be that blackbird be?', the Gloucester's marching song.

A British voice shouted, 'Don't be bloody idiots, there's a flippin' battle going on! Get through here quick!'

Shephard brought his patrol, together with the wounded back through the lines. By now, it was almost completely dark. The Germans had missed their chance and withdrew. Captain Norris immediately recommended Bill Adlam for the award of the Military Medal.

Most British units on the Maginot Line rarely saw their French allies. This was a blessing. The British soldiers reported that they smoked on duty were carelessly dressed and lacked discipline. Men were seen on guard duty in shoes rather than military-order boots. In one case, a man was reportedly seen on guard duty in bedroom slippers. This did not auger well for the fight which would inevitably come.

Tuesday, 9 April 1940, Lorraine

On the Alsace front, the Gloucesters and the whole British and French Armies continued to do little except patrol, fire the odd shot and wait for something to happen. The local church tower continued to be commandeered as an observation post. There were few troop movements on the other side. The odd German reconnaissance plane flew over and was fired upon and flew away again. By now this largely inactive phase of the war had been dubbed 'the Phoney War' in Britain and '*der Sitzkrieg*' [the sitting war] by the Germans. It was characterised in the main by boredom.

The *Daily Express*, having little to report of the war, ran a poll among servicemen as to who was the most popular musical performer. Charlie Kunz, the pianist was a formidable contender. Joe Loss the bandleader had wide support. There was however only one possible winner, Vera Lynn. The uproar when the winner was announced is likely to have led to stern words from Colonel Buxton.

'Adolf would have heard you lot in Berlin! If there is any repetition of last night's cheering after lights out, I will put every bloody man in this battalion on a charge. Is that clear to all of you?'

'Sir!'

It is completely inevitable that a rumour ran around afterwards.

'He voted for Vera Lynn as well, you know!'

'I bet he did, the old bugger.'

As a result of the poll, the *Express* called Vera Lynn 'the forces' sweetheart'. She would always be known by that name.

The advent of radio brought another aspect into the life of the frontline soldier, Lord Haw-Haw's propaganda broadcasts. Haw-Haw was an American of Irish parentage. His name was William Joyce and he had thrown his lot in with the Germans. He had been a member of the British Union of Fascists in the United Kingdom and had left the country just before the declaration of war. There were rumours that his sudden departure was due to privileged information given to him by someone unknown in high places.

'Jarmany calling; Jarmany calling!' Haw-Haw had a rather strange manner of pronunciation.

'Who the hell is that on the radio?'

'It's that British Union of Fascists bloke, Joyce, the CO, said to ignore him.'

This is Reichsender Hambursh, (which is how he pronounced Hamburg) Bremen and DXB transmitting on the 31-metre band. Here is the news from Jarmany.

The government of Jarmany has noted with dismay the British preparations to invade neutral Norway. This is a move typical of British foreign policy and will not be tolerated by the Jarman Reich. This morning, Jarman troops are occupying Norway to guarantee the freedom of that small nation.

British listeners will remember the British invasion of Belgium in 1914 'that small nations might be free'. Belgium was ruined and Jarmany wishes to protect Norway from the same dismal fate.

Early reports indicate that the Norwegian population are welcoming Jarman soldiers with flowers in the streets of Oslo, who they view as liberators protecting them from British aggression.

Representatives of the Norwegian *Nasjonal Sammling* [the Norwegian fascist party], under the firm leadership of Vidkun Quisling, are meeting with Jarman representatives with a view to forming an interim government and maintain peace and order across the Norwegian nation.

This is the end of our news in English. In thanking you for your attention, I would remind you that our next transmission in the English language takes place at a quarter past nine, Greenwich Mean Time, tomorrow morning and will be given by Reichsender Hambursh, Bremen and DXB.

'What the bugger means is that Germany has invaded Norway. Peace and order? They'll be dragging all the decent blokes off to prison.'

It was not the last that they were to hear of Haw-Haw!

Thursday, 9 May 1940, Lorraine

'Hey Bill, did you hear the news this morning?'

'No, I was out on patrol, what's everyone so het up about?'

'They're saying that Chamberlain has resigned.'

'He's done what?'

'Honest, John Snagge just announced it'.

Snagge was a senior announcer on the BBC. His word was the Oracle for the British people.

'It's been on the cards for a couple of days. There's a bloke over in E company got a *Daily Mirror* from a couple of days ago. This old boy called Sir Roger Keyes walked into the commons; he was wearing an admiral of the fleet's uniform'.

'... are you making this up?'

'No, honest, he's an MP as well. He told them that the war in Norway is lost and that Chamberlain had made a mess of it. The entire commons sang 'Rule Britannia' and shouted 'go, go, go!' at Chamberlain'.

'Oh yeah? I should say so!'

'It's true Sarge, I saw it in the *Mirror*, and it came off an RAF transport'.

'Well, I'll be...'

'So, who takes over? Not that silly bugger Halifax? If he takes over, we might as well surrender now.'

'No, they're saying that Churchill is taking over.'

'Now, that would be a different kettle of fish. That is very different.'

But there were so many rumours during that time of the Phoney War that no-one really knew what to believe and what not to believe. During that evening of the 9 May, the pros and cons of Churchill versus Halifax as the new Prime Minister were debated and discussed. Support for Halifax was muted. Churchill would have been the almost unanimous choice.

The last post sounded.

'Right, that's it you lot! Lights out! We can all look forward to another day of fun and games in lovely Alsace Lorraine.'

'I'm going for a walk with Brigitte tomorrow afternoon.'

'Oh, listen to flippin' Romeo.'

'Shut up and put that bloody light out.'

'Ok, sarge!'

Friday, 3 May 1940, Gloucester

The Citizen

Blackout time 9.00 pm to 5.14 am

Glo'ster Sergeant Wins First M.M. Awarded Territorial in France
FINE EXAMPLE TO PLATOON IN EIGHT HOURS' ACTION
WIFE AWAKENED BY NEIGHBOURS TO HEAR GOOD NEWS
SERGEANT WILLIAM GEORGE HENRY ADLAM, THE FIRST TERRITORIAL IN THE BRITISH ARMY TO WIN A DECORATION IN THIS WAR IS A GLOUCESTER MAN BORN AND BRED.

Early this morning excited neighbours wakened his young wife at her home at 18 Carmarthen Street, Gloucester, to tell her that her husband has been awarded the Military Medal by Lord Gort. She had not heard the announcement on the wireless last night.

"I don't know whether to laugh or cry, I am so proud of him" she told a "Citizen" reporter today.

Here is the story of Sergt. Adlam's gallant action, which won for him the immediate award by Lord Gort.

[Note: the newspaper got this wrong. The award was not made by Lord Gort but, as will be seen later, by King George VI].

On the night of April 4th, Sergt. [Note: The newspaper had the wrong date the correct date was the night of the 3rd / 4th March] Adlam was acting as platoon sergeant in a forward position. A raiding party of Germans attacked his post, which was under considerable pressure. A Bren gunner of the British post was wounded and the gun fell over the barricade. It was the only weapon holding the barricade and Sergt. Adlam at once saw the danger of the post being rushed from that side if the gun was not brought back into action. In spite of heavy fire Sergt.

Adlam recovered the gun and opened fire on the enemy. He was under fire again the same night and gave assistance to a patrol.

In the announcement of the award, it is stated that the general bearing of Sergt. Adlam during the action, which lasted more than eight hours, and on subsequent occasions when on patrol, has been the best possible example for the men of his platoon.

Soldiering His Hobby
Sergt. Adlam has been in the Gloucestershire Regiment for over four years. Soldiering was his main hobby. He was so keen on Army work that his employers, Messrs. S.J. Moreland and Sons of Bristol Road, Gloucester, gave him time off to attend special lectures. He studied hard and in 1937 as a lance-corporal he received from the Small Arms School, Hythe, the unusual and gratifying report for a junior N.C.O. of "fit to instruct without supervision".

In that year, also, and in the two years following he won the N.C.O.s Challenge Cup. He also won a cup for cross country running.

He has been employed by Messrs Morelands for ten years and was a gas-plant attendant at the Bristol Road factory. His colleagues there, with whom he has always been most popular, were delighted to hear of the honour bestowed on him, as were his employers who regard him as an excellent employee.

He was married six years ago and has three children. He is 27 years of age.

[Note: the newspaper also got this wrong: it should say 'two children'.]

His wife told the "Citizen" reporter of her husband's enthusiasm and determination to make good in his Army career.

"He always said that he would come back with something better than when he went out. He has made good his word, because I am expecting him home on leave soon", she said. "He studied hard in the evenings from his military books, and I used to hear him to see that he knew it precisely. He always knew every word of his subject he had been learning".

The first Mrs Adlam knew of her husband's achievement was at six o'clock this morning when neighbours banged excitedly on her door waving copies of the morning papers. "It was worth waking up for" she said.

Mrs Adlam was out last night when the announcement was made in the B.B.C. news service.

ALL GLOUCESTERSHIRE IS AS PROUD AS MRS ADLAM AND SERGT. ADLAM'S PARENTS ARE OF HIS BRAVERY WHICH BRINGS THE FIRST TERRITORIAL AWARD TO THE CITY.

Chapter 4

The Road to Ledringhem

Friday, 10 May 1940, Somewhere in Alsace Lorraine

The NCOs and officers from the other platoons were hurrying in the same direction.

'What the bloody hell do you reckon it is, Bill?'

'I have no idea but I flippin' don't like it. It doesn't feel like the normal sort of flap.'

The assembled company came to a smart salute and stood to attention. Colonel Buxton returned the salute.

'At ease.'

The assembly stood smartly at ease.

'Gentlemen, I have no time to beat about the bush. Jerry is invading Holland and Belgium as of 0400 hours this morning. Intelligence tells us that the Dutch Army is as much use as a chocolate frying pan. Holland is expected to fall completely within 72 hours.'

Colonel Buxton paused to ensure that the gravity of the situation was not lost on his subordinates.

'We are being sent into France as part of a defensive line to stop the Germans if they have decided to carry on beyond Belgium and attack France. The Army has a plan for this eventuality. It is called Operation David. This means that the British and French Armies will move north to stop the Germans on the Dyle River.'

'I suppose this means that my leave is cancelled?' Bill must have asked.

The reply, which would have been of a direct nature, is not recorded for posterity.

There was a war on!

'I want everyone fed, dressed properly in full marching order by 0700 hours. NCOs, you know the drill: no stragglers, no barrack room lawyers, no lead-swingers. This is serious. Impress on the men that the Phoney War is over. There are no more cricket matches now and no more chatting up French floosies. We will be seeing lots of gentlemen in grey uniforms and square helmets, and we will flippin' shoot them before they flippin' shoot us. Any questions?'

'No sir.'

'Dismissed! Lieutenant Shephard have reveille sounded if you would.'

'Sir!'

As all the other NCOs did, Bill ran at full speed back to his section.

'Can I say goodbye to Brigitte, sarge?'

'No, you flippin' can't and can I just make it clear to everyone, we have to be ready for the lorries by 0645 hours. Make sure that all of your water bottles are filled up. Draw rations for the journey. Any flash 'Arry trying to draw extra rations is on a charge.'

One hour later, the battalion was speeding through the early morning light. Brigitte and all other flirtations were ceased without notice. The stray dogs who the soldiers had befriended were abandoned. The shirts which were with the ladies in the village to be washed were forgotten and unpaid for.

During the evening at some unidentifiable place, which could have been in France or Belgium, the CO called officers and NCOs for a further meeting.

'Gentlemen, you are to advise your sections that the Prime Minister, Mr Chamberlain has resigned. The new prime minister is Mr Winston Churchill.' A minute later, Colonel Buxton smiled. He smiled at the outburst of spontaneous cheering from up and down the line of lorries.

'What the hell is going on?'

'Winston's back. He's PM!' and more men jumped up and down.

Colonel Buxton's smile faded from his face.

'Sergeants, get your men back on the lorries, we've got a long way to go.'

'It's good news, though, sir, except for bloody 'Itler!'

Progress was slow. The Gloucesters had their convoy, but the vast joint French-British Army of 250,000 men had generated other convoys too, hundreds of them. Bill did not have time to see what regiments they were from, but there were cap badges he had never seen before, shoulder flashes in red and blue and green. Some berets wore cockades, the Scottish regiments wore their Glengarry hats or tam-o'-shanters and now he saw the first of the French Army with their distinctive helmets.

Saturday, 11 May 1940, Auby, France

At Auby, the battalion rested and awaited further orders. While they were there, Churchill made his first speech to the House of Commons in London.

One phrase was to come out of that speech, which would set the tone of the challenge now faced by Bill, the Gloucesters and the whole country. That phrase was 'blood, sweat, toil and tears'. It was all that any of them had. It also said that Britain was not going to give in and would fight with whatever she had.

Holland fell quickly but not painlessly. The Germans had bombed Rotterdam. Now the evil was manifesting itself in the fall of Poland, Norway, Denmark, Holland, Belgium, where next?

Wednesday, 15 May 1940, Waterbosch, Belgium

'Right lads! Get ready! The trucks are coming at 0600. We're on the move again.'

'Where to this time, Sarge?'

'Just south of Brussels, it'll take a couple of hours so make sure your water bottles are full. Draw rations after breakfast and everybody in full marching order by 0545. Everybody got that?'

The convoy stopped. It seemed within minutes that the tents were raised, ablutions organised and a field kitchen was set up. The following morning, the officers left in a truck.

'Where are those buggers going? Are they leaving us in the lurch?'

'No, they're doing a recce of what's up ahead. You will not believe where they're heading for, Waterloo.'

'The railway station?'

'No, you silly bugger, the battlefield! Where Wellington fought Napoleon, it's just down the road.'

'That'll be something to tell your grandkids, you fought in the battle of Waterloo! Well, you can tell them if you come back.'

Bill was now coming gradually closer to the action. He could only hope that he would survive, acquit himself well and maybe take a couple of the evil Nazi bastards with him. Already, at 0730 that morning, the French General Weygand had telephoned Winston Churchill and got him out of bed. 'We are beaten. We have lost the battle.' In one week, the situation had become a crisis and was now headed for a total, unmitigated disaster. Bill Adlam was right in the middle of it and moving more and more to the centre of the action.

Friday, 17 May 1940, Glabais, Belgium

Bill and the 5th battalion arrived at Glabais at around 0400 in the morning. This time, there were no trucks to carry tents and heavy equipment.

'Right lads, just doss down where you can.'

The word came through that the Germans had broken through to the south. The places which Bill had been in just a few days ago were already occupied by the Germans. This meant that they were now faced with Germans to the north and Germans to the south. It was a chilling prospect. The Germans were moving so hard and so fast that it seemed that nothing could resist them. The first complaints were now heard, 'Where was the bloody RAF?'

At 0600 hours, fresh orders came through.

'Right, lads, up you get, we're on the move again. Draw rations and fall in. Come on, never mind shaving, just have a piddle, and get your marching order on. I do not want to hear about blisters. I do not want to hear about anyone being tired. I just want you fell in. Now get fell in!'

'Yes, sarge.'

They grudgingly and rather tiredly formed a marching column.

'Right, this is Trous-du-Bois. Never mind your packs we've got to set up a defensive line. Bren gunners! Where are the Bren gunners? The rest of you over here and get digging with C company and D company.'

At 1700 hours, as the defensive line was nearly ready, the bugle sounded 'all NCOs'.

'What? Again?'

Colonel Buxton addressed the officers and NCOs.

'The Germans are coming at us from the north, the east and the south. We are ordered to the Forest of Soignes, which is five miles to the north.'

'That is where we were supposed to go yesterday.'

'There is a war on, and we obey orders, immediately, effectively and without acting like a load of nancy boy Frenchmen.'

The first of the contempt for the French performance was beginning to arise.

On the horizon, they could already see a dozen sinister dark grey German tanks rumbling towards them. Puffs of grey-brown smoke came from their guns. Shells whistled overhead but missed. A couple of local houses were destroyed in seconds. Civilians were now starting to leave their homes and take whatever possessions they could.

Colonel Buxton organised a rear-guard of anti-tank guns to hold up the German advance.

'Come on lads, sharpish! We've got to get out of here quick. Fall in!'

'Do we draw rations, sarge?'

'There aren't any.'

'Oh bloody 'ell!'

They marched another five miles to the Forest of Soignes, with empty stomachs and heavy packs. By 2100 hours, they had arrived and were preparing new defensive positions. For a moment, there was no further sign of the German advance.

An hour later, another order came.

'Two companies are to advance to the village of Chenois and the rest of the battalion is to proceed to Waterbosch.'

How was Bill to pass this on to his troops? By now they had marched over 30 kilometres with all of their equipment plus weapons and very little food.

'Right, you lot, get fell in. Corp, would you wake up those sleeping beauties over there. Our orders are to proceed to Waterbosch.'

'Waterbosch? That's where we started out.'

'The orders are to go to Waterbosch and that is that. There is a war on, son, and there is no point complaining. I don't like it any more than you do but it is either go to Waterbosch or else.'

'Or else what?'

'Or else you'd better learn the German language fast, lad!'

The distant rumble of shelling had rapidly become a normal backdrop to their day. It was now there all the time. The refugees on the roads had put whatever they could salvage into a handcart and headed west. Bill must have thought that with the rapid advance of the German Army they would soon be overtaken anyway. Then there were the increasing sightings of Luftwaffe planes. For the moment, they were Fieseler Storchs, reconnaissance planes. That meant that the Messerschmitt 109s and Stukas were not far behind.

Bill had seen Fairey Battles, single-engined bombers going from west to east to bomb the German advance. They saw very few come back. These brave bomber pilots were engaging in aerial suicide. The German Army was so good at what it did that the question had to be asked, 'How long would it be before the 5th Gloucesters would be required to make their own valiant but futile attempted suicide?'.

It would not be long.

While Bill and the 5th battalion were spending the day in fruitless, circular marching the 2nd battalion, some kilometres away, were learning the facts of life in a different way. Without warning, sniper fire had come at them from the main street, from the west. This was odd as the German advance was still to the east. The Gloucesters undertook a house-to-house search. The snipers proved to be local youths, firing with sporting guns. Most made off as soon as the search began but three were captured.

The Gloucesters did not speak French, so they handed them over to a French officer for interrogation. He was not satisfied with their answers. He made them stand against a wall. He drew his service revolver and, one by one, shot each in the head and left the bodies in the house.

The realities of war were becoming firsthand experience for all concerned.

Saturday, 18 May 1940, Enghien, Belgium

The next orders were chilling.

Companies were 'to make their own way via Hèrrines and Bois D'Acren to make a new position at Wannebecq, a village close to Lessines'. Given the normal precision and clarity of military orders, this was a surprise. It was woolly and vague. It told the experienced soldier that all was not well at Brigade HQ, wherever that might be. Captain Norris, Lieutenant Shephard, Sergeant Adlam and B company began the trek. A few days ago, there had been a trickle of refugees, now there was a flood of tens of thousands. In one way, you could feel sorry for them, but the buggers were getting in the way of the British troops who were fighting for their cause, or at least trying to. The civilians' faces showed fatigue, dog-tiredness but also a despair, which the soldiers' faces did not yet share. No food was forthcoming. If any soldiers purloined fruit or vegetables from nearby fields, those in authority would be looking in quite a different direction. By 1800 hours, the company had trudged into Wannebecq and reunited with the rest of the battalion. Was this by design or just a lucky chance? No-one was interested in asking questions. They just wanted to sleep, and sleep came quickly.

The bugle sounded. It was 'all NCOs'. Oh no! Not again. Colonel Buxton and the officers were already assembled. There was no discussion as the non-commissioned officers approached his tent.

'Gentlemen, I have some things to say to you and they are important. I know you have not slept or eaten properly in days, and I haven't either. I will be brief and to the point. Firstly, HQ have advised that Jerry has broken through in such numbers and with such force that we cannot hold him back. We are now not fighting to beat the Germans or even to keep them out of France. I want you all to impress on the men that they are fighting to see their wives, girlfriends and children again. The situation is that bad. The Germans are coming down through an area called the Ardennes. The French told us that it was impassable to German armour. They forgot to tell that to the Germans and a complete German corps of several divisions is pouring through with little, if any, opposition.

'Secondly, the French are surrendering in droves. In the last lot they were good soldiers. In this lot we could only wish they were on the Germans' side because we don't want them on ours. Defeat is bad enough, but disgrace is a quite different matter. If any man of this battalion surrenders without my direct order, then I will shoot the bugger myself.

'Thirdly, we have got this far with remarkably few casualties. That is going to change very soon. Men under your command will see their mate's head get shot off and I cannot have them going to water and falling in an ignominious heap. I want the NCOs, especially, to be in charge of your men. I ask you to ensure that under fire they do not wilt and if things get bad – and that is probable – then it will be your job to make sure that the 5th Battalion acquits itself well and behaves like British soldiers.

'Any questions?'

'No, sir!'

'Now, I want you to get your men out of their slumbers. We are leaving immediately to march to Buissenal, the officers know where it was. There is transport there to take us forward. Dismissed.'

'Sir!'

The men had marched 150 kilometres in three and a half days. They formed into lines. There was no wisecracking. There was no attention to uniform, they were all filthy. Their eyes were bloodshot and sunken. Their spirits were sunken even more.

There was a nastiness creeping in. The Tyneside Scottish were holding a canal bridge. They were told to blow it up. The engineer in charge of the demolition refused because there was a stream of refugees crossing and he could not stop them. His colonel pressed home the plunger with people still on the bridge. As the colonel later wrote, 'sentiment comes no-where in war'.

The Road to Ledringhem   25

Sunday, 19 May to Tuesday, 21 May 1940, Bruyelle, Belgium

The transport was not at Buissedael, it was at Frasnes but this hardly mattered. Now, the transport was partly in British army trucks and partly, in trucks from farmers, hauliers, removal firms and any other transport that could be commandeered. Most probably, the legal document that authorised the acquisition was in the form of a Lee Enfield rifle aimed pointedly at the owner. The situation was becoming desperate. The 5th Battalion piled onto the trucks and went to sleep immediately. It is unlikely that a single man even asked where they were going. Destination was of no consequence, only sleep.

The bus stopped on the outskirts of Tournai. All of the other trucks stopped. Colonel Buxton and the senior officers got out and surveyed the smouldering ruin of what had once been a beautiful medieval town.

'Looks like Jerry got here first.'

'Do we try to link up with the other battalions, sir?'

'Link up with what? The place is a burnt offering, man. It's like trying to link up with someone in a forest fire.'

A quick phone call to Brigade headquarters obtained new orders.

'Back on the lorries, everyone, we've to go to Bruyelle. I have no idea where it is but you've all got maps so use them. I'll see you there.'

Bruyelle, six kilometres south of Tournai, did not prove to be a haven of peace. There was almost permanent shelling and enemy patrols tested the flanks on an almost permanent basis. Nevertheless, the battalion was to stay there for three days. Casualties had been few but were clearly on the rise. The first and biggest issue was sleep. The second issue was for the NCOs to get the men shaved and washed so that they looked like soldiers again. The third issue was to bring the battalion into some sort of military formation with discipline, shape and direction.

Colonel Buxton passed the message on via the officers.

'We have no means of feeding you. You will need to live off the land. The NCOs are responsible to ensure there is no wholesale looting but otherwise, take what you can from wherever you can, however you can and eat it. In any case, there are lots of abandoned houses. Just break into them and see what you can find. French houses often have lots of stuff in the cellars.'

German artillery shells were falling among them. Up above, the Stuka dive-bombers were swooping down to drop well-aimed bombs into the ranks of the British soldiers. Where was the RAF to protect them? What was going on? Bill's war record shows that he received shrapnel in his buttocks in Belgium. It would have taken more than that to take him out of combat.

To make matters worse, German tanks had penetrated the line and came at the battalion from the rear. The anti-tank rifles and other small artillery drove the Germans back. Bill began to see casualties in large numbers. For the first time, he would see men with legs, arms and faces blown off. He would see men scream in agony. He would see dead men lie in fields. He would see men crack under the strain and scream in terror. Some he had known back in Gloucester.

The Germans were attempting to cross the River Escaut. It was clear that if they established a bridgehead, then the Gloucesters were doomed. Fusillades of small-arms fire hit the German soldiers but even more importantly, it lacerated their rubber boats. As they sank, it left the Germans in their heavy equipment to drown in the river or be picked off by accurate and deadly Bren-gun fire. The Germans had made an attempt to take Bruyelle but determined resistance had fought them off. The writing was on the wall. The Gloucesters, plus the Oxfordshire and Buckinghamshire Regiment and the Worcesters, certainly lived to fight another day. They were not stopping the German advance, but they were applying a gentle brake to it.

News came through that the Germans had now reached Abbeville on the coast of the English Channel. The British and French Armies were now besieged from the south and from the north. They were caught like animals in a trap. It would be a couple of days before the realities of this situation became fully clear to them.

On the evening of 21 May, the 8th Worcesters appeared. Colonel Buxton passed the word.

'We are relieved. We've to fall back to Wez-Velain. That is here on the map. It's about two miles. Then we are to move to Aix and carry on this road here through Avelin to Herlies.'

'Is there any chance of transport, sir?'

'Afraid not. It's only about 25 miles [40 kilometres] so it's not too far.

'Very good, sir.'

Colonel Buxton did not have to say the obvious words: 'we'll have to march it.'

Thursday, 23 May 1940, Herlies, France

The battalion walked all day and into the night. To their surprise, a fleet of trucks was waiting at Herlies.

'You the 5th Gloucesters?'

'That's us.'

'You're to come with us to Dunkirk. They're starting a big evacuation.'

News spread with all possible speed through the battalion.

'We're going back to Blighty!'

The journey was slow and torturous. They had seen refugees aplenty in the previous week, but the trickle had developed into a flood and now a deluge in their attempts to escape the German onslaught. The narrow roads were packed with these people. The transport drivers beeped their horns to try to clear the way. This raised storms of protest from the men who were dog-tired and having their sleep disturbed. There were no stops for food only stops for calls of nature, which were doubtlessly accompanied by the odd spot of pilfering. The stealing of food was becoming normal by now. The hunger pangs, which caused it, gave an easy moral justification. As the trucks forged on, they would see British soldiers, stragglers, shouting, 'Pick me up, don't leave me for the Jerries.' Orders were clear, 'Don't stop for anyone, we don't have the time.' Men were being left behind. They were being left for the Germans.

Friday, 24 May 1940, Dunkirk, France

It was 1400 hours and at last, the port of Dunkirk was in sight. Ruined buildings showed that it had been heavily bombed. Burned-out Messerschmitts and Stukas, which lay in fields, showed that the British Empire still had some remaining teeth. Up above the dogfights continued. The Spitfires and Hurricanes were getting in among the Luftwaffe planes. The Messerschmitt 110s and Stukas were coming off badly, but the Messerschmitt 109s gave formidable opposition. It was chilling to note that when the British planes disengaged, they always disappeared over the horizon back to their landing strips in Britain. That meant that the British high command had already abandoned all airfields in France. This was an understated but clear indicator of the stark realities which faced them.

Dunkirk was full of thousands upon thousands of soldiers. They were mainly British but with thousands of French as well. Over to the right lay the port installations. They could see Royal Navy ships, British coastal vessels and cross-channel ferries, which were doubtlessly being readied to take them across the channel.

The trucks turned left.

'What the bloody hell? Why are we going left? The port is over there, to the right!'

The realisation came that they were being sent to fight the German advance and to hold them back while some sort of evacuation happened. They were to be sacrificed. Morale and discipline held.

At 1600 hours, they entered the village of Wormhoudt, which at least was a bit quieter.

'Everybody out.'

Everyone found a quiet place and for the first time in days, had a peaceful night's sleep.

Chapter 5

The Road to Dunkirk

Sunday, 26 May to Tuesday, 29 May 1940, Ledringhem, France

At 1330 hours, the 5th Gloucesters were ordered forward to the next village, some three kilometres down the road.

'Where the bloody hell is this?'

'Ledringhem, wherever that is.'

Ledringhem! Bill Adlam was only destined to stay there for three days. He would never forget the name, but he would never mention it. It would never quite leave his dreams. He would never be free of it.

At first, it was quiet.

However, a formidable German force, the 20th Panzergrenadier division, was trundling their way towards them from Saint Momelin, under the austere and determined command of Lieutenant General Mauritz von Wiktorin zu Hainburg.

The 20th Panzergrenadiers were a totally motorised division of 15,000 men. Colonel Buxton had some 800 to hold them back, minus casualties. Colonel Buxton ordered that Ledringhem and the village of Arneke, three kilometres to the south-west, be turned into a fortress. It was clear that these two villages could not be held for long. They could, however, be converted into useful strong points, which would hold up the German advance. This now was their task, fighting a hopeless and possibly suicidal rear-guard action. Every hour of delay represented an hour in which men could be ferried away from Dunkirk and back to England and relative safety. At this moment, the Gloucesters could not expect this for themselves. The limit of their ambition was an unknown number of years in a prison camp. Either that or the eternal peace of a war grave.

Bill's B Company under Captain Norris was to cover the south and east quadrant of the defence line around Ledringhem. HQ Company was to cover the north. Colonel Buxton sent A and D companies to defend Arneke with the orders to fight as long as possible and then withdraw to Ledringhem.

Colonel Buxton ordered that the roads in the Germans' path be blocked with farm vehicles, rocks, landmines and anything else that the desperate 5th Battalion could devise. They set up an observation post in the church tower. They dug slit trenches facing the roadways where the German armour would doubtlessly pass. They were later joined by a platoon from 53 Anti-Tank Regiment, Royal Artillery. They would help keeping the tanks out! It was the calm before the storm and every man knew it. Any man not on guard duty or with other tasks fell into an immediate deep sleep.

Those remaining awake would have been somewhat horrified to see German planes, the Fieseler Storch reconnaissance planes, buzzing around them and radioing their positions back to German headquarters. The German commanders knew the Gloucesters' strength and deployment precisely. The Gloucesters did not know the same about the Germans. They were doomed to be fighting blind. Why were there no British planes doing reconnaissance over the *Boches* [Germans]?

Had they known what was happening in high places the Gloucesters would have been even more horrified. Lord Gort, the British Commander in Chief, was taking orders from the French Prime Minister, M. Reynaud. These were relayed to him second hand via the French General Blanchard. The most worrying aspect was not knowing what the orders were. From their position at Ledringhem, the Gloucesters were mounting a holding operation to let the main body of the British Army escape. In reality, no-one knew, and, in effect, no-one was in charge.

To the south, the 2nd Gloucesters in Cassel were already copping it. Bombers were giving the place a pasting. The sound of gunfire was constant. The smell of smoke was in the air. A Henschel aircraft could be seen landing in farmers' fields to replenish the Germans' ammunition. The *crump* of heavy artillery sent a sick feeling through the stomach of everyone who heard it. Those were Gloucester lads getting blown up down there. To the north, the first sporadic firing could be heard from the Royal Warwickshire Regiment positions at Wormhoudt. That rapidly developed into a battle as well. It was clear that Bill would see action in the next 24 hours if not sooner.

Some slightly odd people, men and women of differing ages, were seen approaching Ledringhem.

'Halt! Who goes there?'

The Lee Enfield rifle was pointed at them, fingers were ready to pull the triggers. They appeared to be civilians.

'Right, you lot come over here and if you make one clever move, I'll flippin' shoot you! Comprendez?'

The figures smiled benignly. They were not threatening. They walked with faraway eyes and fearless smiles to the barricades, which blocked the entry to the village.

'Speak English?' barked the sentry.

The civilians beamed a broad smile and said something in French.

'Right, take them to the lieutenant for interrogation. He speaks a few words of French.'

A few minutes later, the group of civilians were ushered politely out of the village.

'They were peculiar, that lot, sir. What were they? Were they Jerry spies or something?'

'They were inmates from the local loony bin. The staff have all run for it with Jerry coming and left them to their own devices.'

They had to laugh. At least that night everyone got a good night's sleep. It was not clear whether the inmates would survive the next 24 hours. No one ever knew what became of them. It was not clear if anyone would survive. Beyond Arneke, the distant rumble of vehicles gave clear warning of that. They could clearly hear the distinctive music of squeaks, rumbles and powerful engines. A very large number of tanks were moving towards them, somewhere just out of sight.

Something else happened that day, which was rather odd. Bill's record shows him as posted on that day to the Infantry Training Centre. This appears to be a bureaucratic nicety for closing off his record, which meant ceasing his pay and pension entitlements. In other words, the military high command did not expect him – or anyone else in that pocket – to be going home.

Monday, 27 May 1940, Ledringhem, France

As dawn broke, the spotters in the church tower reported enemy troops, tanks and artillery moving to the north of Ledringhem towards Wormhoudt and also south towards Cassel. They were out of range. Common sense said that an attack would have to come along the road via Arneke to Ledringhem. The first attack started in the evening. The Panzers moved forward. Ahead of them, the Germans appeared to be driving civilians as human shields. This was war. The order was given to open fire, regardless of civilians. A number of the civilians were hit, but the German column stopped and took shelter in ditches and behind stone walls. The Gloucesters noticed that rather than commence a firefight, the Germans moved with great speed in rapid flanking movements to the north and the south. Their battlefield drills were evidence of a very well-trained and disciplined force.

Bill could hear it in the distance. He heard the barking of the German tank guns, the rattling of the British Bren guns and the sharp crack of the British artillery. The recently arrived artillery had been deployed immediately to fight the tanks at Arneke. Colonel Buxton ordered a carrier section forward under Lieutenant Shephard. They ambushed a German unit and caused casualties. Bill heard the German attack peter out into silence. One up to the Gloucesters! Then the shelling began. German artillery fire rained down on Arneke. The *crump* of mortars could be heard clearly in Ledringhem. The ripping paper sound of the German MG34s could be heard raking the small village. Bill would learn the next day that a German tank had driven down the main street and fired through the open window of the local pub, which was being used as a firing point. The casualties were terrible but a wall of fire from the light artillery drove off the tank. This was real war not the glorified punch-up of Grindorff.

Friends were being killed and wounded. Arneke did not give in. The grey uniforms could be seen moving further north of Ledringhem and also further to the south. Actually, the uniforms to the north were grey-green and those to the south were grey. Did that matter? *They would find out the next day that it did matter, and it mattered quite a lot.*

Ledringhem was coming under fire now as well. At Arneke, Bill could hear the battle raging on and on. It must be hell down there. There was no time to think of it. Mortar shells were raining on Ledringhem, tanks were rumbling in the distance

Reports to Colonel Buxton advised that the enemy was gradually surrounding Arneke. He ordered A and D companies back to join C company under cover of darkness just outside of Ledringhem.

'We knocked out five of their tanks and five armoured cars,' boasted one of the soldiers as they returned. 'There's a lot of dead bodies down there.'

'Did we manage to bury our boys?'

'Not a hope, we got some dog tags but even that was hard. We'll only really know about casualties when we have a rollcall.'

'Have a lot of our boys bought it?'

'There's a fair few dozen left down there. You wouldn't want to see them; they're blown to bits most of them.'

Overnight, the shelling continued. The Germans had now moved into Arneke. The three extra companies in Ledringhem turned the village into an armed fortress. They were raining shells onto the village. The sight of broken bodies, headless soldiers and men with missing legs or arms or terrible head wounds was now commonplace. By now, Bill would have no doubt as to what war really meant. There were little heaps, covered with blankets. They were men that he had known. Some were cut in two by the shell blasts. The screams of the wounded from the underground first-aid station were constant. The quiet village of Ledringhem had turned into hell.

Tuesday, 28 May 1940, Ledringhem, France

By 0400, the light was just starting to show. The British guns fired back at the places where the Germans were thought to have gathered. They fired round after round against their unseen enemy, hiding in the hedgerows and small copses. The German tanks answered back with explosions from the town, almost every minute. At midday, a runner came to Colonel Buxton.

'From the church tower, sir, we're surrounded. There are Germans on all sides.'

'Thank you for letting me know.'

There was little else the colonel could say. At this point, he had professional pride, dignity and little else. The situation in the fields around Ledringhem was now verging on disaster. The Royal Warwicks were clearly overrun to the north. The 2nd Gloucesters were keeping up a spirited fight to the south, despite appalling casualties. For the 5th Gloucesters, all they could do was keep on firing and hope it would achieve their mission. Worse news was to come. A signaller came to Colonel Buxton.

'It's no good, Sir, we've repaired the landline to brigade three times, but the buggers just keep cutting it. There's too many of them out there. We can't get near it to repair it anymore.'

'Thank you for letting me know; we'll organise a dispatch rider.'

The dispatch rider was Private Joines. He was to make five trips across the fields on his motorcycle to communicate with brigade. Each time, he was the target of a hailstorm of bullets.

A light German vehicle came down the road from Wormhoudt to Ledringhem and crashed into a barricade. A long burst from a Bren gun killed the occupants. One of them lay on the road with his brains seeping out onto the tarmac. One or two soldiers vomited but most were becoming inured to such sights now. The soldiers buried the Germans in the garden of a nearby house. Would the Germans extend the same niceties to the British dead in Arneke?

At Wormhoudt, it was all quiet. The Royal Warwicks had put up a fight but clearly had been beaten. They would now be discovering what it was like to be in German captivity. If they had stayed at Wormhoudt then the Gloucesters would also have surrendered by now. More shells, more mortar fire and more German troop movements were now in evidence.

Midmorning, Major Vigrass appeared with a truck and rations. How on earth had he got through? Few stopped to ask questions. They ate their rations and drank down hot sweet tea with the relish of men being given their last meal. For dozens of them, it would prove to be just that. Major Vigrass would not make it through again.

By mid-afternoon, they could clearly hear the sound of weaponry to the north. This was strange. The Royal Warwicks had already apparently surrendered or withdrawn. There had been no sound of action up there for hours. Then, they heard the sound of small arms. The burst was short and sharp. And again, short sharp bursts.

They sounded like firing squads but surely not. What Bill had heard was the Wormhoudt massacre. Waffen SS troops of the Leibstandarte Adolf Hitler division had herded some 100 soldiers of the Royal Warwickshire Regiment, Royal Cheshire Regiment and Royal engineers into a barn. They had then thrown hand grenades in to kill all of them. The survivors were dragged out in groups of five and machine-gunned to death against a wall. Allegations later identified the German officer who gave the order as *Hauptsturmführer* [Captain] Wilhelm Möhnke. Bill never knew anything about this sinister Nazi officer by name, although he was to come into uncomfortably close contact with him again, some four years later.

Heavy artillery fire commenced on Ledringhem. They all knew what this meant. It was the softening-up process before a main attack. Again, the Fieseler Storch spotter aircraft were buzzing about the sky, giving detailed deployments to the German divisional headquarters. Heavy mortar fire hit the orchard on the east side of the village. There, under camouflage, sat the battalion's transport trucks. They were all destroyed in a single lucky salvo. The camouflage was apparently not good enough to fool the German spotters.

The Germans had surrounded the village and were preparing for the coup de grace. Joines had gone out again on his motorcycle, but it was unclear whether he had got through to brigade headquarters or whether he had been killed in the attempt. A renewed heavy mortar attack started at 1930 hours. This meant that a major attack was coming closer. Then the artillery started with air-bursting shells. The Germans were cleverly out of range for the Gloucesters to reply with their limited range of weaponry. The village of Ledringhem was now on fire. A large windmill started to burn and would burn all evening giving a hellfire aspect to the men fighting and dying in the village. Two figures came out of the smoke and ran for the British positions. This was it, then!

'Fire on my command! NO! Hold your fire! They're ours!'

Lance Corporals Barnfield and Mayo rushed to Colonel Buxton with a dispatch. It had taken them four hours to cover six kilometres through the German lines from Brigade HQ at Rousbrugge. The dispatch, which they brought, was crucial. If Barnfield and Mayo had not got through then Colonel Buxton's orders were, in effect, to fight to the last man and the last bullet. This altered the situation. The orders were from Brigadier Hamilton.

Make your way after dark or when you can to Bambecque via Herzeele.
At Bambecque we will try to contact you. We are hard pressed here and hope to get away after dark to Wylder or Bambecque.

It was his order to withdraw. The 5th Gloucesters were not to fight a suicidal rear-guard action after all. The loss of the motorised transport was academic by now. There was no prospect of driving out of Ledringhem without being annihilated by the Germans, who had surrounded them.

An account by Sergeant Organ describes what took place as the Germans moved into the outer houses in the village.

Suddenly, an officer burst into the room (of a house where some of the Gloucesters were sleeping) shouting that the enemy was attacking. He told us to go down the street as far as possible to the school (which was also the mayor's office). We got to the school, out of breath, and found the best part of the battalion there. There were machine guns and rifles poking out of every window ready to fire. Apart from the glow of cigarette ends, the rooms were in total darkness, and we were squeezed in like sardines. We quickly realised that by setting the houses alight the enemy were going to force us out into the open. We soon saw them running towards us. We opened fire. Each time I finished a round, the enemy retaliated blowing out doors and windows.

Colonel Buxton ordered that the battalion start to make a dash for freedom at 2115. The grey shapes attacked en masse before that could happen. They were moving into the west end of the main street. Every man who could hold and fire a rifle was firing as many targeted shots as he could get off in a minute. The first wave came in from the north and west, followed closely by a second wave from the south and east. Now the Germans had taken over the entire west of the village. Savage bursts of Bren gunfire mowed them down in their dozens as the Germans tried to rush the defences. The worst of the situation was that with the Germans so close, it was not possible for Colonel Buxton to evacuate to Bambecque. The battalion was pinned down. If they tried to make it across the fields with the Germans in those positions, then there would be few survivors, if any. He had to do something to drive them back.

By now, the remnants of the battalion were packed into the school and houses down the main street. There were Lee Enfield rifles and Bren Guns pointing out of every window. The artillery pieces were trained down the street which meant that the Germans could not risk their tanks or armoured vehicles. They did not need to. At some point the Gloucesters would run out of ammunition and surrender would be the only option.

Colonel Buxton could not bring his troops out of the village without being shot at by the Germans at the bottom of the main street. The village was on fire, and the large mill was still burning unchecked with a bright yellow flame. There was no possibility of sneaking out under darkness, the village was lit as brightly as daytime. He looked at his options and decided there was only one thing for it, a bayonet charge 150 yards down the main street.

Colonel Buxton asked for volunteers. Captain Norris volunteered for the first charge. He was accompanied by six other officers and seven other ranks. They worked their way along the main street taking cover where they could until they were within grenade-throwing range. At Norris' command, ten hand grenades hurtled towards the German positions. Captain Norris shouted, 'Up the Gloucesters!' and all 14 charged with fixed bayonets. The Germans fell back, but Captain Norris fell wounded. The rest of the Gloucesters retreated up the main street. As they did so, the Germans moved forward again and began firing. A second bayonet charge was attempted with more men. This one was led by Lieutenant Dewsnap who was also injured in the charge. Again, the Germans fell back. Again, the Gloucesters returned to their lines and again, the Germans retired to their positions.

They could hear a German officer shouting at his men to get back into position. Ah! So, the Germans clearly did not relish the bayonet charges. That was interesting! This time they also set-up a machine-gun position in a house at the bottom of the street. Colonel Buxton called for a third charge. This time 30 men stepped forward. Lieutenant Shephard, who took part in the charge, described the attack. His reference to men who were 'in the Saar' means that Bill Adlam was almost certainly in this action.

This time we had more men. Two more officers were with us and most of the men were those who had been on fighting patrols in France (in the Saar region during the Phoney War), the very medicine for the *Boches*. I think the German officer must have sensed that we meant business this time. We could hear him exhorting his men to meet the attack. The first sense of fear left us, and it was almost thrilling moving down the street to get to grips with those grey-clad infantrymen. So, cheering, thirty odd men and officers moved steadily towards the corner by the church.

The blaze had grown greater, and we could see the figures of the enemy as they waited for us in the cover of walls and doorways. The light of his own making showed us the leader, who was shouting harshly at his men. I saw him at the same time that others did and simultaneously our rifles cracked, and the German went down.

We lost men as we went forward but that did not deter the others. Suddenly the road was illuminated by great explosions as the enemy rolled and threw their stick bombs at us. Our own grenades replied and one, neatly lobbed through a doorway, silenced the machine gun for good. We fired another volley at the shadowy figures and ran in.

On my right, I saw a Tommy bayonet a man. I heard him shout triumphantly. Another Tommy ran past me and round the corner to bayonet a *Boche*, who crouched there with his bombs. Another German ran away and fell at my feet before I realised that I had fired again from the hip. Everywhere our men were doing the same thing, bayoneting, shooting and bombing. Everywhere we were pushing the enemy back from the village. *It was exhilarating*!

The Germans came back up the street after them. They were firing rifles, throwing stick grenades and tried to use a flamethrower, which fortunately failed to ignite. Several of the Gloucesters were covered with vile sticky oil. They had to wipe the oil off their weapons, or they could not handle them. The oil got into their eyes, their noses and their mouths. The flamethrower operator now stood somewhat exposed. He was hit many times and died quickly in a hail of bullets from Lee Enfield rifles.

The Gloucesters continued to reply with rapid and sustained fire. Major Waller led a counterattack but was killed instantly. The Gloucesters' Bren gun and rifle fire drove the Germans back and cleared the street. That was vital if they were to escape. News came now of another German attack from the other side of the village. Colonel Buxton was hit in the leg as he went to investigate it. This new attack was not as severe as the one fought out in the main street, but for the moment, the coast was clear.

At 0015, Colonel Buxton sent a note to all sections. Anyone who could do so was to rendezvous at an orchard close to the blazing mill. The three wounded officers and over 100 severely wounded would be left behind with two medical orderlies to await the Germans. There were many dead bodies of both British and German soldiers down the street. There was no time for rollcalls or niceties. All Colonel Buxton could do was hope that the Germans, as signatories of the Geneva Convention, would act in a civilised manner. There was no alternative. They formed into a single file; many were wounded. All were exhausted. All were terrified as to what would befall if they encountered the Germans. The Germans in the village must have been as battle-weary as they were. There was no pursuit. The remains of the 5th battalion moved in silence following the stream and following a line of hedgerows.

Captain Hauting led the column. He gave clear compass readings to all officers and senior NCOs. Colonel Buxton was being pushed in a wheelbarrow due to his leg wound. At this point, no-one saw any humour in this. They moved slowly, not speaking. They moved in single file, following the lines of streams, behind hedgerows and across the silent fields, foot by foot, inch by inch. Bill did not know who was leading the column, all he could do was to follow the man in front. On several occasions, the silence and the darkness led to the column being broken. Fortunately, Captain Hauting's compass bearings allowed the officers to lead their men back to rejoin the secret, silent column. As they neared Herzeele at around 0200, they were all motioned to lie flat. The column head had come across some sleeping Germans.

Three of them awoke but discovered they were looking very closely at rifles with murderous bayonets on their ends. They raised their hands in surrender. None of the Gloucesters spoke German and the Germans did not speak English. A motion with a bayonet and a murderous look would be sufficient to communicate a simple message, 'If you mess us about, we will cut your guts out.'

They crawled, wriggled and ducked with painful slowness through thick hedgerows and deep brooks until they reached Herzeele at around 0400. A woman was awake in the village. What on earth was she doing there? All the other civvies had run for it. She motioned to the Gloucesters that in that direction there are sleeping Germans. They knew what that meant. If there was a single uncontrolled sound, the Germans would awake. There would be a firefight which they had no chance of winning. The woman must have been terrified. If a fire- fight broke out, she was right in the middle of it. There was only one option available. They gave her the thumbs up and changed direction, to skirt around them. They quietly commandeered two farm horses to transport Colonel Buxton and another man. The colonel gave up his wheelbarrow to a third. It was primitive but effective.

They shuffled on for another two hours across open country. At 0630 it was already light. They noticed that the prisoners were wearing the grey-green uniforms. These were not the men they had fought at Ledringhem who wore grey uniforms. Two other aspects of the uniform were noticeable. On their helmets, there were the letters SS. On a black collar patch, there were also the letters SS. On a black band on the left cuff was the name Adolf Hitler. They did not know the full facts, because at this stage of the war, no-one was yet aware of the fanatical Waffen SS. They did know these men would need to be handled with extraordinary care.

As they neared the village of Bambecque, Captain Bill Haywood, the Adjutant of the 8th Royal Worcesters, tells the story.

> During the early-morning stand-to I saw a wonderful sight. Round the corner as I came out of Battalion HQ appeared the survivors of the

5th Gloucesters. They were dirty and weary and haggard but unbeaten. Their eyes were sunken and red from lack of sleep and their feet as they marched seemed to me no more than an inch from the ground. At their head limped a few prisoners with Hauting, the Adjutant in close attendance. I spotted Major Mason and young Shephard with his head bandaged. The column halted and two of the Germans flopped down exhausted, though the captured officer remained standing and tried to look defiant. I ran towards Colonel Buxton, who was staggering along, obviously wounded. He croaked a greeting and I saw lumps of sleep in his bloodshot eyes. 'I'm peppered all over, Bill, none of it serious.' Our Commanding Officer came running out and told the 5th Gloucesters second-in-command to rest the troops for a minute. I took Colonel Buxton indoors, gave him a tumbler of stale wine and eased him gently to the floor on a blanket, assuring him again and again that his men were alright. In a few seconds he was asleep.

The 8th Worcesters had taken casualties and the group who helped the Gloucesters are best described as remnants.

Wednesday, 29 May 1940, Bambecque, France

In the morning, they ate breakfast like they had never eaten before. They were dirty, dishevelled and desperate. They had not changed their clothes for nearly three weeks. Bill Adlam, however, still had enough spirit to clean his teeth. He carried his toothbrush all the way through the war. Toothpaste was an unimaginable luxury, but salt did a reasonable job. The Worcesters had provided trucks to take them to their next destination, Rexpoëde.

The news came through that the Belgians had surrendered en masse. The King of the Belgians had signed a surrender document without consulting the British or the French. That meant that the northern flank would be that much weaker. Never had getting out of a country seemed such an attractive proposition. Why would those trucks not come? It seemed hours!

The trucks took the surviving Gloucesters the ten kilometres to Rexpoëde. On the way, they passed ashen-faced French people heading for the coast.

'We'll be back! We'll be back!' some of the Gloucesters had shouted.

'Do you believe we'll be back, Bill?'

'Dunno but I do hope so for their sakes. Life under Mr Hitler is not going to be much fun.'

'At least we haven't got to bloody well walk it.'

On the road, there were thousands of stragglers. They were desperate. Every last one was asking to be picked up.

'Stop for us lads! Stop for us, you bastards! You can't leave us to Jerry!'

Ever since the debacle of Brussels, everyone knew the rule. There was no stopping for stragglers, it was now an unaffordable luxury.

The Gloucesters arrived at Rexpoëde late morning.

'Right, everybody out except the wounded!'

'What?'

'We need the trucks to carry the wounded only. Able-bodied men and walking wounded out. Come on! There's no time to mess about. Get off those flippin' trucks when you're told!'

Something else happened at Rexpoëde. Some half dozen of the Royal Warwicks had arrived there earlier. They had been at Wormhoudt, just north of the Gloucesters' position. They were telling of a massacre, which had taken place in a barn. Other British soldiers had been gunned down in the town square, in cold blood. Still others were massacred at a military dressing station. Others had been stripped to the waist and machine-gunned against a wall. They did not know the numbers, but it was clear that over 100 British soldiers had been murdered. These were the sounds of firing squads which Bill and the other Gloucesters had heard from Ledringhem. The Royal Warwicks were able to say something else of importance, 'The ones who did it were the ones in greenish uniforms; not the ones in grey.'

The Germans in the greenish uniforms were the second and third battalions of the SS Leibstandarte Adolf Hitler. These troops, who would later be called the Waffen SS, were different to the regular German army. They were committed and dedicated Nazi true-believers and took a personal oath of loyalty to Adolf Hitler. The ethos of the SS was to give your life for Hitler and to extend the same terms to your adversaries.

You could not reason with these people, only shoot them.

The three German prisoners remained under close guard. What were the Gloucesters going to do with them? The eyewitness histories say they were 'handed over' but to whom?

Thursday, 30 May 1940, Bray Dunes, Near Dunkirk

The Gloucesters left at midnight and arrived at Bray Dunes at 0430. It was wet, it was miserable, and it was cold. Given their state of utter exhaustion, a hike of that length at that speed with full kit is a feat of exceptional endurance. All along the route, there were lorries that had run out of petrol and had been set on fire to keep them out of German hands. Loose French cavalry horses were everywhere. Burned-out fighter planes littered the countryside. Every farmhouse was a blackened, ruined shell, looted and burned. Dunkirk to the north-west was burning, now they were close to enough to smell it. Clouds of acrid black smoke arose angrily to the clouds and beyond. The refugees were more piteous than any they had previously seen. To the south, there were sounds of heavy artillery, to the east and west, there were the sounds of heavy artillery. The Germans were not far away in any direction. They were close to Bray Dunes but that did not mean they were home and dry. It meant that they had to cross the beach, find a boat and then cross the channel.

The town was packed with thousands upon thousands of traumatised British and French troops. They were in the final state of exhaustion. Tired red eyes looked at the beach, which was lined with hundreds of burning vehicles. As the grey dawn rose, Bill could see across the grey murky sea and found something quite astonishing. There were small boats. At first, it seemed as if there were dozens. As the light strengthened, he could see that there were scores. Eventually, they saw that there were hundreds. Beyond the small boats, there were larger boats. Cross-channel ferries, fishing boats, coastal vessels, tramp steamers, Thames barges. Someone had organised this. Someone was actually organising the beach into orderly queues. It was as if someone had gone into that dystopian catastrophe and organised what looked like queues for London buses. It was orderly, it was civilised, and it was all terribly fair. A man from the Gloucesters might be standing next to a Coldstream guardsman, an East Lancashire fusilier or a Frenchman from any one of a dozen French divisions. It did not matter. Order was slowly emerging out of chaos.

The endless snaking queues of men edged their way forward. A small boat might only pick up 20, maybe only ten men. Then, it would shuttle back to a larger ship, offload the men and return to pick up some more. And the queues moved on.

'Right, that's enough for this boat.'

Off it chugged to the mothership. The mothership would wait until it was overloaded but still just about seaworthy and it would peel away for Blighty's shore. This would have been the first time that Bill Adlam thought he would actually make it back to England. He did not know how many of the Gloucesters had been lost, but he did know it was a lot. He had been so sleep-deprived and so traumatised by the endless marches, the house to house fighting and the final desperate withdrawal.

'Right, you lot! Who's for Blighty? Follow me.'

He did not need to repeat the order. The sleeping beauties leapt into action within seconds. The officer organised them into a single column, three abreast. The column moved forwards through the dunes, over the beaches and past sentries posted at a cricket-pitch length apart, their rifles at the ready.

'What are those guys for?'

'They have orders to shoot queue-jumpers.'

From further down the beach, a sharp *crack* could be heard.

'See what I mean?'

Had someone really shot a queue-jumper? He was past caring. Now it was Bill's turn. He had placed his rifle as instructed onto a pile of rifles to be destroyed. He followed the queue into the sea. Now his boots were full of salt water. Now his filthy battle dress was immersed in water up to the waist. It was the first time that water had touched his body in three weeks. Now his nostrils were filled with the tang of seawater, which was very pleasant after the smells of cordite, blood and excrement that he had experienced over the last couple of days. Now the heavy serge material of his uniform felt as heavy as lead with the seawater it was absorbing. Now he was up to his chest and his toothbrush was covered with seawater. Ahead of him, men were being picked up. It was all terribly orderly and British. A small boat approached crewed by a couple of British civilians.

'Right! Next ten!' shouted a voice from somewhere. This included Bill. Hands came from over a gunwale and hauled him into the boat.

'Thanks, lads!'

'Get out of the bloody way, there's plenty more to load up, you know.'

Then he was taken for a quick five-minute ferry ride to the larger ship.

'Come on, bloody move yourselves, get up here quickly.'

Now he was on the larger ship. He was soaked from foot to shoulders. He had lost all of his kit and his rifle. His helmet and gasmask had disappeared, but he was still alive. He was alive. He had to laugh. He was still alive and on a ship that would take him back to England if the Luftwaffe didn't sink them first. The engines of the ship hummed, and he felt the ship lurch and roll and slip its moorings in the roads outside of Bray Dunes. Looking back the horizon was still a mass of flame and smoke. On his right, Dunkirk Harbour was ablaze from one end to the other, but the Navy were still using it to load men onto destroyers. An hour later, he was being shooed off the boat onto a jetty somewhere in England without ceremony, grace or even politeness.

'Come on you lot, move yourselves! We've got to go back. Get off and let's get on with it. Wake up those buggers over there and tell them to get down the flippin' gangplank.'

All around him, other boats were disgorging their thousands of survivors from the catastrophe of Dunkirk. His first footstep onto British territory would have been one of unutterable emotion. For the first time in three weeks, he now felt he was going to survive. It is not known what port he washed up in. The last ten Gloucesters finished up on an ancient wheezing paddle-steamer, the *Glen Avon* and ended up miles from Dover in Harwich. The smoke from Dunkirk still blazed up to the sky. The sounds of battle could still be heard clearly over 50 kilometres of water. His most important agenda on that Thursday morning was sleep. Sleep, what a beautiful word!

In a 1940 letter to his regiment's magazine, now in the Soldiers of Gloucestershire Museum's archives, Major F.W. Priestly of the 5th Gloucesters recalled the events at Dunkirk.

During the day evacuation was commenced by wading out to small boats for conveyance to ships in the 'roads'. For this purpose, lines of men three deep were formed in various areas of the beach and were finally embarked. The last party consisting of the Second-in-command, Captain Mason Berenger (The French Agent de Liaison) CSM Wilcox and ten 'other-ranks' were picked up at 0400 hrs 31 May and were taken to the paddle steamer *Glen Avon* which was moving off for Harwich. Small parties of the battalion were collected in this way and deposited at various ports on the English coast and despatched inland by waiting troop trains.

Back at Wormhoudt, the incoming 20th Panzergrenadiers found seven of the Royal Warwicks still alive after the massacre, despite suffering from appalling wounds. The medical orderlies of the German Army brought them back to health, with the exception of one man who died of wounds. It was the same unit of medical orderlies who looked after the three officers left behind at Ledringhem, Captain Norris, Lieutenant Norris and Lieutenant Dewsnap.

Chapter 6

The Road to Buckingham Palace

Sunday, 2 June 1940, Kington, Herefordshire, England

The 5th Battalion eventually gathered at Kington in Herefordshire, a total of 400. Half the battalion had not made it back. That left a hollow feeling in the stomach.

'Sergeant Adlam, colonel's tent straight away!'
'Oh? What's it about?'
'You been busy on the black market?'
'Chance would be a fine thing!'
'He wants you straight away, at the double, sarge!'

Bill doubled smartly to the colonel's tent in the prescribed manner to find him smiling broadly and several officers present. There was something in the air. He had walked into a lot of officers' meetings before, but they didn't smile like this. He entered the tent, saluted and came sharply to attention.

'You sent for me, sir?'
'At ease, Adlam.'
'Sir.'
'You'd better read this.'

What on earth was going on? The Colonel seemed to hold onto the envelope just a little too long as if he were savouring the moment. The bevy of officers were smiling even more broadly. As he opened the envelope, he saw the words Buckingham Palace. He looked at the Colonel who was smiling even more broadly.

'What the heck?'

Buckingham Palace, London SW1
From the office of the Private Secretary to his Majesty King George VI
To Sergeant William George Adlam, 5th Battalion, the Gloucestershire Regiment.
It is my pleasure to inform you that His Majesty King George VI has graciously awarded you the Military Medal for gallantry of the highest order in an incident at Grindorff in France on 3 March 1940.

> *The investiture will take place at Buckingham Palace, London SW on Thursday 13 June 1940 at 10.30 am. You may bring a relative or friend with you.*
> *Please read the attached notice, which sets out the regulations, under which the medal and ribbon may be worn and the correct use of postnominal letters. You may proceed to use the latter immediately upon receipt of this summons. Please confirm via your battalion's adjutant whether you will bring a person with you.*
> *For Private Secretary to His Majesty*
> *Sir Alan Frederick Lascelles, GCB, GCVO, CMG, MC*

He froze. He read it again. Somewhere in the distance the Colonel said, 'Bloody well done, Adlam, you've done the regiment proud.' The officers were clapping and patting him on the back. There was Major Biddle shaking his hand.

'Well thank you, sir. I'm just totally amazed.'

'Well, I didn't want to mention it before', said the Colonel confidentially, 'because I didn't want to be responsible for your disappointment if it didn't go through.'

'It's been all over the bloody battalion for weeks!' said one of the officers.

They all laughed. The twinkle in Bill's eye said that he had heard the rumour too.

One handshake was of special importance and, later in the war, to be of great significance.

'Well done, Sergeant Adlam!'

It was Major Biddle who spoke.

'Sir!'

'At ease, I heard of your escapade with the Bren gun, I just wanted to shake your hand and say "well done".'

The euphoria of the medal award faded as reality crashed in on his world. The Britain to which Bill Adlam had returned was not the one which he had left. Bread, as he knew it, had disappeared. Unlike other foodstuffs, it was not rationed but there was now only one kind of bread, the national loaf. It was grey and rather solid. Bill's beloved HP sauce had disappeared from the shelves during his time in France. It seemed, now, that if you wanted to get hold of many foodstuffs you had to know the shopkeeper very well and he would keep something under the counter for you.

It was a serious offence for a grocer to sell even a packet of tea to an unregistered person.

Everyone was reminded that they had to carry their gasmask everywhere. The Air Raid Protection people, in their black helmets, would have visited the colonel to remind him of the serious consequences of letting any light be seen after dark.

'The first time, it's a fine, sir, then they send you away.'

After a charge down a village street into German machine guns, being 'sent away' really held no horrors for any of them. Although it would have been unpatriotic to say so.

Having survived, Bill Adlam was now witness to the worst time in British history since the threat posed by the Spanish Armada in 1588. Everything went against Britain. There seemed to be no light at the end of a tunnel or even a tunnel, which was capable of leading to a light.

Tuesday, 4 June 1940, Kington, Herefordshire, England

'Come on, you lot!'

'What's going on?'

'We're all going over to the adjutant's tent. Mr Churchill is making a speech to the nation.'

It was a moment that no-one who was there will ever forget. It was a long speech delivered in the House of Commons. It would have been received in total silence on that muddy field in Kington in Herefordshire. The part, which moved them and which they would never forget, was the last paragraph.

> Even though large tracts of Europe and many old and famous States have fallen or may fall into the grip of the Gestapo and all the odious apparatus of Nazi rule, we shall not flag or fail. We shall go on to the end, we shall fight in France, we shall fight on the seas and oceans, we shall fight with growing confidence and growing strength in the air, we shall defend our Island, whatever the cost may be, we shall fight on the beaches, we shall fight on the landing grounds, we shall fight in the fields and in the streets, we shall fight in the hills; we shall never surrender.

The adjutant turned off the radio. No-one spoke.

'Fight on the beaches? Fight in the hills? Never surrender?'

That is right.
That is exactly right!

Saturday, 8 June 1940, Kington, Herefordshire, England

'Jarmany calling, Jarmany calling.'

'It's that bastard Haw-Haw again, turn that bloody radio off.'

'Hang on; let's hear what the sod has to say.'

'This is Jarmany calling from Reichsender Hambursh and stations Bremen and DXB on the 31-metre band.'

They waited for Haw-Haw's would-be-posh British but sneering tones to talk down to them.

'The Jarman government announces a historic and strategic defeat over those who wish to deny her historic destiny. The British and French forces, who began their attack on Jarmany last September have now been literally pushed back into the sea in the area around Dunkirk.'

The hideous drawl finished. The hatred among the listeners at Kington Camp would have been mirrored many thousands of times over across the United Kingdom. Lord Haw-Haw was to achieve a level of unpopularity, which, if it were possible, outdid that of Hitler.

Thursday, 13 June 1940, London

'Sloane Square… Victoria… St James' Park, this is it, Bill!'

Bill and his older brother, Ossie, an RAF bandsman, walked past large imposing buildings, now minus their name plaques. They were obviously places of some importance, but the requirements of wartime secrecy meant they were now sinister and anonymous. Each one had heavily sandbagged doors and windows taped up to prevent bomb shatter. There were bored sentries with bayonets menacingly fixed to their rifles and with gasmasks over their shoulders. The whole place was on a war footing. Bill and Ossie turned the corner. *There it was!* The palace was magnificent! In front of it was a huge park. This was presumably the park that gave the tube station its name. In peacetime, it would have been a wonder.

Now, it was covered with dozens of tents. These were for the troops who manned the anti-aircraft guns, which were now searching the skies 24 hours a day. More troops operated the barrage balloons which presided over the park and the palace and the whole of London, to prevent the German Heinkel and Dornier bombers coming too close to their target.

The once-magnificent ponds were drained but he was glad to see a truck marked 'NAAFI'. The NAAFI (Navy Army and Air Force Institutes) was the organisation that provided canteen facilities, shops and recreational facilities for other ranks. They made cups of tea, and bacon sandwiches for the troops, who had the same, bored expression on their faces as Bill had seen in Alsace. He hoped for their sakes that they stay bored. Bill was in a position to advise them that boredom was better than the alternative.

They walked through the park and up to the imposing, black-iron railings outside of the palace. To Bill's surprise, a crowd was gathering outside. Some were in service uniforms, some in civvies, most had family members with them. The women, in particular, were massively enjoying the event and had dressed up in their best veiled hats, fur coats and the family jewellery. Many had schoolboys with them, resplendent in neatly pressed blazers and wearing caps. There was excitement in the air.

'What do you suppose the crowd is for, Ossie?'

'I reckon they want to see the heroes get their medals.'

'Well, I'm not a bloody hero.'

'Officially you are, Bill! Er, I think we have to go through that gate over on the left.'

The policeman saluted as Bill and Ossie approached, with the envelope in hand. Bill would have noted that it was a very sloppy civvy salute. He would have died rather than make a salute like that.

'Right, sir, can I just see your summons? Sergeant, you are being presented? If you would go through that door over there and someone will see to you. If your friend will just go through that door on the left, an usher will guide you to the viewing area.'

Bill entered a large anteroom. Soldiers, sailors and airmen were milling around, making light, inconsequential chatter. An equerry entered, he wore the uniform of some esoteric unit and not one, which had seen the muck and action of Grindorff, Bruyelle or Ledringhem. His exotic golden lanyards and expensively tailored uniform marked him as a serviceman different to those that Bill knew.

'Sailors and Royal Marines over here, if you would, gentlemen. Airmen over here and soldiers over here.'

It was clear that of the 50 or so awardees, the Royal Air Force was by far the best represented, with some two thirds of the group.

'Gentlemen,' the equerry continued, 'firstly, I will order you into the sequence in which you will be presented to His Majesty. You will stay in this sequence and an usher will lead you out in groups into the inner quadrangle.'

'The king has just arrived,' whispered a voice.

Bill was now starting to feel tense. People from gritty Gloucester backstreets did not normally get into the inner sanctums of Buckingham Palace to meet the king. He could have pinched himself.

He was there, he really was!

'Ready, everyone, if you would, please. Now, here are the rules of etiquette in front of His Majesty. You will speak only if spoken to. You address him as "Your Majesty", the first time and as "sir", thereafter. You only answer any question which he puts to you directly. It is not your place to continue a dialogue with His Majesty. When you are summoned, you will step forward, salute smartly and come to attention. Is everyone quite clear?' drawled the equerry.

The assembled multitude nodded their assent. A couple of 'yes, sirs' were to be heard.

'Follow me, if you would, gentlemen.' Bill found himself at the bottom of a wooden ramp. At the top of the ramp were several extremely senior officers. He noted that the soldiers all wore the red trimmings, shiny Sam Browne belts and burnished brass of staff officers. Then he saw a most curious-looking man. He was immensely tall and dressed in a morning suit but with a wooden leg. He stood at the top of a ramp, which led to the King's standing position.

Beside him stood a man of modest stature in the uniform of an Admiral of the Fleet, it was His Majesty, King George VI. To Bill's right were some dozen rows of chairs with family members waiting to watch the presentations. Ossie must be there somewhere. Bill did not dare to look for him or the temptation to wave would have been too great, which in turn would incur the wrath of the tall man with the wooden leg and immediate confinement in the Tower of London.

The tall man with the wooden leg read the sheet, whispered a sentence or two to the king and nodded to the awardee to step forward. The awardee, an airman, duly snapped to attention and stepped forward to receive his award. Bill would have noticed that airmen's drill was really a bit sloppy.

It was barely better than the policeman outside the gates. The Brylcreem Boys, as the army called the Royal Air Force, were just not up to it when it came to drill.

A figure moved at a window. He looked up and it was Queen Elizabeth watching the investiture. What could she be thinking? She had to be thinking that these men and a lot more like them were needed to keep her brother-in-law, the former King Edward VIII, out of Buckingham Palace as Adolf Hitler's right-hand man. Would Bill rather die than disappoint her? Yes, he would, and he knew that every man in the investiture that day and every man in Kington camp would do the same.

'Sergeant Adlam!'

It was the usher calling him forward. The 20 paces up the ramp seemed to take several years. His hobnailed boots clattered as he walked up and the sound echoed around the quadrangle. He gave a bravura performance of a salute and came smartly to attention like a British soldier. There was no telling him that the Brigade of Guards were one iota smarter than the Gloucesters!

The man with the wooden leg whispered 'Adlam' to the King and a couple of details.

George VI, King by the Grace of God, Defender of the Faith and Emperor of India presented Bill Adlam, from Carmarthen Street in Gloucester, with the Military Medal for conspicuous gallantry in the face of the enemy.

'Sergeant Adlam, you are a very brave man. Your retrieval of the Bren gun was an act of great courage and initiative. The British people are grateful to you.'

'Thank you, Your Majesty!'

The man with the wooden leg nodded, Bill performed a perfect right-face and marched smartly off the podium. Another usher showed him the way back to the anteroom.

He could hardly believe that it was true. He had just saluted the King of the British Empire with Queen Elizabeth watching from a window. He looked at the medal. It was all so vague; it had happened in an instant and now he had actually been awarded a medal. Would he retrieve that Bren gun again to keep the Nazi bastards out of England, out of Carmarthen Street in Gloucester and out of this place?

Yes, he would, a thousand times yes!

Tuesday, 18 June 1940, Kington, Herefordshire

Winston Churchill again spoke to the nation. Bill heard it again on a crackly radio connected to a generator outside the adjutant's tent. Once again, the speech was of Shakespearean magnificence and once again, the payload was in the final memorable paragraph.

> What General Weygand called the Battle of France is over. I expect that the Battle of Britain is about to begin. Upon this battle depends the survival of Christian civilisation. Upon it depends our own British life, and the long continuity of our institutions and our Empire. The whole fury and might of the enemy must very soon be turned on us. Hitler knows that he will have to break us in this Island or lose the war. If we can stand up to him, all Europe may be free and the life of the world may move forward into broad, sunlit uplands. But if we fail, then the whole world, including the United States, including all that we have known and cared for, will sink into the abyss of a new Dark Age made more sinister, and perhaps more protracted, by the lights of perverted science. Let us therefore brace ourselves to our duties, and so bear ourselves that, if the British Empire and its Commonwealth last for a thousand years, men will still say, 'This was their finest hour.'

At the time, it did not feel like their finest hour. Eighty years later, Churchill was right; this was the finest hour in the history of the British Isles.

Chapter 7

With the Commandos at Weymouth

Friday, 12 July 1940, Oxford

Bill had to pinch himself. His orders had sent him to an address outside of Oxford for assessment into a new unit, for which he had volunteered. He found himself approaching the gracious aristocratic mansion of Headington Hill Hall in Oxford. That was one good thing about the war, backstreet boys were invited into the domains of Britain's elite, perhaps tolerated rather than welcomed. The hall had belonged in years past to one of London's premier and most fashionable socialites, Lady Ottoline Morrel of the Bloomsbury set. She was not only literati, she was glitterati. In a previous peaceful century, Oscar Wilde had danced there dressed as Prince Rupert of the Rhine. Now it was surrounded by khaki-clad grim-looking sentries who hailed from places like Hartlepool, Birkenhead and postal regions of London of which Lady Ottoline had never heard. They carried fixed bayonets, deployed barbed wire and sandbags, manned Bren gun positions and were ordered about by officious officers and hard NCOs. The once spacious gardens were now a car park, sullied with officers' cars, a variety of military transport and motorcycles used by the despatch riders.

As he approached the Italianate stairway, it could have gone through his mind that he may have made a very dubious choice in life. Bill had done the one thing that old sweats (as the army called its veterans) are supposed never to do, volunteer. He had seen a notice at Kington asking for volunteers for a new special duties unit. He was keen to see what it had to offer. There were accounts to be settled with Mr Hitler and his representatives.

'Up the stairs on the left and wait in that room until you're called for interview!'

Winston Churchill had created this new group just ten days earlier. They were to be called commandos although only a few senior officers 'in the know' knew this word already.

The immediate task of this new force was to defend Britain in the case of a German attack. Their immediate job would be to 'spring at the throats of any small landings or descents'. The main long-term purpose, however, was to mount 'tip and run' raids on the European mainland, to undertake small specific raids of tactical and strategic importance. The job of this new commando unit was designed to cause maximum effect against the German war effort with minimum effort to the British war effort. 'Tip and run' raids would shortly evolve into 'butcher and bolt'. This new and, as yet unheralded force was to be made up of a new kind of soldier, technically excellent, extremely resourceful and utterly aggressive. It was to be an elite unit.

Tuesday, 23 July 1940, Weymouth

After his delight at being accepted and posted to No 4 Commando, Bill was given a travel warrant for a train to Weymouth where, to his astonishment, the adjutant told him to find his own billet. He'd never seen that before. This was his first inkling that commandos did things in different ways to the conventional line regiments, and this was just the start. Bill was now to learn about his new comrades in arms. The Commanding Officer, Colonel Legard, had represented Great Britain in the Pentathlon at the 1932 and 1936 Olympic Games. He was one of very few British people who had seen Adolf Hitler in the flesh. One detail from the fabulous propaganda success of the 1936 games had now assumed great symbolic importance. The British Olympic team had only given an eyes-right salute to the Führer. The French, however, had actually given a full-blown Nazi salute.

Bill loved the new sort of comrade in arms he was now teamed with. Over in 3 Commando in Plymouth, Major 'Mad Jack' Churchill, a former model for Brylcreem hair products, was wont to go into battle playing the bagpipes or wielding a Claymore sword. According to rumour, he had been on patrol at L'Epinette in Northern France, two months previously and cut down a German sentry with an arrow from his long bow. Apparently, it had been a personal ambition.

Then there was 'Old' Sir Roger. He was the man who headed up this new sort of army. This was Admiral of the Fleet Sir Roger Keyes. Bill had heard that name before, but where? It came to him. Sir Roger was the man who had walked into Parliament in full Admiral of the Fleet uniform and gave such a critical speech about Neville Chamberlain that Chamberlain had resigned and paved the way for Winston Churchill to take over in the top job. 'Old' Sir Roger was a person of such position, prestige and connection that he was listened to. His access and influence with Winston Churchill were crucial as to how the commandos would be formed and the amount of priority which they received.

In short, Bill Adlam had progressed to the elite of the armed forces. He was surrounded by larger-than-life characters and in an elite unit which made up the rules of warfare as they went along. He was in his element!

The great problem facing higher authority was that they had now assembled this elite branch of the fighting services but no-one seemed to know what 'elite' meant.

This was duly set out for No 2 Commando by Lieutenant Colonel Newman in 'the commando catechism'. It was to apply to all commandos equally. Bill Adlam fitted the concept very well and better than most.

At the other end of the scale 'returned to unit', also known as RTU, swiftly became a badge of shame. It meant that the commandos had rejected you, either for physical or character reasons. Deep in Bill Adlam's psyche was the resolve that the ignominy of RTU was never, never going to happen to him. Death down that street in Ledringhem was far preferable.

Training commenced with what little resources they had. This began with 50-kilometre marches in full kit, in all weathers, by day and night. One of the great ways of organising men to march in time is to sing. 'Roll out the Barrel', 'It's a Long Way to Tipperary' and 'Ten Green Bottles' were great favourites. Bill must have reflected, with bitter irony, that one of the most popular songs, which the Gloucesters had sung in France 'We're Going to Hang Out the Washing on the Siegfried Line' had now disappeared. He had seen the Siegfried Line from the top of his church tower in Alsace. The Siegfried Line had won. The marches went on and on and on.

The 'returned to unit' figures went on an upward trajectory as men failed to achieve the standards. In some units, the RTU figure could be as high as 50 per cent.

The marches pushed on from 30 miles in one day to 120 miles (200 kilometres) over four days. Bill would have heard that over in 2 Commando, Lieutenant Colonel Newman led his soldiers all the way. That put pressure on Bill's Colonel Legard to do the same. Legard was well able to respond. The nights were spent in bivouacs, in barns or sometimes, exhausted soldiers would just flop into a field and fall immediately asleep. Bill's experience in France had already given him old sweat status. He would be able to say with the total conviction of the experienced,

'It was worse than this in France. A lot worse, and we were on half rations part of the time and foraging for food for the rest.'

'What? Worse than this lot?'

'Well, a bit worse!'

Friday, 2 August 1940, Lulworth Cove, Dorset

After three weeks, at last there was to be weaponry training! Lulworth Cove is a beach area in Dorset of outstanding natural beauty. In 1940, barbed wire quarantined it from the public gaze. The local sheep farmers had been removed perfunctorily by the War Office to enable military training to take place. This is where reality began to bite. Transport had to be organised from local truck operators. The battalion had only two cars for officers. No other transport was available. It was now being used by grateful German troops where they had left it behind in France.

Similarly, there was only enough ammunition for 25 rounds per man. So many rifles and so much ammunition had been abandoned or destroyed in the days before Dunkirk, that all material was in short supply. The battalion had a small number of Boys anti-tank rifles. These were so scarce that they were kept in the headquarters troop and only let out on a rota basis. Thanks to Sir Roger's influence and pull, the commandos were not at the back of the queue for munitions, they were at the front. What the shortages were like elsewhere in the shattered British Army was a matter not to dwell on. If the Germans attacked, it was a complete mystery how they could be stopped.

The other great aspect to training at Lulworth was Tyneham. This was a village, which Bill would have noted was not unlike Ledringhem. The villagers had been moved out. Tyneham has still not been reoccupied eight decades later. In 1940, the buildings, streets, shops and offices were a training ground for combat in a closed area. As more weaponry became available, plus the necessary dummy rounds and thunderflashes (grenades without shrapnel) the commandos were able to exercise and develop drills. Bill's experience at Ledringhem would have been invaluable here. Unlike other British Army units, commando officers were not above listening to other ranks.

Bill would have been able to explain to his senior officers how the 20th Panzergrenadiers had displayed a level of drill and manoeuvre, which British soldiers could only gape at in wonderment. Tyneham was the heaven-sent opportunity for the British to catch up to the Germans.

Sunday, 11 August 1940, Weymouth, Dorset

'Oh God! There are bloody hundreds of them!'

It was just after 10 o'clock in the morning. The air-raid sirens sounded. Civilians ran for the air-raid shelters, which in Weymouth were few. Most people ran home and hid in the crude but effective Anderson shelter, a metal shed-like structure half buried in the garden, which gave some protection against bombs and which almost every house in the country possessed. Some just sat under the stairs. Some hardy souls chose to stay outside and watch the raids develop. One aspect of an air raid was quite clear, if a bomb headed in your direction, the makeshift air-raid precautions and especially, the Anderson shelters were not going to save you.

At 10.09, the German escorts arrived. Even though they were high they were identifiable as Messerschmitt 110s and Junkers 88s, twin-engine destroyer fighters. Immediately, the first of some 70 fighters, Spitfires and Hurricanes got in among them. The German fighters were hefty planes, heavily armed but their manoeuvrability did not match that of the RAF planes. The first of the German planes fell to the earth in flames. From ground level, great waves of cheering arose.

The bombers, Heinkels and Dorniers, tried to slip in unnoticed underneath the dogfight. The ploy did not work. Late arriving British fighters got in among them and soon, several were hurtling earthwards with plumes of yellow flame and black smoke behind them. A small number of parachutes wafted gently down.

'I don't fancy those blokes' chances if some of the farmers around here get them before the Home Guard do! You can have a nasty accident with a pitchfork!'

'I wouldn't imagine there would be too much in the way of questions asked!'

Despite the attentions of the RAF, some German bombers were successfully getting through. The targets were clear now, Weymouth and Portland docks. The size of the German bomber fleet could be seen from the ground, but the damage in Weymouth was modest. The German attackers totally missed the docks but they had tragically demolished Messrs Devenish and Grove's Brewery. Some 35 houses were hit and were in various states of demolition. Two vegetable allotments were obliterated.

The Germans were more successful in Portland where burning oil tanks sent plumes of opaque, greasy, black smoke up into the stratosphere. Late in the attack, some squadrons of Messerschmitt 109 fighters appeared quickly over the horizon to cover the retreat. The Luftwaffe had taken a mauling and disappeared over the horizon harassed by Spitfires and Hurricanes firing the last rounds of the day and bringing the last stragglers down into the drink. The siren sounded the all-clear.

That night Lord Haw-Haw was to claim that the German raiders had shot down 57 British planes, including two Curtiss Hawks. That was much talked about in the pubs of Weymouth. Royal Air Force men pointed out whimsically that this was interesting. The RAF only ever used Curtiss Hawks in India and Burma.

The true number of RAF planes shot down was 16, mainly by the Messerschmitt 109s. The total number of German planes involved was fixed at 165, the biggest number yet in what was already being called the Battle of Britain.

One of the commandos was to return home to find his bedroom in perfect order except that one wall was completely missing. Otherwise, the feeling was that the Luftwaffe's raid was a waste of effort.

Tuesday, 20 August 1940, Weymouth

Once again, Mr Churchill was to give a speech to the nation. Radio was the most vital means of communication in war-torn Britain. It helped to take peoples' minds off the nagging and ever-present threat of invasion and the hideous prospect of Nazi occupation. Comedians, such as Ted Ray, Jewell and Warriss and the Crazy Gang, attracted enormous audiences on the airwaves. *Workers Playtime* was listened to by millions at home and was piped daily into factories, barrack rooms and airfields across the country. Singers such as Noel Coward sang songs like 'London Pride' as a morale-booster during the bombing. Others like Vera Lynn sang popular tunes, many with a patriotic overtone such as 'Seagulls over the White Cliffs of Dover' and 'We'll Meet Again'. Marlene Dietrich was massively popular with 'Lili Marlene. This was odd because Ms Dietrich was German, although virulently anti-Hitler.

The British Government and British Broadcasting Corporation were reeling at the popular success of the Prime Minister's earlier rousing broadcasts. They had expected success but not on this scale. By the middle of August, the Battle of Britain was approaching a crescendo. For weeks now, the Luftwaffe had attacked RAF stations and docks along the south coast. Every attack had been repulsed. The thin line of defence had wavered, sometimes tottered but never quite broken. The performance by the RAF Fighter Command had been outstanding in the annals of military history.

This latest speech contained a sentence which everyone, who heard, it would remember for the rest of their lives.

> The gratitude of every home in our Island, in our Empire, and indeed throughout the world, except in the abodes of the guilty, goes out to the British airmen who, undaunted by odds, unwearied in their constant challenge and mortal danger, are turning the tide of the World War by their prowess and by their devotion. **Never in the field of human conflict was so much owed by so many to so few.** All hearts go out to the fighter pilots, whose brilliant actions we see with our own eyes day after day…'

Bill, unfortunately, did not hear the broadcast, he was on a simulated attack to Maiden Castle some 20 miles north of Weymouth. Maiden Castle is the largest iron-age hill fort in England. This fascinating fact was totally lost on 4 Commando, who were attacking it in the role of a German airfield, with the objective of destroying as many of the aircraft on the ground as possible. Those new and sophisticated battlefield manoeuvres were beginning to be worked out and taught.

Chapter 8

Of Cromwell and Cavalry

Saturday, 7 September 1940, Weymouth

It had not been a good day. Two hundred German bombers had bombed the East End of London that afternoon. They had hit warehouses and rail facilities and hundreds of people were homeless. Hitler was changing tack. He was not hitting the fighter stations of Kent and Sussex, he was now hitting the docks, the civilian population of London and anyone who stood in his way.

It was 8.30 in the evening of an otherwise uneventful day in Weymouth. The Billy Cotton Band Show was just starting on the radio.

'Can't beat Billy Cotton,' said the landlord. 'Anything to take your mind off this bloody war!'

'I'm a Jewell and Warriss man, myself,' said Bill.

There was a furious banging on the door.

'Well, we're not showing any lights outside so bugger off!' said the landlord.

'Language!' said the landlady.

'It doesn't sound like the air-raid wardens, I think we'd better answer it,' said Bill.

It was a private from another company, he was out of breath and in great distress.

'Sergeant Adlam, colonel's orders, everyone to muster at the pavilion, Jerry's landed.'

'What?'

'Message from higher command, everyone to anti-invasion duties.'

The private ran on down the street to alert more soldiers who lived in the same street.

'Bill, what do we do?'

'Right 'ang on a minute, I'll just get my kit.'

He ran upstairs as fast as his stockinged feet would take him. What kit was he to take? There were no standing orders to cope with this emergency.

Did he take full service marching order or battle order? He decided on battle order, it was quicker and lighter. What anti-invasion duties had the private talked about? There weren't any. He decided not to reveal that to the landlady and landlord.

'Right, well let's just think while I get my kit on.'

He pulled on his battledress blouse and buttoned it in regulation fashion.

'Well first off, don't panic. Keep the radio on the light programme or the Home Service and listen for any announcements.'

He pulled on his webbing, tightened it and checked how many rounds of .303 ammunition he had. Not many.

'Then, make some sandwiches and get some bottles of water and be ready to leave home if necessary. Do not go unless you have to.'

He blackened his face with a piece of burnt cork, kept handy for just such an exigency.

'If they come from the sea, go up into the hills. You've got some friends in the villages a few miles north, haven't you? Well, be prepared to go to them.'

'We can't just land on their doorstep in the middle of the night, Bill.'

'Oh, yes you can! When you've seen what I saw in France, you'll find it very easy.'

He wiped his hands and checked his grenades. Not yet primed. He inserted the fuses.

'What if they come from the air?'

'Just go in whatever direction takes you away from them.'

'Are they likely to kill us?'

'You can't tell. Some places in France they were OK, some places they weren't. The main thing is not to upset them, or they will just shoot you.'

He checked his rifle. It was loaded with the safety catch on. He inserted his bayonet into the scabbard in his webbing.

'If the balloon really has gone up, I'll try and get a truck to pick you up. There's no promises. I've got no idea where they will send me.'

'OK, Bill, we understand.'

Finally, he pulled on his helmet, grabbed his gasmask, pulled on his heavy boots and ran out of the door.

The hobnails on the soles of his boots rang out as he ran through silent streets all the way to the pavilion. People were staying at home in fear of what might happen if they ventured outdoors. He was very glad to be this fit and managed it within ten minutes. What he found was total chaos.

Colonel Legard had told the battalion that their role, in case of an invasion, was as mobile reserves behind the coast. It now became obvious that the only transport – the colonel's staff car and a small truck – were all that was available to transport 500 men. The colonel was giving appropriate orders about securing the docks, setting up roadblocks and removing civilians from key points but it was all ad hoc, improvised at best and bloody shambolic at worst. The colonel was making it up as he went along. It was clear that there was no contingency plan.

Moreover, at half past eight, at least half of the unit were still in pubs, cinemas, listening to the Billy Cotton Band Show on the wireless or walking with new-found girlfriends. More and more private soldiers were being sent out on more and more call-up errands.

'And if you stop off for a quick pint in any of those pubs I will bloody bayonet you myself when I get my hands on you. Do you understand?'

'Yes, sir.'

The colonel ordered all ranks to assemble on the municipal car park. With the wartime restrictions on petrol, there were very few private cars available, and the car park was nearly empty. What Bill saw there filled him with horror. Some were in full service marching order; some were in battle order; some had no equipment with them whatsoever and were in regimental berets rather than helmets; some were half cut having come out of the pub; some were in civvies. There were very clearly dozens of absentees.

It was clear that the ad-hoc efforts to bring the commandos together were not working.

The colonel's utter exasperation led him to give the ultimate order, 'Ring the church bells!'

By now, it was after 11 o'clock. The cinemas were closed, the pubs were past 'chucking out' time and still the commandos were not assembled.

Ringing the church bells was an extreme move. Everyone in the British Isles was quite aware of the emergency order. Church bells could only be rung in case of an invasion. The townspeople by now were off the streets and sitting at home terrified. Back in the car park, Colonel Legard was seething with rage. It had taken four hours to muster the whole of 4 Commando.

The ranks were told to stand easy and allowed to sit down but be alert.

'Well, I haven't heard any Jerry aircraft yet.'

They all knew the sound of the German aero engines. They had a throbbing sound, which was very different to Royal Air Force types.

'And we haven't heard any of ours going over the sea.'

Silence reigned. Out at sea, a large shape moved silently and without lights parallel with the coast.

'What's that ship out there?'

'That's one of ours. I think it's one of those destroyers from Portland on patrol.'

'Well, they aren't shooting at anyone.'

'Maybe they landed up the coast at Brighton?'

'God knows!'

Silence still reigned.

'Well, I'm going to get some kip. Let me know if Adolf appears down the pavilion.'

Those like Bill who had been in France were seasoned soldiers now and could sleep anywhere, no matter how cold, uncomfortable or unprotected from the elements.

At dawn, a few sleepy heads awoke to see the colonel speaking very pointedly and volubly to the adjutant.

'Atten-tion!' shouted the Regimental Sergeant Major.

The commandos came smartly to attention.

'It's a false alarm, everyone. Everyone on the pier at 0800 in full marching order. We're scheduled to do a big one today, false alarm or no false alarm!'

'Oh Christ!'

'Shut up, you'll get yourself RTUed! [returned to unit!]'

The men's responses, spoken under their breath, were as predictable as they were profane.

Bill wended his way back to his billet. The overall feeling must have been relief, but this had been a good opportunity to prove himself in action again and it had been frittered away. He tiptoed into the house minus boots so as not to awake the landlord and landlady. They were awake anyway.

'Is it alright, Bill?'

'False alarm!'

'Oh bugger! And we missed the Billy Cotton Bandshow for that?'

'Language!'

'So Hitler didn't come shooting his way in, then?'

'We were so badly prepared that he would just have bloody waltzed his way in. We were an utter shambles', thought Bill, preferring not to share that choice knowledge with a civilian.

The next response can be reported with total and complete historic accuracy. 'Never mind, let's have a nice cup of tea.'

In Weymouth, there were sighs of relief. In London, they were still putting fires out from the raid the night before and digging people out of the wreckage of hundreds of houses. Some were still breathing. Some were not.

Colonel Legard put an inquest into operation the next morning. Three things had gone wrong. Firstly, someone in general headquarters had panicked for whatever reason. At 2007 hours, some unknown person had transmitted the secret code word 'Cromwell'. This meant that an attack was underway and that the whole country should stand by to repel the evil Nazi hordes. This was an error and was out of 4 Commando's control. Secondly, the experience of the night had shown that there was no contingency plan in operation. Talking with other COs in the area, Colonel Legard discovered that the shambles at Weymouth had not been the only debacle. There had been hundreds of them up and down the country. Thirdly, if 4 Commando was to be a mobile reserve, then one car, one truck and virtually no petrol was not going to fit the bill.

Simultaneously with Colonel Legard's initiative, his officers scoured the *Daily Mail*, the *Daily Express*, *The Daily Telegraph* and even *The Times*. There was not a mention of the incident anywhere. The BBC radio did not report it. The vast, nationwide imbecility and anti-climax had been airbrushed out of history overnight. Officially, the false alarm never happened.

The farce of the false alarm had led quickly to a profound change in No 4 Commando's routine at Weymouth. The endless marching, occasional weapons firing and operations on imaginary German airfields on iron-age forts ceased. They were replaced by much more focussed exercises on how to repel an attack. There were exercises to set-up independent troop bases, exercises to live off the land, exercises to carry out mock raids against an invader by day and by night. Invasion flaps became very common, one after another and some lasting a full week. There were exercises against the Home Guard, exercises against the RAF and exercises against the Royal Navy. There were exercises on bicycles, exercises in boats, which used commandeered trawlers as landing craft, and exercises on commandeered vehicles. Inevitably, there were repercussions. Some of the bicycle owners appeared in Colonel Legard's office demanding that their stolen bicycle be returned.

'If I get it back, I will withdraw my complaint at the police station. It's a blue one with a shopping basket on the front.'

'Oh, come on, Madam, there's a war on!'

'Well, it looks daft! You wouldn't see 'Itler's stormtroopers blazing up the beach on a lady's bike, would you?'

Many let the commandos keep their bicycles for the duration of the war 'but I want it back as soon as 'Itler's been shot!'

The commandeered vehicles did lend a semblance of mobility to the mobile reserve. Precisely how a German tank commander would have reacted under attack from a vehicle marked Jones's Quality Meats remains unclear. It is possible that he would not have had the heart to open fire.

During this period of high activity, 'Old' Sir Roger was to appear frequently. Bill was amused to discover that the commandos were to use the purloined bicycles as in a 'cavalry ride-past' of Sir Roger. As sergeant, he was even required to give the order 'Eyes, right!'. In response, Sir Roger used his considerable clout for 4 Commando to have the unit insignia of a red and yellow lanyard, the colours of the cavalry. From this point, 4 Commando was known as the Cavalry Commando. In a perfect world, Sir Roger would have used that same clout to provide the commandos with transport, weapons and other equipment but that equipment had all been lost in France and replacement was slow.

Winston Churchill was to have the last word. 'Neither I nor the Chiefs of Staff knew that the decisive code word "Cromwell" had been used… it served as a useful tonic and rehearsal for all concerned.'

For Bill Adlam and 4 Commando, the false alarm had shown the deficiencies, demonstrated what needed to be done and created enough impetus for the necessary measures to be brought into place. It was to act like a locomotive to help 4 Commando take shape and prepare it for action.

Saturday, 14 September 1940, Weymouth

A week later, it was as if the drama of the false alarm had never happened. The route marches were becoming harder and faster. The swimming drills in full uniform were becoming longer and of greater intensity. The morning 'pokey drill' was becoming more imaginative. Pokey drill was drill using rifles. It had always been a part of army training, but now it was becoming much more serious. Now, there was a drill in firing from the hip using a finger and thumb method, which meant that a Lee Enfield rifle could be fired almost like a machine gun. The commando was receiving Tommy guns now with

50-bullet drum magazines. These fired a .45 bullet at a rate of 700 rounds per minute. The commando was excited that these would not merely stop a German, they would cut them in half and splatter them into fertiliser across the British countryside. Similarly, there was training now in firing a Bren from the hip. This was a totally new concept. Bill would have loved to do this when he won his MM at Grindorff.

Other new tactics coming to the fore now were revolutionary. Sergeants were to take responsibility under fire for locating the enemy machine guns and without recourse to officers. The sergeant would give the order to move forward, which direction to move in and give commands by agreed signals as to move forward, outflank the enemy and kill them. At first the manoeuvres were carried out at walking pace, then at running pace, then firing blank ammunition and then with opposition in full battlefield simulation.

This was not merely innovation. In the hidebound and stuffy British Army, it was nothing short of revolution.

Chapter 9

The Road to the Isles

Sunday, 13 October 1940, Goodness knows where

'Where are we, sarge?'

'God only knows, I certainly don't.'

As the train sat in the station during the changing of engines, freight trains clattered through one after another, all pulled by massive hissing steam locomotives. Some carried army trucks going south. Others carried anti-aircraft guns going north. There was energy, urgency, almost frenetic endless activity.

'Snudger, stick your head out and ask the stationmaster where we are.'

'He says it's Carlisle, sarge.'

'Well, ask him where we're going.'

'Right, sarge. He says we're one of the "funnies" and no, he can't tell us where we're going.'

'What does he mean by the funnies?'

'He says he can't ask us who we are, and he can't tell anyone where we are going.'

'Well, why not? We're on the bloody train!'

'He says he doesn't care; don't we know there's a bloody war on?'

'Tell him he should leave his job anyway and join the Army!'

'Don't think so, sarge, he's about 60.'

'The train now standing in platform three is about to depart,' boomed across the glass and metal cavern which is Carlisle Station.

They all went back to sleep.

Bill Adlam had been posted to 4 Commando. They were being sent north (wherever that may be) for further training (whatever that may be). As ever, the powers that be told them nothing. It was better that way. You never knew what German spies were listening to. Families would not know where the men were but could write to them at British Forces Post Office No… All letters were censored. Any letter containing sensitive information was destroyed.

At 0600 hours, the train pulled into a station by a river. It was not a particularly large river but with hundreds of shipyard cranes, hills in the distance and a destroyer going out to sea on patrol duties. Presiding over the whole scene were dozens of the huge barrage balloons, which by now were part of the landscape. The business end of the balloon was not the large floating blimp, it was the cable that it held up. These made it hazardous for enemy planes to descend to low levels to bomb their targets accurately.

'Hey, some of the Jocks know where we are, it's Port Glasgow, apparently.'

A party of grim, uncompromising, military police were waiting. The men formed into ranks and marched through the town where early morning workers looked at them in a vaguely interested way. They marched down to the quay and formed up in front of a medium-sized, scruffy freighter. Bill saw the name *Glengyle*. Indeed, HMS *Glengyle* would be home for the next few months.

Well, it was certainly going to be a bit different. They clattered up the gangplanks and into the bowels of the ship. The cargo holds had been converted to mess decks. Which way was A company? Ah yes, down that ladder.

'Not that way, soldier!' A large burly sailor was talking to him

'Eh?'

'You don't go down a hatchway that way or you'll break your neck in a big swell.'

'What do you mean?'

'Gawd! Look, you go this way. Feet inwards and facing the steps. If you face outwards from the steps you're going to fall and land on your backside.'

'Thanks! There's a lot to learn!'

'There is, mate, a real lot! This is the Navy and it's a whole different world.'

Each man was issued with a hammock and a hook from which to sling it. The mess was now called the galley. Most startling of all were the announcements made by the chief petty officer over the loudspeakers. This was preceded by a loud blast on the boatswain's pipe, which seemed to penetrate your head and loosen all your fillings. Then the chief petty officer would yell, 'D'ye hear there! D'ye hear there!'. At no time was this more disturbing than on waking in the morning. In the Gloucesters, he had woken to the sound of reveille on the bugle. At Weymouth, he had woken to the sound of his own alarm clock.

Now, he was woken to the sound of that damned pipe and the voice of the chief petty officer, 'Wakey, wakey, lash up and stow.' The sailors also had to show them how to correctly fold up the hammocks and stow them away in the lockers. Interestingly, hammocks were quite comfortable to sleep in, although the scent below decks of rancid socks, cigarettes and boot polish made an interesting melange of fragrances. One aspect of life in Glasgow was very different to Weymouth. The shipyards were clattering and banging all night. This made sleep difficult, although it was possible to become accustomed to it. There was no complaining. Everyone understood only too well, there's a war on!

Tuesday, 15 October 1940, Port Glasgow

The ship was humming. He could feel the engines as they pulsed and turned. The deck beneath his feet moved very slightly.

'Hey, sarge! We're on the move.'

They went up onto the deck. The *Glengyle* was pulling slowly away from the dockside. Commandos in various states of readiness lined the railings.

'Where the hell are we going?'

'It can't be very far because we haven't had any shore leave.'

Colonel Legard made an announcement over the loudspeaker.

> We are sailing up the Clyde today to engage in the first training in proper landing craft. We all had fun in the trawlers and other craft in Weymouth. Now we have real assault landing craft, and we can train in how to use them. The ship will proceed to Inveraray and anchor off the coast. We will train in how to enter the landing craft; what to do when you are in them and what to do when you come out of them. The journey will take a couple of hours so enjoy the journey while you can.

Clydeside was impressive! All the way down the river stood shipyard after shipyard after shipyard. It seemed that the forest of dockside cranes went on as far as the horizon. Every shipyard was busy with hurried activity. One was building a large merchantman. Another, a cruiser for the Royal Navy and another, a destroyer. Along the river, he saw yet another destroyer apparently going out on patrol into the Irish Sea and another returning from a similar journey. It was really not too bad at all. The salt tang on the air was energising. The activity in the shipyards was highly entertaining and was a great example of the muscularity with which the war was being fought. At one place, several sinister shapes represented submarines, dark and deadly.

High above them, patrols of Hurricanes kept watch for enemy aircraft. Glasgow had been hit by air raids. The evidence could be seen from the ship. The Luftwaffe had aimed at the shipyards, but the bombs had mainly hit the town or dropped harmlessly into the river. 'They got the *Sussex*, though, the buggers!' said a sailor. 'Bloody big heavy cruiser she was. They got her in the middle of a refit at Yorkhill Quay. We were all told not to talk about it for some reason.'

They were to learn that morning that the Assault Landing Craft were called LCAs. The *Glengyle* carried ten of them. As they neared Inveraray, they were to learn all about them.

Firstly, they had to learn how to assemble at the relevant assembly points in the ship.

'Today, we'll do it slowly and you can see where you are going. Later on, we'll do it in the dark so that you can find your way blindfolded and in battle order. Don't worry about battle order today. Just come in marching order.'

Bill found that his assembly point was their mess deck. Well, that was easy enough.

'Now we have to get you from your mess deck to your boat station without getting in the way of every other bugger. Follow me, gentlemen.'

They followed a predetermined route through the ship.

'Now, notice that you have not even seen another company, let alone got into their way. Access to LCAs is always via this route.'

They lined up against their allotted LCA.

'You will notice that there are three rows of seats in the LCA. Now, notice what position in the line you are standing in. When we do boat drills you will always – always without fail – be in exactly these places.'

'Question, sir?'

'Yes?'

'How do we get the order for embarkation?'

'It will always be by the loudspeaker.'

'What if the loudspeaker isn't working, sir?'

The officer wrote down the question.

'Good question, I'll have a think about it. Now from here to here – to that man there – you go in and take up the central seats. Now, up to that man there take up the right-hand seats. And, finally, to that man there, take up the left seats. Is everybody comfortable?'

'Yes, sir' they chorused.

'This is the point at which I pass on a message to central control and central control gives the order through the loudspeaker to lower away.'

'Question, sir?'

'Yes?'

'What happens if the loudspeaker isn't working, sir?'

'If the loudspeaker is not working, I will personally shoot you because it is the easiest way out of a nasty situation.'

The officer took down notes of the drills, procedures, timings, additional notes.

He slammed the front door shut, sent a private up to the bridge. Half a minute later, the crackling command came through the loudspeaker, 'lower away'.

The LCA swung in the air, lowered down the side of the ship and its flat bottom hit the water with a *splat*.

The powerful engines at the rear of the landing craft started up and the boat headed for the shore.

'Stand by to beach!'

They all braced.

The flat bottom hit the stones on the beach.

The front gate was dropped.

'Now, disembark in the same order in which you got in. Central seats first, then the right-hand seats, then the left-hand seats.'

They crunched up the beach to the designated muster point.

'Well done, everyone. For a first attempt, that wasn't bad. Now let's reverse it and go back to the ship. Do you all remember where you were in line?'

'Yes sir!'

Friday, 10 November 1940, Ayr, Scotland

'Right, you 'orrible lot! Gather round! We're on the move again!' RSM 'Jumbo' Morris spoke to the whole Commando.

'Oh gawd! Not again!' was the most common reaction from the ranks. There were other variations on the theme, but none was printable.

Since leaving the *Glengyle* two weeks previously, they had been sent to Oban. There were no billets available. Then they were sent to camp in tents at Inveraray. Then they marched 16 hours through a rainstorm to Dalmally, wherever that was. It was only October, but it was bleeding freezing, the rain was like a wild animal and the wind was like a creature from hell. Then they had finally been billeted in Ayr. Now they were going somewhere else.

'Listen, everyone!' shouted Morris. 'You will be parading in front of the good citizens of Ayr, so I want to see bags of swank. I want your uniforms, hats and webbings worn correctly and not like that horrible little man there – you with the ginger hair, *pull yourself together*! That webbing looks like a nancy boy's handbag! There will be no talking in the ranks.'

Bill was used to the psychology of marches. You had to find the rhythm and then turn your mind off.

The pipe band struck up. First, the rattle of the drums, then the bagpipes turned on with their uplifting moan. Regimental Sergeant Major Morris gave the order, 'By the left, march!'. The bagpipes took up the tune of 'Bonnie Dundee'. They were used to marching at 140 paces per minute. With this band, they were barely achieving 110, but the intensity of the music was something Bill had never experienced before. Regimental Sergeant Major Morris had wanted swank and swank he was going to get.

And so the entire 4 Commando swanked its way, headed by the stirring music of the pipes and up to their next destination, which turned out to be the pleasant town of Troon.

With Ayr left behind them, talking was permitted in the ranks.

'What're we doing at Troon, sarge?'

'The first thing we are going to do is what is called battlefield inoculation.'

'What the heck is that?'

'They've got some live firing ranges. We have to crawl under barbed-wire entanglements while they fire machine guns over our heads.'

'How close?'

'I've not done it before, but I'm told that if you stick your head up, you'll get it blown off.'

'Christ!'

Bill had been shot at from a distance at Grindorff, at proximity at Bruyelle and at Ledringhem, he had seen the whites of the eyes of the men who shot at him. None of those who had shot at him went home. Being shot at by friends was never going to be as bad as that.

'Who does the shooting, sarge?'

'Bren gunners mostly. Most of the gunners are quite good. Our ones are pretty accurate. There's one guy in F company who is likely to have an accident or two. I think he needs glasses or something. Try not to get him if you can avoid it.'

'You're having a laugh, sarge, those Brens are on fixed traverses, they can't be trained down beyond a certain point so that they can actually hit us.'

'Well, they can if you stick your head up. Anyway, they're funny things those traverses, they've been known to slip, just a bit but just enough.'

Bill was going to have to lead his section from the front. He would have to be the first man under the barbed wire with live rounds flying just one foot over his head.

'Oh, and there's something else as well.'

'What's that, sarge?'

'You'll be in full battle order so make sure that your backpack and your gasmask don't get caught in the barbed wire or you'll really be in trouble.'

Despite all the madness of war, there was method. 4 Commando was being groomed to land on enemy beaches. He wondered when and where it would come.

Wednesday, 25 December 1940, Gloucester

It was possibly the worst Christmas in history. The centre of Coventry had been obliterated some weeks previously. London, Manchester and Liverpool had undergone heavy bombing. As a result, 24,000 had been killed. Thousands more were homeless. 41,000 British troops were in captivity in Germany.

And so it was that Bill Adlam made his Christmas odyssey. The awkward journey from Troon would have necessitated changes at Glasgow, Crewe and Birmingham. Passenger trains were often shunted into sidings to give urgent war materials priority on the rail lines. Restaurant cars had disappeared completely.

On arriving home, Bill's priority was to see his wife and daughters. Without doubt, it was a joyous event. Then came reality. Where was the air-raid shelter? Which of their friends have been killed? One of the girls hasn't seen her man. He never came back from Dunkirk, could you go and see her? Are there enough coupons for a Christmas dinner? Bill's billeting as a commando meant that he had been given food coupons. He had been able to keep some back to put towards a Christmas dinner. The difficult part was finding a butcher or a poulterer who had any meat to sell.

The public were discouraged from giving presents and to give the money to the war effort. One by-product of this was the emergence of bomb-shelter presents such as sleeping bags, gasmasks for girls' dolls and small torches to allow the owner to find the way to the shelter with enough light not to attract German bombers.

Women's stockings had all but disappeared. Gladys probably did what most women did, stained her legs with tea to make them look as though she was wearing stockings and drew a line down the back of the calf to simulate the stocking seam.

The meat rations for a family of four would barely allow the purchase of a chicken. More commonly, people would raise their own chickens or rabbits and eat them for Christmas. This often came as a shock to young children who had assumed unwisely that the rabbits had been pets.

However, the excitement of seeing Gladys and his daughters Poppy and Pauline would have given him the adrenaline to keep going and to have enough energy to celebrate with them when he arrived home.

As they sat down to their Christmas dinner, the inevitable question was 'Are the gasmasks handy, just in case?'

Chapter 10

Lofoten, Here We Come! Operation Claymore

Sunday, 2 March 1941, 0500 hours, On board HMS Queen Emma

The shrill whistle of the boatswain's pipe screeched through his semi-conscious head and prodded him from a shallow sleep. 'Wakey wakey you gang of mincing nancy boys! D'ye 'ear there? D'ye 'ear there?' It was 0500. God! That man's voice was irritating! Bill had now endured six months of brutal, unrelenting commando training, the like of which no soldier from a traditional regiment could have anticipated. He had loved every minute of it! It was now in his power to kill that screaming boatswain with one twist of his well-trained hand. Would a court martial acquit him? Probably not.

He was a sergeant and had to bring his head into some semblance of focus. As soon as the *Emma* had cast off, Colonel Lister had made the announcement that some had already anticipated.

'Men, we are not bound for exercises as your officers have told you. We have a real job to do.'

The men had roared approval.

'Thank you, gentlemen, your enthusiasm is noted but I do need to brief you on where we are going.'

'Calm down, lads, calm down!' insisted the voice of an officer from the centre of the assembled throng.

'We in number 4 Commando together with number 3 Commando are bound for the Lofoten Islands in the north of Norway.'

Men looked at each other and shrugged. No-one had heard of these islands before.

'The islands have factories which produce fish oil which is a vital resource for the Nazi munitions industry. Our job is to hit those factories and put them out of business.'

His immediate challenge on that freezing morning, aboard that bucking, gyrating, pitching vessel, was to be the first one to the heads (as the Royal

Navy so quaintly called the toilet) and the washing facilities and be ready to command his section. As his feet touched the floor, conditions impressed on him again that he was now in a different world. Fortunately, he did not have to dress himself as he had slept in his uniform. It was so hard to tie his boots. The floor tilted, it lurched, it swayed to and fro, it moved up, it plunged down. He grabbed onto whatever handhold he could. The only way he could pull his boots on was to sit on the floor, being very careful to avoid any lurking puddles of sick. He had to get to the heads first. He remembered to lift his feet very high so as not to trip up on the water barrier which ran across the bottom of the doorway.

His eyes were met with the most remarkable sight. The Orkneys could be seen receding into the grey distance and the low grey hills, under the thin dawn light beyond a heaving mountainous sea under a leaden battleship-grey sky. Now he was on a peak and looking down into a dark green-grey, menacing sea. He lurched into the heads hanging on for grim death. There would be no drills today in this weather. Out of the heads, he found the ship in the depths of a dark valley. He looked up at the great watery moving mountains, way above his head.

As the ship rode to the top of the next mountain, there was another ship, dark grey like the *Emma*. It was the HMS *Princess Beatrix*. He could gauge the violence of the sea in the way the two ships moved against each other. Now, one was way above the other, now the reverse. There was another ship, a destroyer. That was comforting. There were more destroyers. Two, three, four, five. There were still bigger ships, further out, there were two cruisers. This was serious stuff, and the Germans would have a lot of trouble sinking them. There were still two more ships. He recognised one from the night before, HMS *King George V*. Good lord! What a brute of a thing it was in the daylight! It was huge and the size of the guns on the for'ard and aft decks were almost beyond belief. He had seen artillery in the Army but nothing like that. There was yet another ship. If the *King George V* was massive, what words could he possibly have for this other ship? It looked bigger than the *King George V* and had three vast gun turrets on the for'ard deck. He stopped a passing sailor, 'What ship is that?'

'It's either the *Nelson* or the *Rodney*, sarge, erm, I think it's actually the *Rodney*.'

'You mean there is more than *one* of those?'

'That's right, there's two of them but I don't know where the other one is. It's incredible to see them tied up, side by side when they're in Pompey.'

Pompey was the affectionate name by which British sailors knew the vast naval dockyards at Portsmouth.

Even these monsters were subject and slave to what the sea was doing. He'd had little to do with the camera team who accompanied them but hoped they would get some pictures of this unforgettable sight of the battleships, the destroyers and the troop transports. The battleships lurched up and down, much as the *Emma* did but in a slower and altogether more dignified manner. The destroyers lurched up and down in a quicker tempo and the troop carriers lurched up and down like corks on the water, although they were substantial cross-channel ferries in peacetime. He should have thought to put his greatcoat on. He was freezing and soaked to the skin in just a couple of steps along the deck. A soldier was vomiting over the side. The revolting technicolour mass sped towards him, he ducked back, it spun away from him and along the deck. That was good! It meant that he would not be splattered. Was it one of his own men? Should he try to help the man? The man's face appeared green. He looked again. The face was actually green. He had seen dead men killed in action, but they had not looked that bad. There was no point in trying to help. The man was beyond it. It reminded him of how he had seen men beyond help in a different way at Ledringhem.

Best not to think of it.

Back on the mess deck, he got his team to straighten their uniforms and look like bloody soldiers after a night's disturbed sleep.

'Right, listen, you lot! Colonel Lister is giving us briefings later this morning as to what our tasks are going to be when we hit the landings. Don't hide yourselves away in secret card schools because you'll be wanted for your briefings. There are no drills this morning; it's too bloody 'orrible! Oh and if you go outside put your greatcoats on or you'll get soaked to the skin. Right, lads, go and get your breakfasts.'

Some of the men looked at him in horror. He wondered what he had said.

'Breakfast?' said a voice.

Some half of his section pushed passed him roughly, exited out of the door tripping over the sill and charged urgently for the comfort of the railing. They stood there and vomited and vomited and vomited. The least smart was the one furthest downwind.

'Couldn't someone just organise a U-boat to come and put us out of our misery?'

'It's no good, mate, you won't get a U-boat coming up in seas like these.'

'Oh bugger! Where is a friendly torpedo when you most need one?'

The rest of that day was spent in hammocks or walking around the ship trying to stave off the remorseless seasickness. It seemed that everyone had a pet recipe how to beat it. If you stayed in the middle of the ship, you could avoid the relentless swaying motion and that should beat it. It didn't. If you walked around the deck, you could evade the awful nausea by breaking the pattern of the up-down motion. That didn't work either. There were other home-spun remedies. None of them worked. A day which should have been spent in important drills was lost.

Monday, 3 March 1941, 0600 hours, On board HMS Queen Emma

'Wakey, wakey rise and shine! D'ye 'ear there? D'ye 'ear there?'

Bill awoke in his hammock. Doubtless, he had thoughts of murder against the boatswain, but something was different. The hammocks were not swinging as much. The groans of the severely seasick were quieter. The ship sounded different; it did not creak so much. Out on deck, he found to his complete relief that the storm had blown itself out during the night. The sea still ran a mighty swell, but it was calm and looked almost benign. The short sharp waves, which had formed vicious saltwater pyramids, had abated. There was less sea foam. It was not physically painful to walk into the wind.

Colonel Lister used the day for embarkation drills. He made the men go through them over and over until they could have done them with blindfolds on. There was something odd that day. Some troops were being issued with large numbers of blindfolds. Why on earth would blindfolds be part of a raid like this? All troops were briefed that all prisoners, German or Norwegian collaborators, were to be lined up in town and brought onto the troopships with blindfolds on. It all seemed very odd. Oh well, orders were orders.

The camera team were busy polishing lenses, making sure that the salt winds had not done irreparable damage to expensive equipment. The two huge battleships turned in a majestic arc and headed for home.

'Oy! Where are those buggers going?'

'If the German Navy hasn't got us yet they won't be able to put together a force to stop us. Anyway, they won't risk the big guns that close to the

Norwegian shore. All it takes is a couple of torpedoes or a couple of bombs from aircraft and they're done for.'

The tension was building now. Their first taste of action was only a day or so away.

'Oh bugger!'

'What is it?'

'Look over there just in front of that big cloud.'

'Christ!'

Some miles off, they could see a dark shape travelling towards them. It banked over and flew parallel to them. It was a plane.

'Any chance it's the RAF boys?'

'We're too far away and anyway, it came from the east. It's a German patrol That is definitely a Luftwaffe kite.'

'Well why aren't we firing at it?'

'You complete nurk! If we fire at it, we are telling them we are British.'

'Aren't they going to know anyway?'

'We might just get away with it.'

'Do you think so?'

'No, not really.'

'They'll be waiting for us?'

'So, it'll be fisticuffs then.'

Morale on the ship had improved in the relative calm after yesterday's storm. With morale, came expectation. Seeing the German plane had sharpened the expectation into a surge of testosterone and adrenaline. They were going to see action. They would need to shoot their way ashore. Without being told, the commandos sharpened knives, checked that weapons were cleaned and oiled and ammunition pouches were filled with the correct ammunition. They counted and recounted the 100 Krone 'pocket money' with which they were issued although none of them had any idea what they might spend it on. Lights out was early that night.

Bill must have thought what all soldiers think before battle. 'Will I still be alive this time tomorrow? Will I acquit myself well?'

In his stomach, there was a mixed feeling of apprehension, fear and determination. It was as though someone had placed a brick in his stomach, and it would not let him rest. On the other hand, the pre-battle tension, which he knew how to deal with, was highly preferable to the awfulness of the seasickness.

Tuesday, 4 March 1941, 0400 hours, Onboard HMS Queen Emma

This morning, there was no chief petty officer to wake them. The loudspeaker could possibly be heard from the shore. There was little talking now. Every soldier knew what his task was, what drills he had to perform and what was expected of him. They all felt that knot in their stomachs. They all felt the same thoughts. Some had written letters home. For Bill Adlam, there was another thought. It was one year today since Grindorff, when he had won his Military Medal. So much had happened since.

The sergeants roused the men at 0400, with 'gunfire tea' served up at 0500. This was strong tea laced with overproof navy rum and was just the thing to warm the troops on a freezing morning. Parade was called for 0600, with each troop assembled beside their allotted landing craft.

All navigation lights were extinguished now. The destroyers and the *Princess Beatrix* were visible some hundreds of yards away, or their shadows were visible in the earliest half-light before dawn. The inescapable seasickness was forgotten now. The inescapable tension had replaced it. After a hot breakfast and as much hot drink as they could imbibe, the commandos picked up their kit, their weapons, their gasmasks and their helmets and shuffled to the embarkation points. Colonel Lister's drills had worked well. Every man knew exactly where to be and what to do.

All of the men were now a different physical shape to when they had first embarked at Gourock, several months into the past. Every commando was wearing every item of clothing, which he had brought with him in his kitbag. The deep, pitiless cold was even more penetrating than the inescapable tension.

Looking over the rails as they filed out on deck, the commandos saw a most awe-inspiring sight. The Lofoten Islands are staggeringly beautiful. They are made up of steep mountains, with almost vertical slopes and snow visible in the gathering half-light. Not one of them had ever seen such a sight of magnificence and awe-inspiring beauty. There was nothing like that in the United Kingdom. Even in the highlands of Scotland, there was nothing remotely comparable to these wonderful, austere mountains. Having looked with awe at their first glimpse of the Lofoten Islands, they all immediately noticed something else.

'Strewth! There's no blackout!'

On shore, they could see rows of twinkling lights. Boats in the harbour had navigation lights glowing. Streetlights were shining. There appeared to be no activity at all. The commandos filed into their landing craft as they had practised, time and time again. The *Emma* ploughed towards the lights of the harbour at the small fishing port of Svolvaer.

The closest of the destroyers to the *Queen Emma* was HMS *Somali*. She was at battle stations with guns at action stations. The white ensign fluttered as it had at Trafalgar, at the Nile and at the Battle of Jutland. And so it did at the Lofotens. A fishing boat ran across the bows of both the *Emma* and the *Somali* at a quarter of a mile distance.

The *Somali* and the fishing boat passed out of sight as the *Emma* pressed on towards their landing ground at Svolvaer. In the large bay outside of the harbour, he was surprised to find an ocean liner. It was the *Bremen*. It was a huge German passenger liner offering the highest level of luxury to the fortunate people who could afford it. It was the fastest civilian ship afloat and was once the possessor of the Blue Riband of the Atlantic, which was awarded to the ship which could make the crossing in the fastest time. Her design was so state of the art that she possessed a catapult from which a small seaplane could be launched. Bill Adlam had ever seen such a ship. There was no time for idle tourism. The Germans could start firing at any moment.

The commandos looked vaguely amused and entertained as the *Somali* chased the trawler rapidly past them and headed for some low-lying islands to starboard.

That desultory chase of this small warship of this even smaller fishing vessel would prove to be one of the most game-changing events of World War II. None of the commandos would ever know this. Bill Adlam never did.

Chapter 11

Bill Sets Foot on Enemy Territory

Tuesday, 4 March 1941, Lofoten Islands, Norway

At 0620 hours, there was an exchange of naval gunfire. HMS *Somali* continued to pursue the uncooperative trawler. The significance of this ship was that the German Navy had a severe shortage of coastal defence vessels. They therefore commandeered fishing boats and armed them. The *Krebs* proved, therefore, to have a sting in its tail. The Somali sent a signal saying, 'heave to'. The *Krebs* disobeyed the order. The *Somali* fired two shots across its bows with its 4.7-inch guns from a range of three kilometres. The *Krebs* was no match for a destroyer, but its own 4.1-inch gun could cause damage. The captain unwisely chose to fight. One of the gunners on the *Krebs* had made an excellent shot. The shell whistled over the head of the Somali's decks and ripped the flag from the radio mast. The crew of this trawler were obviously German Naval personnel and very good at their jobs. This was no heavy-handed treatment of innocent fisherfolk.

The *Somali* began firing in earnest. Almost immediately, one of its shells hit the *Krebs'* wheelhouse. The *Krebs* was out of action. To those who were there, it appeared as if this was only a small detail within a much bigger picture. Everyone had other things to think about.

Colonel Lister ordered landing craft to be lowered at 0700, to make landfall by 0800. The tension in the landing craft was by now even more intense than the cold. Bill, like most of the others, had seen the German forces in action, and they were good. If the German forces at the Lofoten Islands were anything like those in France, there was going to be a battle. Best not to think about it. Think about what the training had taught you to do!

Everyone waited in silence for shore batteries to open up, for aircraft to appear and strafe them with cannon shells and for heavy machine guns from the harbour to open up with tracer bullets. So far, there was nothing. They checked safety catches on their weapons. They checked that their grenades were where they should be. They checked their ammunition pouches. They could hear the swishing of the waves beneath the landing craft. They heard the mournful wailing of the gulls. The duel between the *Somali* and the fishing boat had ended and as far as anyone could see, a boarding party was taking control of it. There were no other sounds. To their surprise, there was no sound of gunfire heading their way.

Could they really be landing unopposed? The landing craft sped unhindered across the morning waves. Then they heard the grating of the landing craft as it slid onto the ice at the edge of the shore. They had, contrary to all expectations, landed unopposed and as far as they knew, unnoticed. The LCA front gate dropped. Bill Adlam clattered out of the landing craft. He ran, Thompson machine gun at the ready. He tensed in apprehension of the barrage of small-arms fire to come their way. *None came*. Now the nerves had gone. Every man had to concentrate on what his task was and carry out that task. Officers gave out orders in hoarse whispers in order to make minimum noise. Keeping quiet was impossible. The clatter of hob-nailed boots sounded like an avalanche in the quiet arctic hamlet. The commandos could not keep on their feet and were sliding around like overdressed, drunken ballerinas as their boots could get no purchase on the ice which was as hard as glass.

To make matters worse, a shot rang out. Captain Cook had slipped on the ice and shot himself in the leg. Some others had grasped the cold steel of the harbourside ladder and lost the skin off their hands. They put gloves on and carried on.

Colonel Lister's headquarters troop took the harbourmaster's office. Captain Hunter with G troop and Bill Adlam secured a bridgehead on the main quay of Svolvaer and sealed off the area with roadblocks.

Lieutenant Webb took over the post office and main hotel. He set about locating the Luftwaffe wireless station, which he was tasked to destroy.

Lieutenant Lewis' troop, assisted by the Norwegians, went to look for the harbour- master and other officials to gather information and vital documents. They were to arrest Norwegian collaborators. There was an interesting officer, Captain Lord Lovat, who was attached to this party as Admiral Keyes' observer. He was notable as a rather charismatic, dashing figure. He was destined to play a major part in Bill Adlam's story.

Captain Emmett and C troop landed near the 'Cuba' fish factory to destroy all factories in the area.

Lieutenant Style and the sappers were to destroy the main fish-oil storage tanks.

Captain Cook and E troop plus Captain Montgomery and A troop were set up as a reserve force. This was of extreme importance. Colonel Lister did not know the strength and willingness that was needed to fight the German forces. His reserves could be crucial in case of a fight. They were also to provide anti-aircraft support using Bren guns. Because of Cook's injury, however, he was unable to move very far or very fast.

Major Kerr with one section of F troop landed a little later on Brettesnes and established a bridgehead with anti-aircraft capability and also was ready to assist Captain Duveen if required.

Captain Duveen and the remainder of F troop together with sappers were to destroy oil factories on Brettesnes and also capture any Germans or collaborators in the area.

All of this logistical plan had been brought perfectly into operation and there was not even a sign of the Germans. Were they asleep or was this part of some devilish manoeuvre to lull them into a false sense of security before hitting them with a devastating attack? Bill knew the German armed forces were quite capable of that.

There was still no firing. Even Captain Cook's involuntary discharge of his weapon had not woken anyone. The few local fishermen who witnessed the landing appeared to be totally bemused, but they also appeared to be very friendly to the British soldiers. Within an hour, all target areas were secured and under armed occupation by the British and Norwegian armies. Intelligence officers aided by Norwegian personnel were rifling through the files in the town hall and harbourmaster's office. Early rising locals came out and proved also to be very friendly to the soldiers.

As German personnel emerged, sleepy-eyed and astonished, they were arrested at gunpoint and put into the holding pen which had been set up by Regimental Sergeant Major Morris. Prisoners were blindfolded according to orders. The soldiers also asked the villagers to point out which of their own people had been collaborating with the German occupiers. They were immediately arrested, blindfolded and put into the pen. As the light became stronger, the camera team began to film.

Back on shore, there were three main streams of activity. The assorted engineers and sappers got on with blowing-up the fish factories and storage depots. In all, some 11 fish factories and 800,000 gallons of oil went up in spectacular fashion, to the glee of the camera team. Secondly, the Norwegian soldiers went around the village and offered a free trip to Britain if any of the Norwegian fishermen wanted to leave the joys of the Third Reich. Three hundred and fourteen took up the offer, including eight women who went on to join the Norwegian Red Cross in London. Thirdly, roundups continued of German soldiers. In the end, some 225 were arrested, as were 60 Norwegian collaborators.

The raid was proceeding exactly according to plan.

Just after 0900 hours, Lieutenant Webb clattered with his heavy boots into Colonel Lister's command post.

'We've found where the Luftwaffe's radio station is, sir. It's about five miles away.'

He pointed out the location on a map on the wall. As far as we can see, sir, it's a straightforward journey. The locals say there are no defended positions between here and there.'

'Well done, Webb, dismissed.'

'Sir!'

'Signaller, send a message to Lieutenant Lewis's troop. I want Captain Lovat over here, immediately.'

'You sent for me, sir?'

'Lovat, strictly speaking, you are here as an observer, but if I read you right, you are rather hankering after some action?'

'Absolutely, sir!'

'Thought so!' said Lister with a twinkle in his eye. I want you to take Lieutenant Veasey and Lieutenant Banks and their men across to this position here' – showing Lovat the map – 'smash up the radio transmitter and bring back some more candidates for Regimental Sergeant Major Morris.'

'Very well, sir, we should be back in a couple of hours.'

'You'd better be, otherwise, we're back to Scotland without you. We're off at 1100.'

'We'll be back before 1100, sir!'

Outside Lister's command post, Lovat spun into action with authority, relish and enthusiasm.

'Right, A troop, over here at the double.'

The 50 or so soldiers of the reserve, who had had surprisingly little to do, gathered around with enthusiasm and anticipation. They wanted to play their part as well.

'Right, chaps, this is how it is. Colonel Lister has ordered me to take you over to the Luftwaffe radio station, smash it to bits and bring back some

Huns. Now, I need you, you and you to commandeer enough vehicles to get us over there. It's about five miles.'

'Right sir, transport coming up!'

'Now, who are the Bren gunners?'

A couple of hands were raised.

'Right, well we'll need those and as much ammo as you can carry. Look, bring magazines rather than belts, otherwise, we'll have some jams just when we don't want them.'

'Mags it is, Sir'

'Now, we don't know if Jerry will come quietly, and he may need some friendly persuasion. Now, we'll need some Norwegian speakers. You there.'

'Sir!'

'Go and find a Norwegian to come with us.'

'Sir!'

The transport was arriving, a fish delivery truck and about a dozen private cars.

'Right, well I'll ride in the truck and everyone else follow me.'

Lieutenant Dunning-White drove the fish truck. Two commandos had placed a Bren gun on the roof. In the cab, Lovat and a Norwegian officer with drawn revolver crowded in beside Dunning-White. The remaining commandos piled into the cars and the ragtag convoy set off for the Luftwaffe base.

There was a problem. This was Dunning-White's first attempt at driving a left-hand-drive vehicle. The truck lurched and weaved as he tried to learn how to handle the gear lever on the right-hand side. At any rate, off it bumped and ground towards the Luftwaffe station. The Bren gunners peered into the freezing cold of the morning with safety catch off and trigger finger ready. The Norwegian officer eased the safety catch off his service revolver and was ready to fire at the first sight of a grey uniform.

'Oh, look!' said Lovat with excitement, 'there's a flock of snow buntings!'

He had apparently observed them on his estates in the Scottish Highlands and was fascinated to find them at the other end of their migration in Norway.

He wound down the window and leaned out, to observe the snow buntings more clearly. Then the truck turned a sharp corner and lurched to a sudden halt. It had run straight into a column of grey-uniformed Germans coming in the opposite direction. The Norwegian officer's service revolver discharged involuntarily, the truck swerved and hit the parapet of a bridge. The three in the cab were gasping for breath as the narrow confine was now filled with cordite fumes. The Bren gunners had been knocked off the roof and were lying in the snow among a much-damaged Bren gun, several clips of ammunition and the number one gunner lamenting his broken dentures. Given that 4 Commando were reputedly elite soldiers, the whole routine had more the atmosphere of a *Crazy Gang* sketch.

The speed and suddenness of it had an immediate effect on the Germans. One or two of them ran for it up the hillside, but two thirds immediately put their hands in the air and surrendered.

The Germans gave no pretence of a fight but one of them dropped a canvas satchel into a stream just below the road. Clearly, these were important papers. Lovat had been trained at the commando training centre at Lochailort in how to kill a man with a single blow. It was a manoeuvre that could not be practised without killing someone. This was Lovat's chance! He gave the man a massively powerful karate chop, designed to kill him instantly. Nothing happened and the German merely stood there looking perplexed. Lovat hit him with a boxing punch which knocked the man clear over a parapet wall and into the river below. This resulted in hearty laughter from both the Germans and the British who witnessed it. The German tried to swim away. The Bren gunner with the broken dentures was on the point of shooting the hapless man but was restrained by other commandos. The other Germans were shouting at the Bren gunner.

Sergeant Goyne, who spoke German, reported to Lovat that the other Germans were shouting that the Bren gunner should shoot the man in the river.

'They say he's an ardent Nazi, sir, and they don't want him back.'

'Right, one half section, take this lot to Regimental Sergeant Major Morris, usual drill.'

'Shoot 'em if they give any trouble, sir?'

'Good lord, yes. There's a war on! Off you go!'

'Sir.'

The remaining ragtag convoy proceeded until the radio station was in sight, some three hundred metres away. It was easily identifiable by the swastika flag, which flew above it, plus the obvious radio aerials. The fish truck pulled to the side of the road, followed by the cars. The building was a converted police station. To Lovat's trained eye, this would pose a formidable defence position if the Luftwaffe personnel chose to fight. There were some locals walking on the road. The Norwegian who accompanied them asked what personnel were inside.

'They say that it is only technicians, sir.'

'Thank them and tell them to get the hell out of here.'

'Sir!'

'Lieutenant Veasey!'

'Sir!'

'Take a dozen men and a Bren. Dig in on that hillside and when I fire a red flare, rake the building with fire. It doesn't matter if you hit anything, just rake the building. For God's sake, keep your men's' heads down because this lot must have heard our burst from the Bren.'

'Sir!'

Lovat sent a heavier patrol around the back of the radio station. He signalled Veasey to commence firing. The Bren and the rifle fire broke windows and sent clumps of concrete ricocheting through the morning sunlight. After some thirty seconds, a flare went up in the air from a Very pistol flare gun. Veasey's patrol ceased fire.

A dozen or so Luftwaffe personnel in rather smart uniforms but looking extremely crestfallen appeared from behind the radio station. They had not had time to put their warm coats on although the fear of being shot won out against the numbing cold. Behind them came a commando reception party. As the Germans had run out of the back door, they had run immediately into their hands. Whether they understood the niceties of 'put your hands up or I'll blow your flipping head' off remains unclear. At any rate they complied. Lieutenant Banks and his section entered the Luftwaffe radio station and found an iron bar. They smashed the radio equipment with glee.

'It's all done, sir, no-one is sending a radio message from here today.'

'Well done, Banks. Right, well first of all get some of your chaps to pinch every document they can get their hands on. You never know what they might contain. Also, you might want to send one of your chaps up and bag that Nazi flag, though. That will make a lovely souvenir to take back to Troon.'

'Right, sir. Troon, sir? Are you joining us then?'

'If it's all as much fun as this, I definitely am. Come on, let's get moving, the Colonel says he can't wait for us if we're not back in time.'

They waited at the radio station just long enough for Michael Dunning-White to help himself to a very nice Leica Camera. Lieutenant Banks came into possession of a superb Luger pistol. Lieutenant Veasey, his black moustache covered by now in icicles, helped himself to a pair of high-quality binoculars. Lovat liberated a fleece-lined rawhide coat and pair of excellent Luftwaffe flying boots. The other ranks were not forgotten, and a case of Schnapps was brought back to help them with the return journey.

Arriving back at Svolvaer, the commandos found G troop in the town surrounded by an almost carnival atmosphere. The locals had come out and were plying the British and Norwegian soldiers with bread and ham and German ersatz coffee. It was made from acorns, tasted abysmal but was, at least, warm.

Without warning and certainly without any British naval action, a puff of smoke was seen from the *Bremen*'s mighty figure. Then came another and soon a pall of brown smoke was pouring out of her and forming a smoke cloud, which rose quickly through the cold, clear air.

Colonel Lister signalled the boarding party which he had sent onto the *Bremen*.

'Make sure she bloody well sinks.'

Naval ratings had gone down into the engine room and opened the seacocks. The freezing water poured into the mighty engine room like a fountain. They ran for the boats, it was not possible to say with any certainty how long the *Bremen* would take to sink. For good measure, they had attached limpet mines below the surface, which had caused the brown smoke. On returning, the Navy men reported that the *Bremen* was being used as a floating oil-processing factory. What a terrible comedown that was for a great lady of the sea. The destroyer HMS *Alfridi* put a few rounds into her to help her on her way to the bottom of the sea.

The morning was now clear and bright. The commandos were totally in charge of Svolvaer, as they were at Brettesnes around the corner. The commandos were by now giving the villagers some food and clothing, which they had brought from Scotland, plus some confectionary for the children. The villagers were very touched by this. They wanted to give the commandos presents. If Bill had found conditions to be spartan in Christmas-time Gloucester, times were much worse in German-occupied Norway.

All the locals had available were woollen mittens, which were hand-knitted and in very attractive Fair Isle patterns. The islanders took them off their hands and gave them to the commandos. As an exercise in propaganda, it was wonderful, a circumstance which the cameras did not fail to record. The backdrop to all of this was that the various fish-processing and storage facilities were burning brightly, and the mighty towers of black smoke went to the sky. Meanwhile the *Bremen* was listing and was clearly on her way to Davy Jones' locker.

On one side of the square, there was a queue of those Norwegians who wanted to return with the commandos to the UK.

'No, we cannot take women! Men only!'

All the women were turned away, at least that was the intention.

At 1100 hours, Colonel Lister gave the order to re-embark. Bill's task was to decommission the roadblock and line up his men for re-embarkation. The team from Brettesnes passed by in their landing craft. Over the hills, the results of their work were quite clear, more columns of black oily smoke. Re-embarkation took place in an orderly manner. However, there was one incident where a German officer was boarding, and British troops had to save him from being attacked by islanders. It was not clear what he had done but if the islanders had got him, he was going headfirst into the harbour. In those freezing waters, that was an effective death sentence. Whatever the Germans on the Lofoten Islands had done, they had by no means appealed to the hearts and minds of the vanquished Norwegians.

Back on the *Emma,* spirits were high. There was no time for delay. Three red star-shells from a Very pistol were the signal for all ranks to return to the ship. HMS *Alfridi* heeled tightly over to the *Emma.* Her master used a loud hailer, 'get the hell out of here and join the *Beatrix* and *Somali* in open water'. On the high seas, out of range of the Luftwaffe aircraft, a battle group of HMS *Rodney*, HMS *King George V* and the light cruisers HMS *Nigeria* and HMS *Dido* waited to give cover and protection against the threat of the powerful German battle cruisers *Scharnhorst* and *Gneisenau,* should they choose to appear.

The discovery of eight women stowaways on the *Emma* caused consternation. Sleeping quarters had to be found for them, as well as special segregated ablutions. One of the Norwegians on board was tasked with putting up signs to say, ladies only. In Norwegian, this translates as *bare dame.* This did not go unremarked among the several hundred testosterone-fuelled commandos on board. Further hilarity centred on Captain Cook, the single casualty who had shot himself in the thigh. The Germans and Norwegian collaborators were kept blindfolded, somewhere out of sight in the depths of the ship under heavy guard. The ship's radio officer picked up the 6 o'clock news from the BBC that evening and relayed it via the ship's loudspeaker.

This is John Snagge reporting. This morning our troops mounted a raid on the Lofoten Islands in Northern Norway. The targets were munitions factories, some 11 of which were destroyed. This was a highly successful raid with no casualties.

Well, 'no casualties' was almost true.

The camera team shot miles of film, which proved to be wonderful propaganda material in cinemas across the United Kingdom. The two major newsreel producers, Pathe News and Gaumont British News dedicated whole news programmes to the celebration of the raids. The best part for Britons, battered by the Germans, were the shots of humiliated German soldiers being taken blindfolded onto the ships and into captivity in Britain.

This had been a small raid against an obscure outpost of the German Reich. The Lofoten raid may have been a pinprick to Hitler's '1000-year Reich' but it was a morale-building success story when success stories were rare and seldom seen. If it had only been this, it would still be a success. But it was more than that.

As the *Emma* and the *Beatrix* came under the protection of the huge natural harbour at Scapa Flow, the escorting vessels peeled silently away and left them to enter the harbour on their own. As they did, so the crews of the huge battleships, cruisers and aircraft carriers emerged onto the rails of their respective ships. Each ship's company came smartly to attention as the two cross-channel ferries steamed silently by. Each ship's company raised their hats in the air. A massive roar, like a vast football crowd, echoed around the harbour as the commandos were cheered to their moorings.

In the pubs at Scapa, one story was told, time and time again. Lieutenant Wills of 3 Commando which had occupied Stamsund sent a telegram. It was addressed to A. Hitler of Berlin. It read, 'You said in your last speech that German troops would meet the British wherever they landed. Where are your troops?'

The German commander, who had witnessed this, complained about the un-soldierly deportment of the British troops and said he would make sure that the Führer would get to hear of it.

Also in No 3 Commando, Lieutenant Kimmins had taken his skis with him, in case he got some spare time during the raid. This he did and reported to anyone who was prepared to listen that the ski conditions were absolutely excellent. Pride of place in the bragging rights department, however, went to an unidentified member of 4 Commando who spent 30 of his 100 Krone pocket money in buying the services of a particularly friendly young lady in Svolvaer. He was destined to spend the remainder of his service in commandos with the nickname of Thirty-Krone Jack.

In every pub on the shoreline, sailors, airmen and soldiers from other regiments queued up to buy the commandos drinks. There was no inter-service rivalry now. Nos 3 and 4 Commando had done the country proud at a time when victories were few. It was good to be appreciated.

Back at Gourock, the *Emma* and the *Beatrix* sidled into their moorings on a miserable cold grey night with the mist rolling in from the Clyde. Captain Vaughan of 4 Commando was waiting on the quayside. Vaughan was standing in the glare of the lights from a car on the quayside. From the ship, Vaughan's voice could clearly be heard.

'Douse those lights, that dopey man on the dock! Don't you know there's a war on?'

It was good to be back. Of Vaughan, Bill would hear more, a lot more.

Chapter 12

Bill's Raid is Reported to the Führer

In writing a history of this kind, the author searches for reliable source information on which to base the developing narrative. If there is any existing evidence as to Adolf Hitler's response to the Lofoten Raid, then it is buried deeply in the uttermost recesses of military documentation. It is worth mentioning that vast swathes of German documentation did not survive the war.

However, it is not difficult to imagine the dialogue between Adolf Hitler and General Afred Jodl, his Chief of Operations. It is to Jodl, the task would have fallen to advise Hitler of this raid. We could imagine Jodl setting out the facts that several hundreds of these new gangster-like British commandos had undertaken a raid on fish-oil factories at some remote islands, 150 kilometres above the Artic Circle. They had found the German luxury liner *Bremen* in a harbour and sunk it.

Hitler's initial response cannot have been other than stark bafflement. On this day, 5 March 1941, Hitler and Jodl had the most pressing of matters to attend to. They were immersed in long relentless days planning an attack for 3,000,000 men to invade Russia in eight weeks' time. In contrast, the best that Britain could offer was this escapade. What was it? Was it a side show? Was it some sort of stunt? Was it some symbolic act of defiance? Hitler certainly understood actions of that type.

As a military man of considerable ability, we would imagine that Jodl would have advised Hitler on two aspects. Firstly, this raid did not fit any known British strategy. Secondly, it made no obvious sense, tactically. The battleship escort was evidence that Churchill had personally ordered it. Hitler and Jodl may have pondered whether this was a ploy to lure Germany's huge and menacing battle cruisers *Scharnhorst* and *Gneisenau* into the open sea to sink them? Another report, that morning, had indeed advised that the ancient but formidable British battleship HMS *Malaya* on convoy protection duties had engaged the *Scharnhorst*. The contact had been brief and neither side had scored a hit.

More tellingly the *Abwehr* [Military Intelligence] had picked up a message from Churchill to the Commander in Chief of the Royal Navy Home Fleet. Jodl would have shown the transcript to Hitler.

'I am so glad you were able to find the means of executing Claymore (the code name for the raid). This admirable raid has done serious damage to the enemy and has given an immense amount of innocent pleasure at home.'

Churchill was satisfied that the raid was successful. They were not after the battle cruisers.

How was the raid 'admirable'? What on earth was the 'serious damage', when all they had done was to blow up tanks containing fish oil and sunk a beautiful ship? We do not know but can guess that Hitler and Jodl decided that the answer to this absurd riddle lay in the words 'innocent pleasure'.

They could not spend too much time on this escapade; they really needed to get back to planning Operation Barbarossa, which was the biggest military operation in history. 'Innocent pleasure' seemed to say it all. It was easiest (we can assume) that they wrote off the Lofoten Raid as a propaganda stunt and morale booster for the consumption of the British public.

They were wrong.

The true story behind the Lofoten Raid would not surface until 30 years after the war.

Chapter 13

What Adolf Hitler and Bill Adlam Did Not Know

Neither Bill Adlam nor Adolf Hitler, nor anyone else outside the tightly restricted coterie of privileged people, knew about 'Ultra'. This was a project to break the hitherto unbreakable German 'Enigma' code. 'Enigma' was indeed unbreakable by any known method. The difference was that the Ultra team had devised 'Bombes', the world's first programmable computers. Given the requisite amount of 'blood, sweat and tears', the team was capable of using the new technology to make the vital breakthrough. The ability to read the German operational orders would give the British an inestimable advantage in the war.

The first problem was that the team needed an actual Enigma machine (or at least part of one). This would allow them to program the Bombe to create their own virtual Enigma machine. They also needed the code books which told operatives how to set up the machine.

The second problem was how to get that possession without the Germans knowing it. That is where the Lofoten raid came in.

After the event, the Lofoten raid had been given maximum propaganda coverage in cinemas throughout the UK and was presented to the British people as a military raid and propaganda exercise. It was a smokescreen and one of the greatest deceptions in military history. It was Alan Turing, the chief codebreaker at the Bletchley Park spy centre who had pressed MI6 for a 'pinch' of a shipboard Enigma machine plus code books. Operation Claymore had pulled it off. It was not a perfect pinch but it was the best breakthrough to date.

If Turing could get his hands on one of these vital 'Enigma' devices, then U-boat orders could be decrypted and convoys could be routed away from them. That would have cut down the massive losses of shipping in the Atlantic Ocean. These, Winston Churchill would later admit were the losses that worried him most throughout six years of war. It would give Britain a vastly better chance of avoiding the defeat which had stared her so clearly in the face in late 1940.

The borderline between the real world, as Bill Adlam knew it, and the looking-glass world of espionage lay in the exchange of fire which Bill heard between HMS *Somali* and the armed trawler *Krebs*. The *Krebs* had fired at *Somali* at 0620 and in the exchange of fire, had been hit by a 4.7-inch shell on the bridge.

The *Krebs* had floated out of control from the point where it was hit and had beached on a small islet opposite Svolvaer. Lieutenant Warmington, signals officer of the *Somali*, suggested to Captain Caslon that he might take a boarding party and search the *Krebs*. Warmington was most definitely not in the Ultra secret. His orders were that where possible German ships should be boarded and anything which looked like communications equipment or code books should be taken back to Scapa Flow and given to Naval Intelligence.

A Norwegian trawler had moored alongside the *Somali*. Warmington commandeered it and took a three-man boarding party to the *Krebs*. He also took Lieutenant Harper-Gower, a commando officer and Major Aslett, a signals officer from Force Headquarters. They found the *Krebs'* captain and two sailors lying dead in the wheelhouse. It cannot have been a beautiful sight. The 4.7-inch shell which hit the wheelhouse had mutilated the men horribly. The five surviving German sailors did not put up a fight. Some were injured, but their main interest was to have their wounded comrades attended to. Warmington told his boarding party to secure the German personnel, while he went to search for communication equipment. He did not find an Enigma machine, which suggests that the crew had already thrown it overboard. Warmington did, however, win a highly acceptable second prize.

His suspicions aroused by a locked drawer, Warmington pulled out his service revolver and fired at the lock as he would have seen done in the countless cowboy films of the day. He immediately ducked. His bullet ricocheted around the cabin. For a moment, he thought that he had shot one of the others or himself. The drawer opened. It contained two rotor wheels. He did not know the significance, but they looked as though they came from some sort of coding device. They were from an Enigma machine and were to be of great use to Alan Turing in breaking the German coding method.

Warmington also came across something else. It was a book with the opaque title of *Schlüßeltafeln M-Allgemein Heimische Gewäßer Kennwort HAU Prüfnummer 1566*. He had no idea what this book might be, but instinct told him it might be useful. It was. He had in his hands the Enigma settings for German home waters. This was exactly what Alan Turing had asked for when he had gone to MI6 and asked for a 'pinch.' Next to a complete Enigma machine, this was the crown jewels. The task force arrived back at Scapa Flow on 7 March. The rotor wheels and code book were handed to Bletchley Park and Alan Turing on 12 March. The settings were for February, which had just passed. This, however, gave codebreakers the method by which the settings were made. That was to take them a long way forward.

Admiral Doenitz's diary records that in the next few weeks the British were unaccountably routing their convoys away from the U-boat ambushes.

On 27 March, a Royal Navy battle fleet, consisting of three battleships, four cruisers and an aircraft carrier, stumbled 'as if by chance' on an Italian battle fleet off Cape Matapan in Greece. The Italians lost five cruisers, two destroyers and the battleship *Vittorio Veneto* was badly mauled. British casualties were two naval aircraft. The action led to the Italians keeping their fleet out of the Eastern Mediterranean, which was crucial some months later when British and Australian forces were evacuated from Crete to North Africa. This victory was directly attributable to codebreaking which flowed from what Turing had called 'the Lofoten pinch'.

The ball was rolling. The Lofoten pinch was by no means the end of the cat-and-mouse game between the German *Abwehr* intelligence arm and the codebreakers at Bletchley Park. It did, however, represent the tipping point where advantage moved away from the Germans and towards the British.

The Germans were not to know that their codes had been broken nor how it was achieved. This also applied to the men, including Bill Adlam, who played their part in it. There is a detail in the newsreels, which gives the game away, seven decades later. It is a detail which Bill and his commando colleagues may have wondered about on the journey back to Scapa Flow. It was the blindfolding of the German prisoners. It was not to humiliate, although that was a popular aspect at the time. It was to prevent them seeing that the German ships were being searched before they were sunk. The raid was a spoof which had been devised by the Secret Intelligence Service, later known as MI6. Planning had taken into account that a German prisoner could have written home and encoded in his letter 'ships searched'. That would have been enough to tip off German intelligence that the raid was after the code machines, not merely to blow-up fish-oil factories.

The story does not quite end there. In the 1960s, Bill as a keen cinemagoer doubtlessly went to see the James Bond films. The MI6 officer who had devised and planned the Lofoten raid was none other than James Bond author, Ian Fleming. It would never have occurred to Bill that the plot of *From Russia with Love* – retrieval of a stolen encryption device – bears more than a passing resemblance to the Lofoten raid.

One of the three men, upon whom James Bond is reputedly based, was none other than Ian Fleming's cousin, Lord Lovat. Bill had seen Lovat for the first time on the quay at Gourock and he was the man who had had shown such dash and verve on the Lofoten raid. That same Lord Lovat would play a great part in Bill's life for the next two years.

Chapter 14

Operation Pilgrim – Bill Goes to Africa

Saturday, 27 June 1941, Inveraray, Argyllshire

The training went on and on and on. 4 Commando were doing endless amphibious training in Loch Fyne and Inveraray. On one typical day, the rain poured down, the commandos sloshed ashore. The pack mules carried the live ammunition as usual. They had now become so inured to carrying hundreds of rounds of live ammunition and mortar bombs that they had long ceased to remember that they were taking death-defying risks. Someone noticed an LCA (landing craft assault) lurking down at the loch. The only occupants were the three-man crew and a couple of oldish looking officers.

'You know who that is, Bill?'

'No, what? You mean in that LCA over there?'

'Yeah, it's bloody Churchill.'

Bill and other soldiers peered out of their landing craft through the murk.

'Good God! I think you're right.'

Lovat was leading the assault in the exercise.

'OK, everyone, up to the Duke of Argyll's Castle, it's just 20 minutes up there. When you get there, get fell in sharpish, you're going to be inspected.'

'What, sir, by the prime minister?'

'Er, yes, it looks very much like it, oh and that other elderly officer is Sir Roger.'

Half an hour later, 4 Commando fell in in front of the huge highland castle. A car crunched up the gravel. An equerry opened it and there in all his glory was Winston Churchill.

James Dunning, who knew Bill in 4 Commando, wrote,

Winston went between the two ranks. The awful 'Scotch mist' weather prevented the great man from speaking to any of the men, but we were enthralled to see Winnie in the flesh. There he was, with shoulders hunched, cigar in mouth, blue naval-type peaked cap on head, and as he marched between our ranks, staring into our eyes with those almost-twinkling blue eyes of his, he seemed to strike a bond with us. It was a memorable occasion.

It was also the last time they saw 'Old' Sir Roger. He was replaced by Earl Mountbatten as Head of Combined Operations. There were rumours in the officers' mess of power struggles in high places. 'Old' Sir Roger had lost and Dickie Mountbatten had won. It was not only in high places that the winds of change were blowing.

Saturday, 13 September 1941, Troon, Ayrshire

There were a couple of crucial changes in the commandos during this time. Captain Charles Vaughan who had welcomed 4 Commando home from the Lofoten Raid was now Major and had taken over as second in command. Captain Lord Lovat, who had been a supernumery on the Lofoten raid, had joined the commandos as training officer. At the time, both appointments appeared to be routine, but both men were to play a profound role in Bill Adlam's future.

From the point of view of Bill Adlam, frustration was not the flippin' word for it! He had had word on Wednesday that his wife, Gladys had given birth to a daughter, Ann Patricia on 9 September 1942. He was delighted. He was also screaming in an agony of despair.

'Permission to return home, sir, on compassionate leave,' he had asked Major Vaughan in hopefulness.

'Refused, Adlam, and before you ask, I can't tell you why.'

'Very good, sir.'

Bill's record shows that he had been sent for training in the Orkney Islands but on returning to Troon, he never disembarked from the ship, the HMS *Royal Scotsman*. Some 26 members of 4 Commando were assigned to a task, as yet unspecified. Then without warning, on the quayside, troops appeared. Some were from other commandos; some from the Royal Marines, some from other units of the British Army. Four days later, on September 17th the *Royal Scotsman* weighed anchor and sailed south by the Isle of Arran. The 26 men from 4 Commando were led by Lieutenant Style and the two operational sections by Sergeant John Groom from the Royal Engineers and Bill Adlam.

'So, where the hell does he think we're going?'

'Search me, but I counted the landing ships, there's ten of them and with the escort that makes 14 ships.'

'Are we back to standing orders and wearing those bloody Mae Wests at all times?'

'We certainly are, it's your life jacket you silly bugger. And don't forget that if you're sick you have to do it on the leeward side of the ship. And you can't wear hobnailed boots or else they'll carve up the wooden decking and the chief petty officer will keelhaul you.'

The Irish Sea was calm. They slid past St Bees head, past the Isle of Anglesey and then past Land's End. Now they were into the wide expanses of the Atlantic. They all had to line up for shots from the medical officer and were given some little yellow pills to take. Ominously, no-one told them what the injections or the pills were for.

The *Royal Scotsman* anchored just off the dockside at Gibraltar. Scrambling nets were run over the sides. This was wonderful! It meant that they could spend a lot of time swimming in the warm Mediterranean water, which was extremely enjoyable. The way into the water was easy, over the side for a gravity-assisted descent. The re-emergence out of the water was painful on the soles of the feet and up the rough rope nets, but they were commandos, they could take it. They were only allowed a single day on shore and that was for a route march to the top of the rock where they saw a wonderful vista out to sea plus some extremely scabby monkeys. It was noticeable that they were not allowed into town on their own, unsupervised, where they might say something of interest to the many Spanish pro-Fascist spies who were known to infest Gibraltar.

Saturday, 27 September 1941, Gibraltar

The force left Gibraltar in the small hours, quietly and unobtrusively. They were heading south but the destination still remained unknown.

After a week, Lieutenant Style called all 26 of 4 Commando together.

'We will be arriving in Freetown, Sierra Leone, tomorrow. Our mission is to establish a base camp and training facilities for the rest of the commandos, who will arrive later. We will live in a tented camp. Further standing orders will be put out after we arrive regarding fraternising with the locals and the things you should and should not do, such as not drinking unboiled water.

This is not Troon; this is the tropics and we need to take precautions against a whole range of nasty bugs. Dismissed.'

'Can we ask questions, sir?'

'No. Dismissed.'

Sunday, 5 October 1941, Freetown, Sierra Leone

It rained! They had never seen rain like this. As the *Royal Scotsman* was guided by tugs into the harbour of Freetown, the rain that came down resembled a solid wall of water. Dozens of vendors in colourful clothes and equally colourful boats rowed out to meet them.

'Buy my bananas, buy my oranges.'

To the men on The *Royal Scotsman*, this was a rare opportunity. They had not seen tropical fruit for years. In wartime Britain, it had almost disappeared.

'There's a guy selling pineapples, I hear they are lovely, never had one myself!'

The notion of an eight-kilometre hike to commandos, even carrying full packs, ammunition, and weapons, was not a daunting prospect. At least, it was not daunting in theory! After only a couple of hundred yards, they began to sweat profusely, their khaki drill uniforms were already saturated from the rain. Their hobnailed, leather boots were waterlogged and becoming heavier by the minute. The whole depressing scenario was, however, brightened up by the local Africans, who smiled and waved in a manner very different to the dour Scots of Ayrshire or Inveraray who had watched their marches previously. The children were especially striking with lovely open faces which expressed such joy at seeing these huge khaki-clad giants with white skin marching in impeccable step, down muddy African streets.

They duly occupied Wilberforce camp and in short order, organised a firing range and begun weapons training. Lieutenant Style began a routine of route marches. Under the African sun, this was very different to marching around Ayrshire or Inveraray. The temperature was above 30 Celsius and made worse by the humidity. Mosquitoes were a constant problem at dawn and dusk. The first cases of malaria were encountered, despite the little yellow quinine tablets. Unlike the arrangements at Troon, where the lady of the house did all the cooking and cleaning, the men now had to draw rations and cook them themselves.

The *Royal Scotsman* remained at Freetown harbour during all this time. All stores were kept in the ship safe from pilfering fingers and it acted as a floating headquarters for all the hapless troops in their various tented camps around Freetown. After some eight weeks Lieutenant Style brought the detachment back to the *Royal Scotsman*. Rumours abounded that they were going home. There was to be no such outbreak of good fortune. The troop had to transfer all of the stores from the *Scotsman* to the HMS *Queen Emma*, she of Lofoten fame, who had entered the harbour a couple of days previously.

The *Royal Scotsman* was then used for training in landings. They did several landings on nearby Banana Island. The landings were similar to the crash landings, which they had undertaken in the Orkneys before they left but this was in the full summer sun. It was a moot point which was worse, the all-enveloping blackness and cold of the Orkneys or the debilitating heat and mosquitoes of Freetown.

Wednesday, 10 December 1941, Freetown, Sierra Leone

Lieutenant Style had reveille sound early, very early.

'Everyone into full marching order, we're boarding the *Emma* this morning. There will be a full briefing when we are on board.'

The troop came alive! This was a real job, another one like the Lofotens. You could feel it. Morale soared. Was this it? Was this what they were brought here for? And just what was the reason they had done this training and brought into this mosquito-infested swamp?

Style called the troop to order.

'We are part of Operation Pilgrim, heading for Ascension Island. HMS *Devonshire* intercepted a German raider which scuttled itself. The crew were reported to have been taken off by two U-boats, which were heading for Ascension. The garrison there is very small. If the Germans were determined and had the right training, they could take Ascension Island, which is, of course, British territory.'

The ranks buzzed. At last, they were faced with a real job.

'Right, I want all weapons in perfect order. I want bayonets as sharp as scalpels but do not prime grenades until I give the order. There will be a kit inspection each day before we arrive, which will be in three days' time. As ever, you do not need your gasmasks, but you are to wear Mae Wests at all times.'

The *Emma* and the *Beatrix* headed southwards through the night with a complement of men eagerly anticipating another punch-up with the Nazis. It was so fitting that it should be these two ships that would carry them.

These two ships were the heroines of the Lofotens and were a good omen for the attack, which was becoming closer.

'Now hear this, now hear this,' came over the loudspeaker.

'All ranks to assemble aft for an important announcement.'

'It's a false alarm, chaps. We're turning back.'

Bill's record shows that he was no longer officially posted to the first ship the *Royal Scotsman*, he is now posted to the *Queen Emma*. It was all academic as they returned to Wilberforce camp. They were, however, 26 useful pairs of hands. They helped the local authority build a roadway through the countryside. They took part in exercises with the West African Frontier Force. Then they were back on the *Emma* in the role of gunners in a journey down to Lagos, Nigeria and Takoradi. It was uneventful. They had still not been told why they had been brought to West Africa.

Monday, 9 February 1942, Freetown, Sierra Leone

Lieutenant Style called all ranks to order.

'The action for which we were brought here has been cancelled. We leave for home today.'

We can only imagine the jollities and the celebrations which ensued. Style impressed one major thing on them.

'As it happens, this operation has been cancelled. If it had gone ahead, it would have been of incalculable importance to the war effort. I have to impress on all of you that you can never tell anyone that you have been here. You cannot tell a living soul that you ever came to Sierra Leone or what you did here.'

'Is that clear?'

'Sir!'

As a footnote to history, it is notable that in *March Past*, Lord Lovat's autobiography, Operation Pilgrim is described as something which only happened in the Orkneys but never got off the ground. He omits to mention that a task force of some 14 ships including 26 men from 4 Commando went to Sierra Leone to organise a base camp for an attack on the Canary Islands in case the Germans had attempted to occupy them. That is what they were there for. The Germans did not attack, but the men were left there for 159 days. They were never told the reason for being there.

Bill was sad to hear of rumours that were circulating that 'Old' Sir Roger's son, Lieutenant Colonel Geoffrey Keyes had been killed in action. It was not known what operation he had been on, but as he was in No 11 (Scottish) Commando, this was not unusual. What was unusual was that No 11 Commando had been immediately disbanded. It was one of those things that you just did not ask about. Some six months later the plot would thicken.

Having left the tropical heat of Africa and back in the grey mists of Scotland, Bill Adlam had discovered that many of the Troon-based commandos had been to train at the new Commando Basic Training Centre at Achnacarry, which had replaced the narrow confines of Lochailort. They could not stop talking about it. There was weapons training on British and German weapons, which included live firing ranges. There was fitness training the like of which was beyond imagination. There was mountaineering training, boat training, opposed landing training. Bill felt definite pangs of jealousy. He knew he was a good soldier. The stories about Achnacarry told him that this was the stairway to his own particular heaven of military Nirvana. He had missed out on a training course there because he had been stuck in flaming Sierra Leone with its mosquitoes, snakes and the never-ending boredom.

Well, there was only one thing to do, bloody well get on with whatever he was getting on with.

Chapter 15

Under Starters Orders

Sunday, 16 August 1942, Weymouth.

It was not lost on troops that a motorcycle despatch rider arrived at Lovat's headquarters with a box of documents 'for his eyes only'. In the last few months, Lovat had been promoted to Lieutenant Colonel and was now the officer commanding number 4 Commando.

HMS *Prins Albert* had slipped her moorings from Weymouth Harbour and quietly put out to sea for no apparent purpose and without fanfare. Nevertheless, there was a certain atmosphere in the air. They could smell it. Some thought it was another job, although this time, preferably more active than the anti-climax in the tropics. The word went around that a new consignment had just arrived from Sheffield, hundreds of bayonets. A brigadier called Head was working in a closed office with Lovat. Who was Head? Where was he from? Why did he monopolise the CO's time? It was all very strange.

Monday, 17 August 1942, Weymouth

The alarm clock rang. Bill turned it off with sleep still in his eyes. He came to. He looked at the time, it was 0500 hours. He was due on parade in an hour but hoped he would be able to leave without disturbing the family, with whom he was billeted. He had told them that he would be away for a few days. There was a light tap on the door.

'Are you up, Bill?' came a whisper through the door.

'Yes, but there's no reason for you to be.'

'Come on, lad, we've got a cuppa for you.'

'Oh, you daft lot, you didn't have to get up.'

Five minutes later, he shared a cup of tea with his landlord and landlady. John Snagge on the radio reported that a bomber command raid on Düsseldorf had damaged hundreds of war factories and the outlying town of Neuss had its city centre destroyed. Four of our aircraft failed to return.

'Poor buggers, hope they did some bloody damage to Jerry, though.'

And he drank his tea.

'Any idea where they're sending you?' asked the landlady.

'No, they never tell us. It could be anywhere or nowhere. He had a good idea that this was going to be the real thing. Even in his dozy early-morning state he remained on guard enough to be circumspect in talking with civvies.

'Well, thank you both for putting up with me for the last couple of weeks. I'm sorry it's been so short. Tell you what, I'll leave my ration book here.'

The possession of an extra ration book led directly to a path of utter bliss. It meant extra butter, eggs and now, even more soap in the house.

'Oh, we couldn't, Bill, especially not after those treats you brought us. The pineapple slices were so nice. They're the first we've seen in, what? Three years?'

'You might as well take it because if I don't come back, it doesn't matter and if I do come back, they'll give me a new one. If it is a raid, they turn our pockets out to make sure we have nothing that can give the Jerries any information.'

'Well, thank you very much but you take care, we want to see you back and all the rest of you lads.'

'Mornin', Sergeant Adlam.'

Lieutenant David Style caught up with Bill as he walked.

'I heard Düsseldorf got a pasting last night, sir. We're making the bastards sweat at last.'

'Oh, that's good! A few more dead Germans is all to the good. I don't feel sorry for them underneath five or six hundred Lancaster bombers, do you?'

'Not in the slightest, sir.'

In so saying, Bill spoke for a complete generation of British people.

'It really is incredible, Adlam, who would ever have thought that civilised men would say they didn't feel sorry for a city full of civvies getting bombed?'

On one side of the square a convoy of Bedford 3-ton trucks waited in silence to take them to wherever they were going. From Weymouth, they found themselves 60 kilometres away at the small town of Ringwood.

Bill overheard Lovat talking to the mysterious Brigadier Head.

'I shall expect a despatch rider at Ringwood Post Office to check on someone's damned fool arrangements.'

This was not a training exercise.

'Where is the commanding officer from Transport Command?' asked Lovat of Morris. 'I've absolutely no idea, sir. I don't think we've seen him.'

One of the drivers interjected with, 'the commanding officer is here, sir.'

A scruffy-looking officer emerged from the shadows with his greatcoat collar turned up and a cigarette dangling from his lips. He did not look like the kind of soldier that Lovat would take to. This proved to be correct. Lovat punched him across the face, which sent the cigarette spinning into the gutter and the scruffy officer after it.

'Sergeant Major, put this man on report for being late on parade. I'll take it up with his CO.' Matters were clearly becoming tense.

Later, at Southampton, a voice said 'Good God! Look at that!'

'What is it?'

'It's the *Prins Albert* and we're heading right for her.'

The departure of the *Prins Albert* from Weymouth had clearly been a deceptive move to confuse any lurking German informants.

As they stumbled up the gangplank at Southampton docks onto the *Prins Albert*, one aspect of the embarkation became immediately clear. Military police were guarding the gangplanks and were patrolling the whole area. Once they were on, they were not getting off until… until what?

Tuesday, 18 August 1942, Southampton Docks

'Now hear this!' the voice grated from the loudspeaker. 'All ranks at 1730 hours to the main assembly point on the boat deck for an important briefing.'

The message was repeated.

'Now hear this! Now hear this! All weapons are to be checked and cleaned in daylight. All magazines are to be filled in daylight. All hand grenades are to be primed in daylight. All equipment is to be checked in daylight. All non-commissioned officers are to check all troops' equipment and ammunition in daylight. Troops are not allowed to carry rations or water.'

As they shuffled to the assembly point, the word went around, 'It's Mountbatten.'

'It's important then.'

Bill's stomach tightened further.

Lord Louis Mountbatten was born His Serene Highness, Prince Louis of Battenberg. Despite the impeccable German lineage, Mountbatten was firmly part of the British establishment, which had resulted in him acceding to several extremely high-flying positions. He had replaced Sir Roger Keyes as Commander of Combined Operations and so was Bill Adlam's ultimate boss. It is worth mentioning that in the world of blue blood, Mountbatten greatly outranked Lovat, who inhabited only the bottom ranks of that rarefied world as a mere baron.

Mountbatten opened with a couple of saucy stories to build a rapport with the troops. Then he came to the business of the moment.

'As you shouldn't know but have no doubt guessed by now, there's a party on tonight.'

He waited for the spontaneous cheering and applause to die down.

'It will be the biggest raid to date. 4 Commando has an extremely important part to play. Tonight, you will attack a battery which overlooks the approaches to Dieppe. Your mission in 4 Commando is to attack and destroy the Hess Battery. This is a complex of six large naval gun emplacements in the village of Varengeville to the west of Dieppe. This battery must be annihilated at all costs. Your role is vital if the raid is to succeed. If you are not successful, then it will not be possible to carry out the larger raid, which is planned for Dieppe. The six guns at Varengeville have the firepower to blow our entire fleet out of the water. I don't give a damn what Germans you kill and what Germans you don't, but don't forget that you have to get the guns.'

'I wish you all luck.'

In saying this, he departed.

Bill was now feeling very tense and very tight in the stomach. He had felt tense before the Lofoten raid but what had transpired now seemed to be almost like a student prank. Dieppe would not be a prank. It would be a tough job, with mates getting killed. He hoped that if the bullet hit him, it would be quick. He did not fancy a shot to the spine that would leave him in wheelchair for the rest of his life. The graveyard would be much better.

After Mountbatten's short address, Lord Lovat spoke next. It is fair to say that the men of 4 Commando were in awe of Lovat, perhaps more so on that early evening in the Solent than at any other time. Lovat's voice has been described as a little high-pitched and with that pronounced drawl affected by intra-war graduates of Oxford and Cambridge.

'Your mission is simple and straightforward, destroy the battery at Varengeville.'

From somewhere behind a screen, unseen hands pulled a cord. A map of the raid was disclosed. Aerial photographs were displayed as was a model showing the countryside in three dimensions. Lovat let them study it for a moment.

'I want you all to understand. This is not a battle. It is a bank raid. We land. We do the job. We leave.'

He outlined the raid.

Lovat was right, it was a bank raid.

'Well, you all said you wanted to have a go at Jerry and who am I to deprive you of that particular delight? Now, you will notice that we have with us some friends from overseas.'

Lovat introduced the French commandos.

'These are a present from Colonel Lister at 10 Commando.'

Once again, there was a round of applause. Lister, Lovat's predecessor at 4 Commando, was still popular with the men.

'We also have with us some American Rangers, who, I am reliably informed by a friend of mine called Colonel Vaughan…'

Again, there was cheering from the ranks. Vaughan had been a captain, then a major, in 4 Commando but was now the commanding officer at that training establishment at Achnacarry, which Bill was still very keen to visit.

'… have actually passed out through Achnacarry.'

'Achna – bloody – carry,' Bill must have thought. 'Everybody in commandos has been through there and I wasted all that time stuck somewhere else.'

'We will all wear cap comforters,' Lovat continued. 'Helmets were a great idea in World War I but we are not fighting trench warfare, we are engaged in a smash and grab raid. Helmets are nothing short of an encumbrance and we are very unlikely to get any shelling from enemy artillery.'

He looked around to ensure that everyone understood what he was demanding of them.

'Now, by the same token, Captain Walker will establish a Regimental Aid Post at the top of the cliff above Orange Beach 1.'

He pointed the place out on a large map hung just behind him.

'If you see commandos get wounded, you are not to fall out to help them. I repeat that. You are not under any circumstances to fall out to help fallen commandos. Walking wounded will make their own way back to the aid post. For more severely wounded, we will improvise. Please note, there will be stretchers in the landing craft, I am not having those stretchers brought ashore until late in the attack.'

This was such a radical departure from normal arrangements that it brought a silence over his men. There had been stretchers used in training, but this was different. They would have to carry injured or dying men.

'There will also be a three-inch mortar at the top of the cliff to hit the enemy position once the fun has started. I must also point out this gentleman here. He is Mr Austin of the *Daily Herald*. He is a newspaper reporter and non-combatant. He will land on Orange Beach 1.'

'I hope he does not get in our way,' thought Bill.

Lovat continued, 'We have assurances that his fitness level is up to this job. He will not be provided with any armaments. If he is hit, then the same orders will apply.'

That meant that he would be left for medical orderlies or would be left to the Germans.

'I also have to point out that Sergeant Langland… where is he?'

'Over here, sir.'

'Sergeant Langland will be our official photographer. He has a rather snazzy German Leica camera to take snaps with.'

'Where did you acquire the camera, Sergeant Langland?'

'It was donated by a kind German Lieutenant in the Lofotens, sir.'

This brought forth a burst of laughter and applause.

Lovat continued, 'When the guns have been blown, C troop will form a perimeter around the cliff top at Orange Beach 1. At this point, I will move up stretchers for the severely wounded. All ranks will proceed through the cordon, climb down the gully to the beach. As the landing craft come in, embark on the first available, regardless of rank, unit or wounds. I will fire a single red Very-pistol shot, which will signify 30 minutes before the final withdrawal. When you see the red signal, wherever you are, you will run split-arse for the beach. The rear party will organise Goatley boats [collapsible boats made of wood and canvas] to ferry you to the landing craft if necessary. The final thing for me to do is to give you the password and reply. Tonight's password is 'monkey' and the reply is 'nuts'. If anyone gives an incorrect reply you are to shoot them immediately.'

Lovat looked around the assembly to ensure that everyone understood what he was saying.

'Gentlemen, what is the password?'

'Monkey,' they chorused.

'And the reply?'

'NUTS!' they shouted with glee.

'And nuts to you, as well, you gang of desperados!'

Lovat asked for questions. The tension in the assembly point was now at fever pitch.

This is what they had trained for, what they had lived for, a crack at Jerry. It was now over two years since the debacle at Ledringhem. The Fifth Gloucesters had fought like lions and had done brilliantly well. They did not have the sheer military talent, the equipment, the training or the brilliant leadership of 4 Commando. He had started as a lowly reservist, had regular promotions, won a medal, fought and survived a bloody battle. Now, he had been accepted into an elite unit in which he felt proud to serve.

The ship rocked a little. She was slipping her moorings. It was 2030. He felt as if someone had placed a building brick in his stomach. He had seen action three times now. He knew the horror of it, the butcher's shop redness of smashed-up corpses and the awful bereavements of good friends.

Bill swung into his hammock and hoped he would be alive at this time tomorrow. If he was not still alive, he wanted the epitaph to read, 'He did his bit'. He could not do more. He knew that if it was necessary then he would go down fighting and take as many of the German bastards with him as possible. The ship rocked in the gentle swell, it was almost like a millpond. It was silent now, blacked out but through the darkness he could feel the locked-up tension of men about to risk their lives. He fell into a shallow sleep.

Chapter 16

Dieppe – Operation Cauldron

Wednesday, 19 August 1942, English Channel

'Wakey, wakey, sarge! This is reveille.'

The first thing was to overcome the terror inside. As he swung out of his hammock, he had to grab the initiative with the section and make sure that he communicated calm professionalism, controlled emotion and strict following of what they had been trained to do.

'Get out!' the inner demons screamed at him once again.

Once again, he suppressed them. His watch showed him it was 0115.

'Right, you lot, I want you in fighting order in five minutes. Be ready for inspection.'

'Right, sarge!' said a weary voice, which had only just returned from the land of nod.

'Right. Let's see your fighting order.'

He knew that he had to find a fault somewhere to impress on them his control of himself and his control of the troops.

'Oy! Evans and McAllister! I said, "fighting order".'

'Sarge?'

'Well get your cap comforters on! Bloody hell! If the CO sees my lads are that bloody sloppy, he's likely to shoot me himself and blame it on Jerry.'

They laughed and the two offending men did as they were told.

'Sorry, sarge.'

'Right, first of all, what is the password?'

'Monkey' they chorused.

'And the response?'

'NUTS!' they replied.

'And if someone gives an incorrect password or reply?'

'Shoot them, sarge!'

'Good lads!'

'Right, now have you all got at least five number 68 grenades?'

'Yes, sarge.'

'And are they all primed?'

'Yes, sarge.'

'Right now, I want each of you to turn to the man on your right and go through his pockets. I want to know if you find anything. You can keep your fags and matches but that's all.'

'Have you all made your wills out and written a last letter to your families?'

Most had but a couple of commandos were silent.

'Have you two made your wills out?'

'No, sarge.'

'Well, you were told to and it's too bloody late now.'

A smell of warm food wafted through the mess deck.

'Right, well, let's get some breakfast.'

All meals were served and eaten in total silence. Someone mentioned that stewards had been pestering officers to pay their mess bills. Officers used credit in the mess to purchase food and drink. At the end of a month, they would be presented with a bill to settle the account.

The clear implication was that some would not return. Normally, such an observation would have led to corny jokes, smart comments, and gallows humour. This morning, it was met with complete silence. In three hours' time, some of the men he was now talking with would be dead. He hoped he would not be one of them.

At the end of the meal, Bill organised his men to don their black and dark-green face camouflage.

'Right lads, the CO has seen enough of your ugly faces so slap it on.'

'The CO wants to see everyone on the main mess deck.'

The word was passed around in a hoarse whisper. The ship was coming closer to the enemy coast. The engines slowed and stopped. Z hour was approaching.

Colonel Lord Lovat gave only a short address before embarkation.

'This is not the hour for a speech. None of us feel very strong at this hour in the morning. But I'd like to say this is the toughest job we've had, and I expect every man to contribute something special.

'Those of you who are going into action for the first time, remember that noise always sounds worse than it is, and that if you're hit in the dark, it's just bad luck. I know that you'll come back in a blaze of glory. Remember that you represent the flower of the British Army. We certainly expect casualties tonight and they may be heavy. If a man is wounded, then my clear order is to leave him behind for the medical orderlies.'

He looked around to ensure that everyone had heard the order. Lovat then proceeded,

'The German soldier is not at his best at night.'

Bill Adlam must have chuckled quietly at that strange utterance. He had seen Jerry at close quarters in the middle of the night, which Colonel Lord Lovat had not, the German soldier had been pretty darned good.

'… and therefore, the Commando has an advantage. The first part of the raid will take place just before dawn at 0430 hours. Remember, everyone, I want a little extra from each man on this occasion. Best of luck to all of you. Sergeant Major Morris, please dismiss the men.'

'Battalion, DIS-MISS!'

'Alright, you lot! Get cracking!'

So, this was it then, the moment of truth.

Bill put on the last of his black and green camouflage paint and swung his Thompson machine gun over his shoulder.

'My section, with me, starboard side first boat.'

All five companies moved as if in a trance. They all knew exactly where to go and took their places. It was going to be a bright morning. There were no clouds. The French coast could be seen some 15 kilometres away. Ah! There was the lighthouse they had been told to look out for, the lighthouse of Pointe D'Ailly.

The inmates of the seven landing-craft heard a whine of winches and saw the ship's huge hull pass above them. They touched the water with barely a splash. Bill looked at his watch, it was 0300 exactly. They were exactly on time.

'Let's go!'

He heard Lovat's voice from the landing craft behind him. The engines fired and they moved towards the lighthouse. The landing craft were in two lines travelling across the calm sea at seven knots. The left hand three were destined for Orange Beach 1. The right-hand four aimed for Orange Beach 2 (with B company and Bill). A Motor Torpedo Boat (MTB) lay off Bill's landing craft far to the right and a corvette, HMS *Grey Goose* astern as escort.

Also to the right was HMS *Fernie*, a Hunt class destroyer. There was someone of extreme interest on board, Ian Fleming. The MI6 man was wearing the uniform of a lieutenant commander. Fleming's role in the Dieppe raid was to watch a covert operation happening behind the scenes.

This was yet another example of the smoke-and-mirrors nature of much of World War II.

SPLASH! A wave broke over the craft and awoke Bill from his doze. He was aware that his arm and leg were dead from cramp, and he did not have the space to stretch out. There was something else. He could hear staccato reports of naval gunfire. From his position, uncomfortably seated on the bottom of the landing craft, he was only able to see a wedge of sky.

'Where's the action?' a voice asked. 'It's about five miles [eight kilometres] away' said a sailor, 'there's another lot going ashore and they're getting shot up pretty badly. There's a load of star-shells and tracer.'

They would learn later that this was Number 3 Commando who had run into a German patrol and were being severely attacked. It was now 0340. It was frustrating not to be able to see what was happening, but it was also comforting that there was no ordnance coming their way and the lighthouse continued to shine for five minutes every quarter of an hour.

Bill did not require the situation to be spelled out. A single shell would sink their landing craft and there would be no survivors. The course of the landing craft lurched suddenly to starboard.

By now the light from the lighthouse was falling right across them. The sailor said, 'Don't worry, lads, it is very hard to pick out low-lying craft at night. They still haven't seen us.'

'There's lots of gunfire' said the sailor, 'but there's none of it coming our way and they don't seem to have seen the major's group either. Right, we're approaching the landing ground.'

The white chalk cliffs were now clearly visible in the moonlight. The sea was still calm and with an untroubled glassy surface. The landing craft was filled to overflowing with barely the space for each man to cuddle his Thompson gun or rifle. The grenades on Bill's chest pressed into the back of the man in front of him in the sardine-like enclosure. All ranks were silent.

'Has anyone got any gold teeth?' asked a voice.

'Yes, I have,' said a couple of voices.

'What's that got to do with anything?' asked a third voice.

'Well, if you get shot, I'll come around and pick them out. I could get a few bob for those down Hatton Garden.'

'Shut up!' said the voice of authority.

Though the dawn light, he could just see that the dark shape of the leading landing craft, with Veasey's section beached. He was impressed with the speed and quiet efficiency with which they disappeared off the shingle and into the cover of the chalk cliffs.

'They've seen us!' shouted a sailor.

Red and white tracer bullets began to hiss and snarl some three metres above the landing craft. Bullets pinged against the metal side of the craft. Fortunately, it was made of stout stuff and was bulletproof.

'Everyone, keep your heads down, for flip's sake!' shouted the Royal Navy boat master.

'Their aim isn't too good; they can't quite get our range.'

At once, they heard the grating of their own landing craft as it made its way onto the hostile shore. Immediately they heard the *thud* of German mortars. The shells began to explode in front of them on the beach. The ramp was dropped. He acted according to a trained reflex. His legs were wet up to his calves just as he expected. Bill ran, crunching across the shingle and into the cover of the massive chalk cliff in front of them. The training had seen to it that no-one even had to think about what to do, it was automatic. It was now 0540.

Immediately behind them, a third landing craft ground up the beach and came to a sudden juddering halt. A mortar shell exploded some 30 metres away. The first man down the ramp clutched his shoulder, hit by a mortar fragment. He ran over the beach ducking into the cover of the cliff.

'Are you OK?' Bill asked. With the lack of rank badges and the blackened face, Bill had no idea who it was.

'Adlam?'

He recognised the voice of his section leader, Captain Webb.

'It's just a flesh wound but could you organise someone to put a dressing on it?'

'Oy, you two, see to Captain Webb. Do you need morphine, sir?'

'No, just a flesh wound I think, but there's a lot of warm sticky stuff going down my arm.'

Behind him, Lance Corporal Flynn, Lovat's radio operator lay unconscious.

HMS *Grey Goose*, a kilometre offshore, returned the fire with several rounds from its three-inch gun.

'A company this way.'

Bill realised that the voice came from the massive frame of Lieutenant 'Fairy' Veasey.

'Come on lads, there's two pillboxes up there and we've got to sort them out.'

They disappeared into the dark to put an end to the gunfire and if required, some men's lives. Bullets snapped and whined overhead. Mortar shells crumped around them. The first section of A company was halfway across a wire entanglement when Bill heard a sickening thump, as a bullet slapped into a dark shape beside him. The man fell immediately and screamed and then stopped screaming.

'Medic! Medic!'

Bill knew that he could not stop. He forged ahead into the darkness. Bullets whizzed and whined around him but clearly the German defenders could not see what they were aiming at. The dark uniforms and dark face make-up were doing their job.

'It's Heckman,' said a voice. 'He's bought it.'

'What, he's dead?'

'He's a goner.'

'Hell, he was only married a couple of weeks ago.'

'Well, she's a widow.'

This was not a time for sympathetic reflection.

'Come on, you bloody lot, get cracking or there will be load more widows!'

The voice came from Veasey's enormous shape.

It was now the turn of B troop with the unmistakable figure of Captain Webb at the forefront, his right arm hanging limp by his side. In the middle was Lovat with his private team of adjutant, runners and signalmen. Despite the inconvenient fact of engaging with the enemy, he maintained his customary Scottish grouse moor look. Bullets continued to whine overhead, the section was taking casualties – Bill thought there were about a dozen already – but Lovat looked imperturbable, as if the whole thing were an abstract concept in a concrete world. A commando's witty comment brought him back to reality.

'It's not as bad as Achnacarry, sir!'

Lovat and several of the men around him laughed. Bill had little time to think about it but the mention of Achnacarry, where virtually everyone except him had been for training, was decidedly irritating.

Behind them came a sudden roar similar to that when a London underground train enters a station. 'TAKE COVER,' shouted a voice. They all ducked into the comforting embrace of Mother Earth. Three low-flying aircraft swooped above them barely higher than the treetops. They

'Terriers' shooting event

WE can't be 100 per cent certain about our facts but, as far as we know, these chaps were all members of the territorial army and posed for the picture following a shooting competition around 1930.

One thing for certain, however, is that the winner holding the cup is Leslie Hauting, father of Una Dowding who very kindly brought us the photograph.

Leslie was born in 1905. His mother and father were lady's maid and butler/valet to Sir Percy Marling and his family who lived near Stroud.

Leslie was educated at Marling School, founded by Sir Percy, and then at Gloucester Technical College.

At the time this picture was taken he was works' manager at Collett's in Bristol Road, Gloucester.

Una believes the shooting competition might have been held at Fiddlers Elbow where the TA had a range which might explain why one of those photographed is still wearing clips on his trousers – cycling was a popular means of transport in those days.

Inevitably as a TA soldier Leslie was called into service with the 5th Gloucestershire Regiment as war loomed in 1939.

He took part in the regiment's retreat from, Dunkirk and wrote an official history of the event.

It was mainly thanks to their gallant stand that 300,000 men were evacuated from the beaches and brought back to Britain in order to fight another day.

Later in the war Leslie, who had also taught at Gloucester Technical College, was sent to West Africa to train local regiments, but sadly died there.

Bill, third from right, achieves a write-up in the *Gloucester Citizen* newspaper circa 1936.

'The Bren Gunner of Grindorff': Bill's exploits were celebrated in this comic book in 1971. Bill did not receive the medal from Lord Gort; he received it from King George VI. He did not have a moustache (Courtesy of DC Thomson & Co Ltd, Dundee, Scotland).

William Joyce 'Lord Haw-Haw' made broadcasts on behalf of the Nazis. He was universally loathed.

Dunkirk – British soldiers packed onto a destroyer to escape Hitler's armies.

Jack Birmingham and his mates from the 5th Battalion The Glosters are pictured here after their return from Dunkirk. Jack — he's the one holding The Citizen caption — remembers when our Photographer snapped the scene at Kington in Hereford.

Members of the 5th Gloucesters at Kington Camp in the English midlands. They were not smiling like this a week ago!

MEMBERS OF THE GLOUCESTERSHIRE REGIMENT WHO SERVED IN "G", LATER "B" TROOP IV COMMANDO - TROON, AYRSHIRE. NOVEMBER 1940

The eight members of the Gloucestershire Regiment accepted into 4 Commando. Bill is on the back row, second right.

HMS *Glengyle*: Bill's home from home moored in the Firth of Clyde.

Members of 4 Commando sample the bracing, freezing air of the Lofotens.

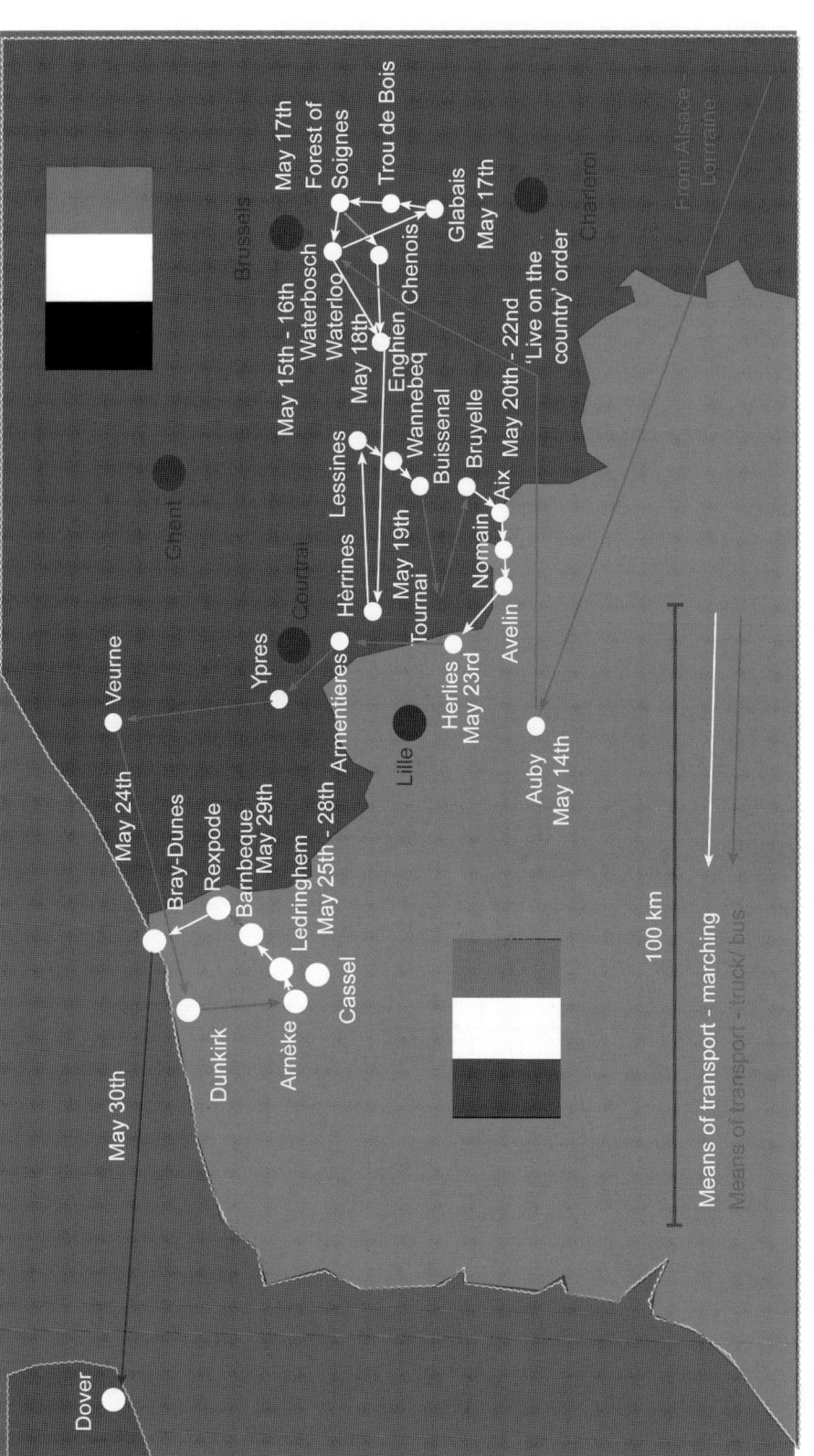

The Road to Dunkirk: the circuitous route of the 5th Gloucesters across Belgium and France shows the confusion and panic of the British senior commanders.

The luxury liner 'Bremen' sent to a watery grave for fun during the Lofoten raid.

British commandos return to Scotland with trophies of war.

The brains behind the Lofoten Raid: Ian Fleming.

The man for whom the Lofoten Raid was carried out: Alan Turing.

The real purpose behind the Lofoten Raid: an Enigma Machine for code-breakers at Bletchley Park.

Picture Post magazine features the Dieppe Raid. The fact that the major part of the raid was a dismal failure was not officially admitted until a decade later.

Preparing hand grenades for the raid on the guns at Varengeville.

Lord Lovat. He was Bill's commanding officer in 4 Commando and leader of the assault on the guns at Varengeville. He was also Ian Fleming's cousin and allegedly one of the templates for the fictional James Bond.

Lord Lovat and Brigadier Laycock inspect 4 Commando at Barassie Street school in Troon, Scotland. This was the morning when the famous green beret was first given to commando personnel. Bill is in the ranks.

Achnacarry House in the remote Scottish Highlands: the top-secret commando training school where Bill was sent as instructor.

The dreaded commanding officer of Achnacarry, Colonel Vaughan (centre) with Lovat and a senior US officer.

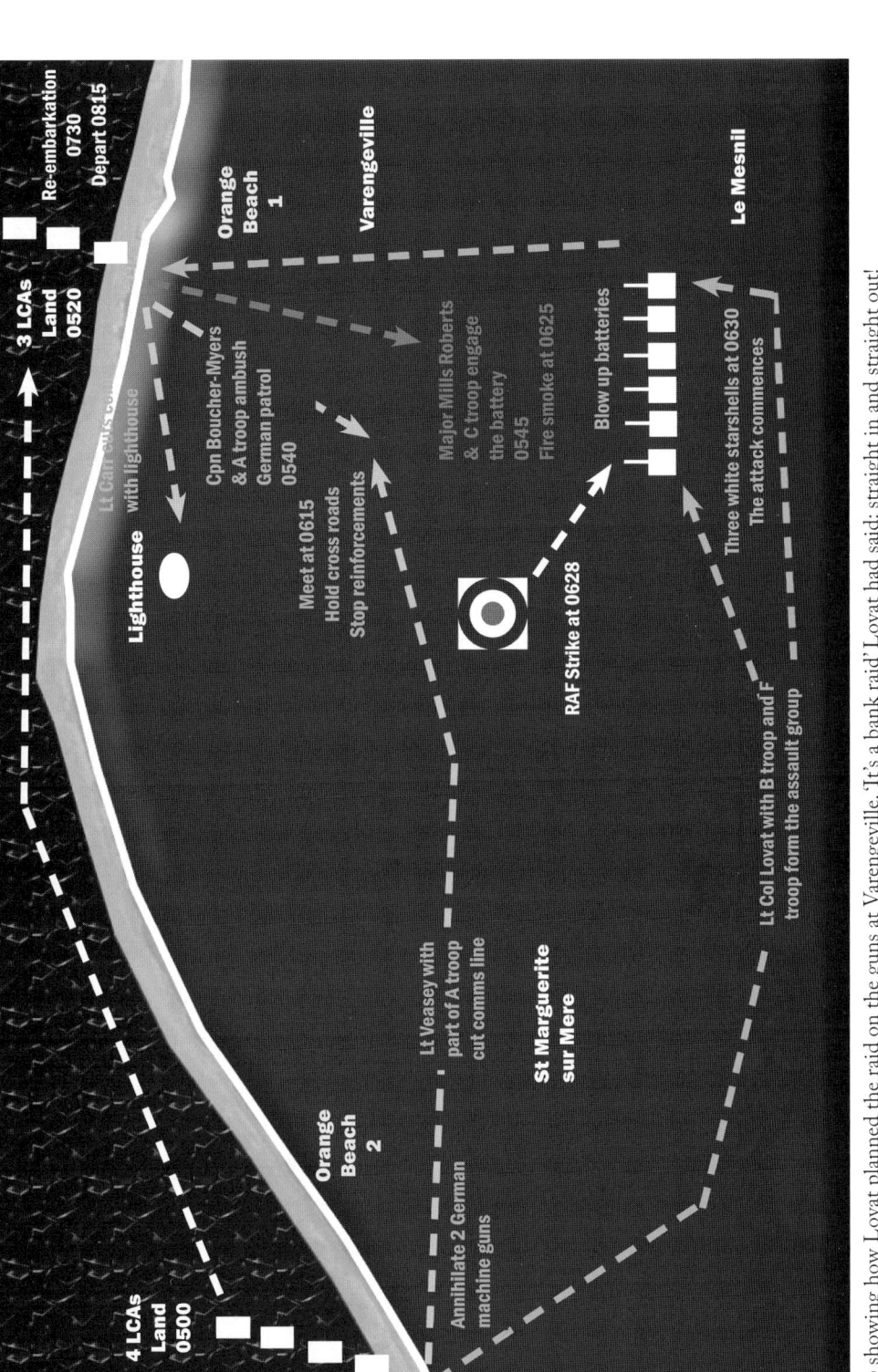

Map showing how Lovat planned the raid on the guns at Varengeville. 'It's a bank raid' Lovat had said: straight in and straight out!

Achnacarry training – not for the faint hearted.

2nd Lieutenant Bill Adlam at Achnacarry. In the stratified British Army for a non-commissioned officer to reach officer status was a considerable achievement.

More Achnacarry training.

The Fairburn and Sykes Fighting Knife: the commandos' weapon of choice.

Johnny Ramensky: safe cracker turned commando.

Ariel view of Gold Beach showing Bill's landing craft.

1st Lieutenant Bill Adlam 2nd Battalion the Gloucestershire Regiment.

A landing craft packed with troops waiting to land on the beaches.

'Storming ashore' on the beachhead in Normandy.

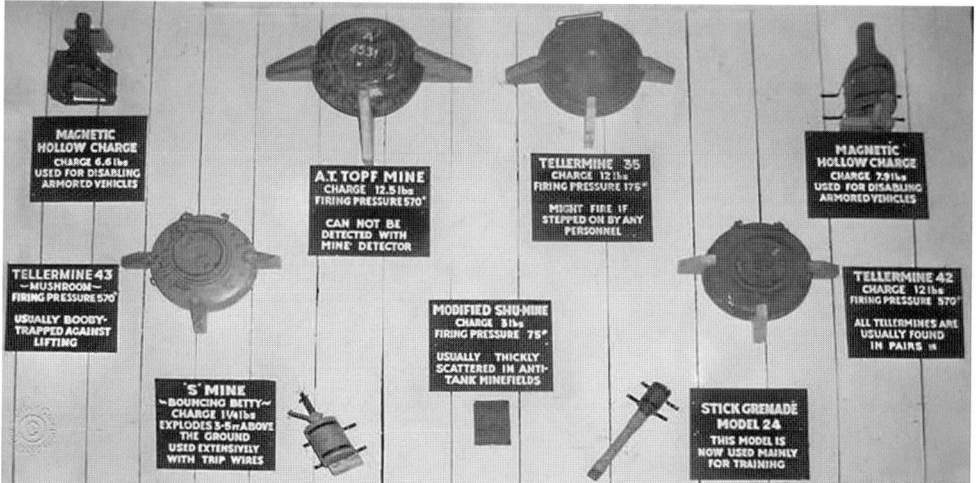

A display of German mines of the kind that Bill's platoon rendered safe. Casualties were high.

After the liberation of Bayeux, General De Gaulle arrives in France to raise morale and take his country back.

A British soldier brings in a captured German. The 12th Waffen SS, against whom Bill fought, mainly consisted of boys of 18 years-old immediately out of the Hitler Youth. They fought fanatically but took some 80% casualties.

Sweeping for mines in the town of Tilly sur Suelles.

Happier times: Bill and Linda at the seaside, Weston Super Mare near Bristol in the early 1950s.

Even happier times: Linda reunited with her father's Military Medal after 60 years.

were Royal Air Force Douglas Havoc night fighters, strafing the German positions, each with four 7.62-mm Browning machine guns.

They watched as a German soldier panicked, broke cover and ran. The hail of bullets caught him, lifted him in the air as it ripped his body apart and deposited him in several pieces several yards away.

'Glad they're on our side!' said a voice as the German positions erupted in a violent sea of fire, exploded masonry and body parts.

At this point, Lovat noticed that Captain Webb, halfway through having a wound dressed, was in a state of undress and moving only with difficulty.

'Webb! Look at you! You're a bloody shambles! When I get you back to Blighty, you're on a charge!'

This was incredible! An officer was wounded by a mortar round and was about to be charged for a state of undress?

'B troop follow me!' shouted Lovat. 'Now, you all know what you have to do. Just follow me up the valley of this stream and we come out behind the battery. We do not expect to find any *Boche* but if we do find a patrol, just take your cue from me. Come on, let's get the bastards.'

They took off at a fast rate. Bill understood now why they were carrying only the minimum of equipment. He carried no supplies and no pack, only a Thompson machine gun, his grenades, and some spare magazines in a pouch. Speed and movement were paramount if this smash and grab raid was to be effective. Away to his left, a firefight had started. That meant that A and C troops were engaging the Germans.

The massive guns of Varengeville spoke with a series of ear-splitting blasts. The Germans were now aware that a raiding force was lying off the coast and they were starting to fire ranging shots. Six times, they heard the massive reports and saw the livid orange flashes light up the surrounding countryside.

'Come on, keep bloody moving!'

It was Lovat's voice again.

The firefight to the left was intensifying.

In the eerie morning light, they found a troop of soldiers in front of them. They were Germans who were outflanking A and C companies. The Germans were taken completely by surprise. After several bursts from Thompson and Bren guns, they posed no further threat. They hardly got a shot off in retaliation. It was interesting that one man was firing a Bren gun from the hip. That was yet another sign of the Achnacarry training that Bill had missed out on.

Up ahead now, they could see an anti-aircraft turret up on a high gun platform was also now training its guns on A and C companies who were hunkering down somewhere below the line of hedgerows and farmhouses. They were being raked with rapid-fire exploding shells from the turret's 20-mm cannon.

Bill chilled to his boots. A single one of those cannon shells could bring down a Lancaster bomber. What it would do to a human body was unthinkable. A loud report rang out and an audible *ting* could be clearly heard. The turret went quiet.

'Oh, bloody hell! They've hit it with the Boys.'

'Nasty, very nasty!' said a self-satisfied but unidentified source.

The Boys anti-tank rifle was in its own way a mighty weapon which fired a half-inch round. Its original purpose was to stop tanks but with the improved armour on enemy tanks it was by now obsolete for this task. However, its tungsten-tipped bullet was perfect for punching a hole in such a turret as they now faced. The bullet would have pierced the metal armour and would have flown around inside the turret rendering all human bodies within into something that looked like something from a butcher's shop. The small-arms fire went on.

A German appeared from inside the turret. A sniper shot him immediately. The man fell twenty metres to the ground where he was killed instantly.

The turret began to revolve again. There was someone still alive in that abattoir up there. They were brave soldiers, alright. The turret again fired a string of cannon shells. Again, they heard the *ting* sound. Another high-powered, tungsten-tipped bullet from the Boys anti-tank rifle had reduced the surviving occupants of the turret to splattered meat.

'*BANG!*'

A massive explosion rent the cool morning air.

Bill saw a livid orange, red-gold flash and a mighty black mushroom cloud arose above the battery.

'The silly German buggers! That must be their ammunition dump going up. They've stored all of their ammo in one place. Herrenvolk? Oh dearie, dearie me!'

It was now 0607.

B company, with F company behind them, carried on up the stream, protected from view by the steep sides of the shallow valley.

The battery was suddenly covered in dense grey smoke. It was now 0625. An RAF Spitfire appeared at treetop height and raked the battery with 20-mm cannon shells. The stuttering explosions around the battery were a scene from Dante's 'Inferno'. Another Spitfire appeared and raked the battery and another and another. In all, 12 Spitfires put several thousand rounds of cannon shells into the battery. The scene of carnage within it was beyond the imagination of any sane person.

'Company halt!' shouted Lovat in a hoarse whisper. 'Pass it on.'

The word to halt passed down the line.

'Sergeant Major, are both companies ready?'

'Both companies ready, sir'

'Sergeant Major, issue the order "fix bayonets".'

The metallic sound of 200 bayonets being clipped onto rifles split the peaceful morning area.

Lovat took out a signal pistol and hid himself behind a clump of trees. He fired one white star shell, then another and then another.

It was now 0630.

According to the plan, C company ceased firing.

B company and F company formed into a wide arcing line then ran at full pelt into the buildings around the battery, screaming as they went. Those with Thompson machine guns fired a spray as they ran. Those with rifles stopped from time to time to fire a bullet towards the German positions.

Later, Lieutenant Gilchrist would write,

With fixed bayonets, F troop attacked, yelling like banshees. In too, came B troop led by Gordon Webb. His right hand was dangling, useless, but he had a revolver in his left. Razor-sharp Sheffield steel tore the guts out of the Varengeville Battery. There is probably nothing more frightening than British troops with the bayonet – Sheffield steel guaranteed.

The carnage carried on for five minutes. Bill was in the middle of and taking part in a massacre. The barbed wire, which formed a perimeter to keep people out of the battery, now formed a cage to keep the German soldiers in. Anyone who was not wearing commando uniforms was shot or bayoneted. No questions were asked. There was no quarter.

Lovat was to write,

… considerable numbers of Germans who hid in tunnels… in the battery office, under tables, in the cook-house and outbuildings were either bayoneted or shot at close range by submachine guns. Two officers including the military commander were also killed after a rousing chase from one house to another.

Now they saw the gun pits. There were six of them, each some 20 metres wide and two metres deep. The guns were of 150-millimetre calibre. A single round could sink a battleship. F troop's explosives men, led by Sergeant Bill Hardman, rapidly placed tailor-made charges into each of the gun barrels.

'Take cover! Get your bloody heads down!'

Six massive explosions completed the scene, which might have fitted the twilight of the gods.

'We've got them, sir! We've knocked off the guns.'

The scene was quiet. Lovat could take stock. The guns of Varengeville were a smoking ruin. They were now just blackened heaps of scrap metal. The anti-aircraft tower was out of action. Some 200 Germans lay in various states of butchery around the surrounding buildings. Lovat's soft Scottish-Oxford drawl was now replaced by an ancient battle cry of a Scottish warlord.

'Set the buildings on fire! Burn the lot!'

The battery buildings were alight. Someone tugged Bill's arm and pointed to the flagpole. They had not noticed but the swastika had been taken down and the Union Jack now fluttered at the masthead.

'Nice touch', said Bill. 'That is a very nice touch.'

From time to time, a gun report was heard from the battery where some surviving snipers were still at work. Each shot was met with the rattle of Thompson machine guns. Then all was quiet.

A woman appeared on the road with a basket of eggs. This was insanity.

'Madame! Get off this road! You could be shot!'

'But I have brought you all some eggs,' she said with a disappointed face. 'We hear that you have nothing to eat in England and want to give you something.'

Several commandos took the eggs and ate them raw.

'Very nice, madam, now please go home and shelter in your cellar.'

As they moved towards the C troop defensive cordon, an old man appeared. He wore a black frockcoat, striped trousers and carried a tray with several glasses of champagne. This raid was developing into a strange mixture between a horror show and a comedy.

'Sir,' insisted Boucher-Myers, 'this is a raid, not an invasion. Don't be too friendly to us or the Germans will make reprisals against you.'

The old man looked terribly disappointed but withdrew indoors with his dignity and glasses of champagne intact.

'Lads, look! Apples!'

The trees were full of loads of delicious French apples, hundreds of which found their way into the pockets of the commandos' uniforms.

'Christ! I haven't seen apples like these in years!'

B and F troops now came down out of the slaughterhouse that the battery now resembled. They had brought some 15 or so very dejected prisoners for interrogation purposes as ordered. They joined A and C troops. Captain Webb with his gammy hand had nevertheless managed to loot a couple of very fine Luger pistols.

'Not as good as the Lofotens, though,' he said. 'I got some fox furs there.'

Several other officers carried as many of the battery papers as they could carry, in holdalls, haversacks and whatever shopping bags they could find in the battery office.

Ominously, they could hear a battle of large proportions, which was taking place down in the town beyond their sight. They could not actually see the main battleground of Dieppe from their position but just hoped the raid was going to plan. It sounded like they had found more opposition than they had expected.

At 0730, Bill and B troop passed through the defensive cordon and filed down into the gully, which led to the beach, the landing craft and home.

Lovat gave a further order.

'Sergeant Adlam, tell your lads to watch out for mines. Go down the right-hand side of the gully. When you get down there just tell your lads to jump into the first landing craft.'

At 0744, the troops were half embarked. Bill took his section past the Hotel Terrasse, gingerly down the cleft in the cliff, through the opening of the barbed wire. He froze as the sound of small-arms fire and the *thump* of mortars started up again. The firing was coming from the lighthouse. To his relief, the firing was inaccurate and did no damage.

'What the hell were that lot doing during the raid?'

'Keeping their heads down, I would say.'

'Very sensible, but they're not very good, are they? Oy, you lot! Keep to the right down the gully. There's a load of mines on the left.'

On the beach seven landing craft were waiting, half of them already full. Just offshore stood the motor torpedo boat, which had escorted them in. The beach master Lieutenant Commander Mulleneux RN was organising the lines of commandos into the tiny vessels, much as a diligent schoolteacher might organise schoolchildren on an outing. A minute later, a single star shell flared up into the sky, it burst out in a red star, half an hour before the last landing craft was to leave. At 0815, the final soldiers from C troops filed down onto the beach.

Lovat gave the order to embark, 'Let's get to the hell out of here.'

Meanwhile, the troop was filing into the boats to make their getaway.

'Oh, come on!' Lovat shouted to the boatswain of the final landing craft, 'Come in a bit further, I don't want to get my flippin' feet wet!'

The last men to arrive on the beach were Lovat's headquarters troop. With them were four German prisoners under a very sinister armed escort, carrying Captain Porteous on his makeshift stretcher fashioned from a door. Porteous had one arm and one leg very badly shot up. Captain Dawson saw them on board. The small-arms fire continued from the lighthouse, but the trajectory of the bullets winged harmlessly away into the morning sky.

'I doubt if any of those Herrenvolk would make it in 4 Commando' said Lovat without a trace of irony. 'Are we all aboard Dawson?'

'All aboard, sir.'

The flotilla of seven landing craft set off at seven knots through the gap in the minefields for Newhaven, Sussex. The small-arms fire followed them for two kilometres to sea but made no hits at all. Firstly, they rendezvoused with the destroyer HMS *Calpe*. The more seriously wounded were transferred.

Like most of the others, Bill fell into a deep sleep. They had been ashore at Dieppe for just three hours. They had made their objectives. The battery at Varengeville was no more. Lovat sent a message via the team of Phantom signallers which he had been given. Back in England, the message would have been seen by the Phantom signaller's Officer Commanding. He was a commando RTU by the name of Major David Niven. In Civvy Street, he was a very high-profile British actor in American films.

0859 TO CCO FROM CO 4 COMMANDO. EVERY ONE OF GUN CREWS FINISHED WITH BAYONET. OK BY YOU?

As their landing craft pulled away from the French coast, they had a fleeting view of the main landing on Dieppe. The Germans did not seem to notice the small flotilla of landing craft, which was heading back to the English coast. Austin, the press reporter described what they saw above them, 'All through the afternoon, I watched fighters scribbling their quarrels across the sky.'

From the depths of the landing craft, Bill could see the aerial dogfights above but could not see the events at sea level. A sailor told them that the Canadian battalions were taking a terrible beating and a lot of tanks were stranded on the beach, unable to move. Grim though it was, Number 4 Commando had nothing left to react with. They had all been under fire. They had all fired their weapons. Some had bloodied bayonets. Some had the blood of the German defenders all over their battle dress. All were mentally, emotionally and spiritually exhausted. They offered cigarettes to the four German prisoners. One of them had no shirt and was given a blanket.

Austin, the reporter talked to them and was intrigued by their names. Wesierski, Kussowski, Samuelowitch and Marsiniak. They were Poles! They belonged to the very nation that Britain had gone to war over. In fact, the entire battery was Polish. Many had been given a choice of going to a concentration camp or joining the German Army. One of them had attempted to join the Polish Army in 1939 to fight against the Germans, had been turned down but was later conscripted by the German Army. This led to the uncomfortable truth that many of the men who they had just butchered were not fighting for Hitler or Germany at all. They had been fighting for their lives! Overhead, they witnessed a battle royal between Royal Air Force fighters and Focke-Wulfs of the Luftwaffe.

At 1300, a sailor shouted, 'Land Ho! I can see the white cliffs! Blighty here we come!'

'Wake me if we're sinking, lads, otherwise just let me sleep.'

The landing craft entered the harbour of Newhaven with their motor torpedo boat at the head. The townsfolk had turned out en masse to welcome the commandos back. The four Polish prisoners were taken off the quay by Canadian Military Police.

Troop Sergeant Major Williams had been severely wounded and was clearly going to be in hospital for some time to come, which meant a vacancy. Bill must have wondered if he might get the job.

The flotilla in general and Lovat in particular were welcomed back by Brigadier Laycock whose immaculate service uniform formed a sharp contact to the filthy, sweaty, blood-stained commandos.

'No-one is to talk of this escapade,' said Lovat. 'In particular, anyone talking to the press will be sacked.'

They had seen death at close quarters that morning. The threat of a summary RTU remained a severely worse sanction.

'You cannot talk about this raid while hostilities are still going on. You cannot even say that you were here. You will find that your personal records will be amended accordingly.'

He handed his rifle and pistol to his batman and disappeared in a staff car bound for Combined Operations headquarters and a debrief with Mountbatten in London. Bill was given a meal in a tent and then taken by truck to a country house somewhere near Newhaven. He was allowed the luxury of a bath. It was not just any bath. This bath had fresh bars of soap for the use of troops. Bill could not say that his nation was ungrateful for risking his life! He was given pay, a fresh uniform, a seven-day leave pass and allowed to send a telegram home.

Sunday, 23 August, 1942, Gloucester

'Jarmany calling; Jarmany calling'

'Oh, is that bloody Lord Haw-Haw still on the radio? He wants bloody shooting!'

'Bill! Language in front of the girls!'

'This is Jarmany calling from Reichsender Hambursh and stations Bremen and DXB on the 31-metre band.'

'Oh, turn it off, love, for God's sake!'

'Oh, hang on, Bill, he sometimes comes up with the odd thing that the BBC forget to tell us.'

'The government of Jarmany is now counting the cost of the ill-conceived raid on Dieppe. Counting, that is, the cost to the British and Canadian war effort. We do hear with some alarm that the BBC is claiming this raid as a victory.

'The government of Jarmany is most disturbed at this gross distortion of the truth. They have omitted to mention that some 4000 Canadian troops who will not be returning to Canada.

'As you go about your business in the United Kingdom look around, if you would, for the Royal Hamilton Light Infantry, or possibly, the Royal Regiment of Canada or even the Fusiliers Mont Royale. I am afraid that you will not find them. Most were shot in the landings and the rest are prisoners. Those who got away will not be talking about it.'

'Is that true, Bill? Was the Dieppe Raid as bad as that?'

'They told us not to say anything about it, love.'

Bill had really hoped for but did not get the Troop Sergeant Major job left from the vacancy by the wounded Troop Sergeant Member Williams.

Bugger!

But every cloud has a silver lining.

Chapter 17

Adolf Hitler's View of the Dieppe Raid

Unlike the situation regarding the Lofoten Raid, more is known about Hitler's response to the Dieppe Raid. At this time, Sunday, 23 August 1942, Hitler was in his secret headquarters, codenamed Werewolf, near Vinnytsia in the Ukraine. He was not in a good mood. His special train, oddly codenamed America, had taken a massive 34 hours to arrive in Vinnytsia from the Berlin Charlottenburg station. The temperature outside of his bunker was approaching 40 degrees Celsius. Hitler had been caught in an outbreak of influenza which had plagued the camp. He did not have the luxury of a day's sick leave.

Life was not all bad, though. His armies were progressing satisfactorily through the Ukraine; they had taken Kharkov and Sebastopol and were pushing on to Rostov on Don deep into Russia. That day, reports had come to him that his armies were starting to mass outside of Stalingrad. He would need one big push to take that city, then the hinterland of Russia, Moscow and the whole Soviet Union were his for the taking.

He also had some good news that his soldiers kept on finding mass graves of 1000s of people who had been murdered by the brutal Soviet dictator Josef Stalin. Grim though this was at face value, politically, it was a gift from the heavens. It meant that many of the local Ukrainians saw the German Army as liberators and not as unwelcome invaders. The practical bonus was that Adolf Hitler was receiving a stream of willing and cheerful volunteers to bear arms against the hated Stalin.

Then came the report of the Dieppe Raid. General Jodl, Chief of Operations, once again would have been the bearer of the news. The essential point was that Allied forces, mainly Canadian, had landed in Dieppe. It was self-evidently an armed reconnaissance rather than an invasion. Unlike the Lofoten Raid, the purpose was clear. The main news for Hitler was that the German army had won in almost every respect. Of the 6000 who landed, 4000 were killed or taken prisoner. German casualties numbered some 600. The Royal Air Force had lost some 100 aircraft, the Luftwaffe 50.

Adolf Hitler's View of the Dieppe Raid

Hitler was so overjoyed with the stunning victory at Dieppe that he decreed that the victors, the German Army's 302nd division should be known henceforth as 'the Dieppe Division'.

Inevitably, there were matters arising. British Commando raids on the protecting gun batteries had resulted in mass German casualties with no survivors. Furthermore, a Canadian colonel had been found to carry orders which said that any prisoners should be bound with their hands behind their backs, in violation of the Geneva conventions. The colonel had nothing to do with commando forces, but Hitler appears to have conflated this with other commando raids where there had been allegations of mistreatment of German prisoners.

Some six weeks later, Hitler was to make his Commando Order. The relevant parts of this order are, as follows.

Hitler wrote,

> 'For a long time now, our enemies have been employing in their conduct of the war, methods which contravene the International Convention of Geneva. The members of the so-called Commandos behave in a particularly brutal and underhanded manner… From captured orders it emerges that they are instructed not only to tie up prisoners, but also to kill out-of-hand unarmed captives who they think might prove an encumbrance to them, or hinder them in successfully carrying out their aims. Orders have indeed been found in which the killing of prisoners has positively been demanded of them.
>
> I order, therefore:— From now on, all men operating against German troops in so-called Commando raids in Europe or in Africa, are to be annihilated to the last man. This is to be carried out whether they be soldiers in uniform, or saboteurs, with or without arms… no pardon is on any account to be given.
>
> Should individual members of these Commandos…. fall into the hands of the Armed Forces through any means – as, for example, through the Police in one of the Occupied Territories – they are to be instantly handed over to the *SD* [the SS security service].'

All German personnel would understand that this order meant that all captured Commando personnel would be sent to a concentration camp to be killed.

The game has now changed. If Bill Adlam, or any other commando is taken prisoner, they will be executed without trial.

Chapter 18

Apotheosis and Beyond!

Saturday, 5 September 1942, Barrassie Street School, Troon

It was a day that none of them would forget. On the face of it, it was just another parade. Brigadier Laycock had been at Newhaven to welcome Number 4 Commando back from Dieppe. Now he was to review the troops, this damp wet morning, on the shining wet concrete of the school's playground, in the damp mist of western Scotland.

There was something special. They were to be given a badge of honour. It was not something you could buy. It was not a thing to be inherited. It could only be given to those who had earned it. Earning it was for the few. It was a simple beret of dark green. Later, the dark green beret would be recognised as an unimpeachable badge of honour and military excellence. On this morning, it was as yet unknown. It is likely it was the first time the green berets were presented. This means that among Bill Adlam's other military achievements he was one of the first to wear the commandos' green beret.

There would be other proud moments in the life of Bill Adlam. There were the births of his daughters. He had shaken the hand of the King at Buckingham Palace. There may well be other proud moments ahead, but this moment was one of the greatest in his life. It said more than almost anything else, 'You aspired to be a commando and you made it.'

The earning of the green beret possibly rated higher than the award of the Military Medal. The Grindorff incident had been worth a gong, but it was all over in 15 minutes. He had retrieved the machine gun and later on, the Germans had retreated. The award of a green beret was altogether different. It said that a man had volunteered for excellence. He had attained the highest level of military excellence known in the British Army, and his peers and the powers that be had attested to that.

What could he now do for an encore? There would doubtlessly be some opportunity to prove he was worthy of that green beret. Some weeks later, however, he was to receive a shock, which he would never forget in the whole of his life.

Saturday, 7 November 1942, Troon

He could read immediately what was in Lovat's eyes, pain and trouble.

He saluted impeccably as always in the presence of his battalion commander. He barely heard Lovat's 'at ease'. There was something badly wrong. The CO asked him to be seated. This was unheard of. His mind raced. Gloucester had not been bombed; he would have heard about it.

'Adlam, I have some very bad news for you, which we have just received five minutes ago by telegram.'

Bill's heart and mind chilled.

'Your baby daughter has died. I am so very sorry to be the bearer of such tidings, Adlam. I can show you the telegram. It merely says that she has died but does not give any detail. You are to proceed back to your wife and family in Gloucester immediately. I have already reallocated your duties. There is a three-tonner standing by to take you to the station.'

Bill was a man in a trance. He barely noticed that Lovat gave him two slips of paper.

'The adjutant has drawn you up a rail pass. Here is a leave chit for a week's leave.'

'Do you have any more details at all, sir?'

'Only that it happened yesterday, Adlam. You are dismissed. You do not need to hand over any of your duties at all. That is being taken care of at this moment. Pack up your things and go home. Your wife needs you more than Mr Churchill does. Bill, please accept the condolences of myself and Lady Lovat. We cannot imagine the grief that you will feel at this moment.'

'Sorry, sir, this is all difficult to take in. When do I need to be back?'

'Next Saturday, Bill, there is a war on, and the battalion needs you back by next Saturday.'

He was sharply aware that in the normal course of events, Lovat would have shrieked at him for not having absorbed information, which his commanding officer had clearly given to him. It also went through his mind that Lovat had called him Bill.

Sunday, 8 November 1942, Gloucester

Patricia was laid out on the kitchen table. The house was full of women fussing. Who were these people? Some proved to be neighbours that he had never met, so long had he been away. Some proved to be relatives, on Gladys' side, who he had never met. His lovely daughter Ann Patricia, just 14 months old, had died of gastroenteritis. Now, she lay like a doll, a pale waxwork or a fairy princess, on the kitchen table. There had to be some possibility that she was just asleep. She looked so peaceful, so beautiful and so quiet. The words that the neighbours and the relatives had said confirmed that she was not just sleeping. He had not heard the words but was grateful for the companionship of sadness.

There had been a companionship of sadness after Ledringhem, but the grief was never anything like this. At Ledringhem, he could take his rifle and avenge death quickly, conveniently and easily. There had been a relief, a reasoning, and a logic in that revenge. Now there was no logic and no revenge. He was faced with a death without reason, without remorse and without explanation. Why had she died? Why had a malevolent universe taken his daughter from him? For the death of a child, there is no explanation. He would spend the rest of his life pondering on that. There was no explanation either, why a family legend was to pass down that Patricia had choked on an apple core. His golden-curled daughter. He had lost her and would never get to know her. He had lost his golden-curled daughter.

A few days later, the war called him with a stronger need than that of his grieving wife.

Monday, 23 November 1942, Troon

'The colonel will see you now, Sergeant Adlam.'

He entered Lovat's office and snapped smartly to attention.

'You wanted to see me, sir?'

'At ease, Adlam. Is everything going OK at home? How is your wife bearing up?'

'As well as could be expected, sir. The family are rallying round, and she is getting all the help that she needs.'

'I am very glad to hear that. It will be so difficult for her. And how are things going in your troop?'

'Fine, sir, except the lads would like a bit more action.'

'Wouldn't we all, and how are you all enjoying your new head gear?'

'Everyone is very taken with it, sir. Some of the lads say it is quite good for attracting the ladies.'

Lovat laughed in his sparse, laconic way.

'It's more than that, you can tell them all, it's their apotheosis.'

'It's their what, sir?'

Lovat laughed again, 'In Greek literature, when a man is elevated to the status of a God, they call it apotheosis.'

The CO might be in a good mood but the gulf between the aristocratic Oxford graduate and the machinist from the match factory was still there.

'Anyway, sir, you wanted a word?'

'Yeah, there's something we need to talk over.'

His spirits dropped momentarily. Did this mean that the CO was not happy with some aspect of his section? Lovat's eyes met his. The aristocratic confidence, customary detachment and understated superiority were all there, but so was the usual twinkle. Bill felt relief that he was not going to get a rocket. He also had to reflect that he was relieved that the chilling sympathy, which he had so recently seen in Lovat's eyes, was not there either.

'Now, let me give you the background to this situation.'

Bill was intrigued.

'I owe Colonel Vaughan a favour, Adlam,' Lovat paused for effect, 'and it is a big favour. As you know, he is now commanding officer of the commando training school at Achnacarry. After we lost all those lads at Varengeville, he gave me first choice of all of the best recruits at Achnacarry. I took in all those policemen that he recommended, and they are excellent, are they not?'

'They're some of the best recruits we've had, sir, all the NCOs are delighted with them.'

'To make matters worse, Number 3 Commando lost a lot more men than we did, and Vaughan still gave us first pick. That means that I owe him a favour and it is a favour that I very much wish to repay.'

This was becoming stranger and stranger.

'Colonel Vaughan has vacancies coming up for trainers at Achnacarry. He is asking for some sergeants from Number 4 Commando, and I feel honour-bound to respond to his request. Three names have come up and your name is one of them. Now, you have been to Achnacarry, haven't you?'

'No, sir, when most of the lads went up there last year, I was on Operation Pilgrim.'

'... of which, the less said the better!'

'Quite so, sir.'

'Right, well I see from your record, that you have a training bent and I have seen you in action at Lofoten and Varengeville. For me, you are just the man that Colonel Vaughan needs and that appears to be his view as well.'

'Well, I'm very flattered to be considered, sir.'

'That brings us on to the nasty stuff. Have you ever stabbed a man?'

'I used the bayonet at Ledringhem, sir, I've killed men in mucky circumstances. I must have got a dozen or so at Varengeville with the Thompson gun, but I haven't actually stabbed anyone as such with a knife. I would have to say though, that anything unpleasant on the Hun is alright by me, sir'

'You were at Dunkirk, I think?'

'Yes, sir. 5th Gloucesters. We had an absolute bloodbath at Ledringhem, and we saw action somewhere in Belgium and I was close enough to hear the SS massacre at Wormhoudt.'

'Christ! I wasn't at Dunkirk but when I talk to someone who was there, they seem to have curiously little difficulty in butchering Germans. Right, well please think it over and let me know by this time tomorrow if you wish to volunteer for the job. I could just post you, but these training jobs can only be done by men who actively want to do it.'

'I can tell you right now, sir. I would love to do it. I'll hate leaving the lads here, but I was born to do the job at Achnacarry. I won't let Colonel Vaughan down and I won't let you down, sir.'

Lovat smiled in his vague, lazy way, once more.

'I was rather hoping you would show that sort of spirit. Right, well that being the case I had better tell you the rest of the job. The vacancy, for which Colonel Vaughan has you in mind, is that of being in charge of a training troop. I can now tell you that the vacancy is for a second lieutenant, and I have no hesitation in recommending you for an immediate emergency commission.'

Lovat waited to see the impact. This was quite enjoyable. He savoured the moment as the truth dawned. Sergeant Adlam was about to become Lieutenant Adlam. He had been confident that he would make sergeant major, but this was beyond his dreams.

'What was that word that you used, sir? Apotheosis?'

Lovat laughed and nodded.

'That's wonderful, sir, it had never occurred to me that I might join the brass.'

'There is one other thing as well. I think you will remember Colonel Vaughan from his time in 4 Commando. He will expect you to be at 100 per-cent top fitness on the day you arrive. You will need to sort out a fitness regime for yourself in the officer training course at Dunbar. That would mean a 10-mile [15 kilometre] run before breakfast or something like that. Is that clear?'

'Perfectly, sir.'

'Dismissed.'

'Thank you, sir.'

'Sir! They will be calling me "sir"!' he realised.

Chapter 19

The Road to Achnacarry

Friday, 26 March 1943, Queen Street Station, Glasgow

He laughed at his mistake and closed the third-class carriage door without entering. He was an officer now and officers went first class. That was something that he would have to get used to. It should not prove too difficult. He walked along the train to find a first-class carriage. This was starting to feel good.

Up on the rack went his kitbag, gasmask, helmet, and Enfield .38 revolver. Precisely what use this weapon would serve in the face of German machine guns remained as an unanswered question. Up on the rack also went the smooth fabric of the officer's tunic which replaced the rough serge of the battledress blouse to which he had become so accustomed. Now the world was different. The sergeant's stripes were gone, and a brand-new single pip was attached to each shoulder epaulette to counterbalance the red, white and blue Military Medal ribbon sewn onto the left breast. Finally, he threw up his swagger stick, the short straight stick, covered with leather and bestowing upon him the authority of his king's commission. It was the final touch of his officer's uniform and marked him, more than anything else, as no longer of the other ranks.

As the train passed through ugly Glasgow suburbs, he had some time to think. Lord Lovat had been right. He had completed the officer training at Dunbar without undue stress. It had not been at all difficult for someone who had acted as a sergeant on active service in commandos. It had been a month where nothing that they threw at him had been especially challenging. The fitness tests were frankly trivial. He passed them without breaking a sweat. The various exercises, which were designed to show his leadership capabilities, were less than what he had been doing in Number 4 Commando for the last two years. The classroom activities were not really up his street – being a practical man – but he had passed all of the tests without any great strain and had received his substantive promotion to Second Lieutenant.

As Lovat had mused, there was some additional training in the etiquette of which knife to use for formal meals in the officers' mess. 'Doubtlessly this will come in handy when you're pushed up against some Waffen SS tank formation,' Lovat had drawled.

Bill smiled at the memory. He would miss Lovat. He would miss Number 4 Commando but as Lovat had said, 4 Commando was going to change a lot. It would not be the same unit. It was going to be reorganised for the invasion, whenever that would be. Many of the officers were due to be posted out. Invasion? It was the first time that Bill had encountered the word. This presumably meant the invasion of Europe in some form or other. It was too far away to even dwell on.

He opened the *Daily Record*. As ever in a wartime newspaper, there was a mixture of the good and the bad. The good news showed that bomber command were reaching further and further into Germany. Berlin was copping it regularly now.

'They bloody deserve it, too,' most Britishers would agree.

Essen, Cologne, Frankfurt, Munich were being bombed almost every week. Over on the Eastern Front in Russia there was still a lull in the fighting. The Soviets had failed ignominiously at Stalingrad but they had lost and then retaken Kharkov but that was not a surprise. The city on the far side of the Ukraine (wherever that may be) seemed to change hands every couple of weeks. In North Africa, the Germans were pulling out of Tunisia. Monty and his Desert Rats had broken through and had Rommel on the run!

Then came the bad news. Austerity measures were increasing. The faceless bureaucrats of the Ministry of Supply had now decreed maximum numbers of pockets, pleats and even buttonholes which were allowed to be on garments. These new regulations would come into force in the next few weeks.

'Better get some pleats put into my green beret, quickly,' he mused.

However, German U-boats had sunk no less than 27 ships in the last week in the North Atlantic. A report had come out of Germany that a student group called the White Rose had been captured by the Gestapo. They had been caught, apparently, a month ago. The group had stood trial and were taken straight from the courtroom and had been executed – *by guillotine*. They were 20 years old! Oh, the vicious, German bastards! He felt sick. No, it was good. This reminded him why he had been in that bayonet charge at Ledringhem. It reminded him why it was actually alright to shoot all those Germans or Poles or whatever they were at Varengeville.

The train puffed on and left the grim Glasgow suburbs. Surprisingly quickly, the scenery had changed from completely industrial and ugly to completely green and breathtaking. There were mountains whose summits up in the clear blue skies were still covered in snow. There were clear flowing streams, which were still in flood from the melting snow. There were charming farmhouses, which must have been there for centuries.

The stations wound on... Tulloch, Roy Bridge... Spean Bridge. This is it! The train ground to a creaking, groaning halt.

A sergeant stood on the platform and bellowed at them.

'All service personnel to remain on the train until told to disembark. Oy! You, over there! Shut that bloody door and keep it shut until you're told.'

There was silence on the platform.

'Wait for my signal!' bellowed the sergeant.

A lance corporal opened the door to Bill's first-class carriage and came to attention smartly.

'Lieutenant Adlam?'

'Yes.'

'Colonel Vaughan's compliments, sir, I'm to drive you to the castle.'

Bill alighted onto the platform. His newly acquired officer's uniform and status as a trainer had rendered him invisible to the bellowing sergeant who stood waiting to give his order. The engine driver and fireman had clearly seen this performance before and were standing outside their locomotive watching the proceedings with an air of detached amusement.

'All ranks are to alight from the train on the line side of the carriage. Not the bloody platform side. I repeat, all ranks to alight on the other side of the carriage! On my order, sunshine, on my order. All ranks, ALIGHT!'

The railway driver and fireman were having a chuckle as several hundred soldiers opened the doors on the railway side, jumped down out of the train and clambered up the platform on the other side. Bill noticed with relief that there was no-one on the platform waiting for a train. If a train had come along now, the carnage would have been of pre-Dunkirk proportions.

The lance corporal loaded his helmet, gasmask and kitbag into the boot of the staff car.

Three sergeants had emerged from inside the station and were haranguing officers, non-commissioned officers and other ranks who had just emerged from the train.

'OK, you lot! Achnacarry is that way. It's seven miles [11 kilometres]. There's no pub to stop for a drink. It'll take you about an hour and a half to walk it. No slackers and no bellyachers! Is that clear?'

The car crunched onto the gravel outside of Achnacarry Castle. Colonel Vaughan was waiting for him. Bill snapped to attention in the highest military style. Colonel Vaughan smiled and returned the salute.

'That was a smart bloody salute, if I might say so.'

'Colonel Lovat's orders, sir. He said that when I got here, I was to give you the best salute that one soldier ever gave another soldier, and it was from him as well as me.'

They both laughed. Vaughan took obvious pride in the delivery of the compliment, as did Bill in the delivery.

'Smooth bastard, Lovat, good soldier though!'

Vaughan was clearly a man from whom a compliment was a valued achievement. His accent said East London. How interesting it was that a man from the East End could dare to bestow a compliment on a man born to the aristocracy. The world was changing.

'Anyway, we are called the Commando Basic Training Centre, but the training we do is very far from basic. Now, you've read that paper I sent you?'

'Yes sir.'

'I expect you're wondering where you fit in?' He did not wait for a reply.

'I am appointing you as Section Training Officer. You'll have a couple of sergeants working with you and a couple of corporals to keep the trainees in order. Having said that, you will lead from the front at all times.'

'Just like 4 Commando, sir!'

They both laughed. Colonel Vaughan passed a piece of paper across to Bill.

'These are the standards.'

Bill read the paper.

7 miles [11 kilometres] in under 70 minutes, followed by digging a defensive position.

9 miles [14 kilometres] in under 90 minutes, followed by a firing practice, usually at falling plates.

12 miles [18 kilometres] in under 130 minutes, followed by a drill parade on the square.

15 miles [21 kilometres] in under 170 minutes, followed by an assault course and firing.

'Now,' continued Colonel Vaughan in his pronounced cockney accent, 'you've been swanning off to some poncy training course at Dunbar for the last four weeks so I need to know right now if your fitness level will let you lead these speed marches.'

'There's only one way to find out, sir. I'll be up at 0500 and do the big one. I'll be back by 0800. Will you have someone time me?'

'No, of course not. If I needed someone to time you, you wouldn't be here. Your word will suffice quite nicely, thank you.'

'Now,' said Colonel Vaughan, 'there are a couple of other areas where I want to use your skills. For a start, this will include the weapons training and the unarmed combat. For weapons, we have all the usual ones plus German MP 40 Schmeisser machine guns, MG34, MG42 and Sturmgewehr 42. Oh, and we have some Mauser pistols and I think there's even some Lugers somewhere which were left over from World War I. Obviously, we've got a whole load of Karabiner 98Ks, the *Boche* Lee Enfield equivalent. Some very forward-looking people brought them back from Dunkirk.'

Bill's eyes widened. Vaughan smiled.

'I thought you would like that.'

'Quite honestly, sir, I wasn't that far-sighted at Dunkirk, I was just happy to get out with two of everything that I was supposed to have two of and one of everything that I was supposed to have one of.'

The Colonel laughed.

'Now, as regards the unarmed combat, we have some unusual techniques here, which you will have to learn. Later on, I will introduce you to Company Sergeant Major Frickleton, Sergeant Bellringer and Sergeant Bissell, who will teach you everything that you need to know about unarmed combat. You'll like Bissell, he's actually a London copper. He came to train at Lochailort before this place opened and we nabbed him as an instructor.'

'I hate to mention this, sir, but Colonel Lovat told me you had let him have all of the London coppers who came through here.'

'Almost all of them, Bill, almost all of them. I hung on to Bissell and Jock Holland.'

Bellringer was to prove an interesting colleague. He suffered from a terrible stutter but was fabulously fit. His claim to fame was that he was one of few survivors from the St Nazaire raid when Number 2 Commando had blown up the only dock on the French Atlantic coast capable of servicing the giant German battleship the *Tirpitz*.

'You're to meet the adjutant, Captain Gilchrist, at 1600 and he will show you to your quarters. You will be living in the castle, which is one of the perks of the job. You'll be sharing a room with three other blokes, and you'll just have to hope they don't snore. Tell you what, though, it's better than sleeping in those bloody freezing Nissen huts or the tents!'

Bill smiled. 'I think that's the first job perk I've ever had, sir.'

'Right, well the first thing is that you cannot tell anyone that you are here nor what you are doing.'

'Not even my family, sir?'

'You can write to them that you are "sitting the war out on a depot in Scotland". Your return address will be a British Forces Post Office address. You cannot mention Achnacarry. If anyone outside the camp asks you what we do give them a fob-off sort of answer. You know the sort of thing. Tell them that you are in an accounting office. That will bore the pants off anyone.'

'I understand, sir.'

'Secondly, you will need to know how to deal with some of the upper crust that we get through here.'

'How do you mean, sir?'

'Well, your emergency wartime commission is actually not going to impress some people. We get some of the Blues and Royals, you know, the Household Cavalry upper-crust types through here. Their ancestor fought at Ramillies, or Waterloo and they have centuries of breeding. To put a point on it, they will look down on you if you give them half a chance.'

'We had guardsmen in 4 Commando, sir, and not a hint of bother.'

'That's because Colonel Lister and I got them early and we got them brought to heel. Now what I want you to do is this. If any of these Hooray Henries give you any bother, do not bring them to me. The way to sort them out is on the speed marches. Don't do anything too sadistic but just run them off their feet and then when they are all in, you show them that you are still as fresh as a daisy. At your level of fitness, that should be child's play. Got it? That way, we earn all due respect without any punch-ups. They may be toffee-nosed shites, but they are still good soldiers or potentially good soldiers.'

'I understand, sir.'

'Then, there are the lot at the other end of the social scale. You will also be dealing with the scum of the slums in Liverpool and Glasgow. When you are doing unarmed combat with them, they will want to erase your face or castrate you with their hobnailed boots.'

'That's nice of them, sir. Actually, Colonel Lovat said that as well.'

'No, Bill, it's not nice but it is precisely what I want them to do. Your job is to let them kick out at you in whatever vicious way they want. And I'm telling you now, it *will* be vicious. If they can put a commando trainer in hospital, can you imagine the prestige among the other slum-dwellers from Liverpool and Glasgow?'

'Well, sir, they can always try.'

'Well, your job is to sit them on their bottom looking silly. As I mentioned, I am arranging for some additional training for you and when you've been through that, you will be able to kill any man alive in several different ways, break any bone in their body that you want to break and throw them in whatever direction you want. Once again, I don't want silly buggers with broken backs, I want silly buggers turned into soldiers, into commandos.

'Oh, I assume the adjutant took your ration book off you when you left Troon?'

'Yes sir, I feel absolutely naked without it.'

Vaughan laughed.

'Well, you won't need it up here. Officers dine in the dining hall. Other ranks cook for themselves. Unlike on civvy street, there is plenty to eat. Oh, that's top secret as well. We've had spivs up here trying to buy surplus eggs and bacon and so forth. If you come across any of those, report them to the adjutant. He will hand them over to the civil police. And there is another thing that I have to tell you about. There are various agencies that you will come across up here. Your job is to know the names but to make sure that the trainees don't ask any questions about them.'

'What are these organisations and what do they do?'

'Who knows? Some of their people come up here wearing regimental badges, some don't. You can take one look at them, and they've clearly never seen a barrack square in their lives. And their kit is a bloody disgrace, you've seen shit order before but not like some of these geezers. At least the Germans look like bloody soldiers. Have you ever heard of Special Operations Executive or the American Office of Strategic Services or Number Thirty Assault Unit? Alternatively, have you ever heard of the Joint Technical Board or Inter Service Research Bureau?'

The Road to Achnacarry 143

Bill looked blank and shook his head. 'Never heard of them, sir, what do they do?'

'We don't know; we don't care; we don't ask. However, we have standing orders from Brigadier Laycock. No-one is to give anyone from these organisations a hard time for obviously not being soldiers. No-one asks them what they do for a living. If anyone here or any civvy asks too many questions about them then you tell the adjutant, and he will bring in the military police without any hesitation whatsoever. My orders are clear, Bill. After arrest, anyone who has shown a curiosity about these various agencies will not be handed over to the civil police. MI5 will come and pick them up and after that, we have no idea what will happen to them.'

'Oh my God!'

'There are a couple of army units that we don't want discussed as well. Have you heard about the Long-Range Desert Group or Popski's Private Army?'

'Popski's what? No sir.'

'Do you know anything about 10 Commando and X troop?'

'10 Commando, sir, isn't that where Colonel Lister went after he left 4 Commando?'

'That's right. Well, he is indeed in 10 Commando, and you will be seeing some of his X troop boys. Now, I cannot emphasise this too much. You cannot be pally with them and ask about Dudley's health. You have never heard of him. Also, if anyone starts to discuss X troop or any of the others or talk about them it's the same thing. Stop the conversation at once. Tell the adjutant and he will take action. Look, any of these non-military people, just think of them as the funnies and leave them alone. OK?'

Vaughan looked at Bill gravely.

'That's all for now, Bill, there's a lot to take in. Go and get settled in. Any questions?'

'Just one other question sir, where can I find a Staff Sergeant Davidson? I have orders from Lord Lovat to give him his regards. He was very insistent about it, too!'

The Colonel laughed.

'Davidson is one of the ghillies off Lovat's estate. It's one of these feudal things, which I don't understand. Anyway, just go down to the sergeant's mess and ask for him. He'll be glad. He thinks the sun shines out of Lovat's bottom. Actually, Lovat is very impressed by him too, Davidson is one hell of a field craft instructor.'

Bill was destined to enjoy some very memorable experiences with Sergeant Davidson.

Bill did indeed get unpacked and meet his new colleagues, it seemed there were about 25 instructors all told. They all looked fit, with extremely positive outlooks and were clearly men who could inspire. Bill was flattered to be considered part of this very adept-looking team.

Chapter 20

The Dark Mile, the Death Slide and the Opposed Landing

Saturday, 27 March 1943, Commando Basic Training Centre, Achnacarry, Scotland

He pulled on the dark green beret with the badge of his own Gloucestershire Regiment backed by the Clan Cameron tartan. This was his uniform headdress as a member of the Achnacarry training team. They said that people who went to work at the elite Harrod's store in London were never actually told that they were the best in the world. They were simply expected to know it. And so it was at Achnacarry.

Bill would have had to admit that of all the places where he was ever posted to, Achnacarry Castle was the high point. It was not only the high point of his army career it was one of the high points of his life.

Achnacarry Castle was set on the scenic banks of the River Arkaig between Loch Lochy and Loch Arkaig. Its history was suitably warlike. It was the hereditary seat of the head of Clan Cameron, Sir Donald Cameron, known as Cameron of Locheil. In 1745, the estate had been ravaged by the rabble of the Duke of Cumberland on his way to sort out the 'young pretender' Bonnie Prince Charlie for once and for all at Culloden.

In the distance, there was the towering mass of Ben Nevis. Sergeant 'Sonny' Bissell had been deputised to show Bill the training centre. Sonny's job title was Close Combat Instructor.

'So, what exactly does close combat entail, Sonny?'

'It means rough, dirty fighting, essentially,' Sonny smiled at him. 'If you're close enough to a Jerry to smell his breath, then you really are not going to worry too much about the niceties of life, are you? I mean, really, you're going to kick his bollocks off, rip his throat out and break his neck and then move on from there.'

'You know, Sonny, I'm starting to like this place more and more.'

They smiled at each other with that certain unabashed smile of two men who knew they were going to get on very well together.

'You can see Ben Nevis today, that means it's going to rain.'

'What if you can't see it?'

'Then it's raining.'

They both laughed.

'That was the joke in Troon about the Isle of Arran.'

Between Ben Nevis and the training centre were processions of pine-covered ridges and peaks with deep valleys and swiftly flowing streams. It was perfection for commando training. Stan 'Sonny' Bissell was impressing Bill as well on that misty morning. Bill was intrigued that, despite the soldierly stature, Sonny was in Civvy Street, a physical training instructor from the Metropolitan Police, as was his fellow physical training instructor, Jock Holland.

'The colonel tells me you're a copper? Well, you look like a soldier to me.'

Bissell was tall, strong, with a military bearing and infectious enthusiasm. Bill made a mental note about that enthusiasm. It was something, which Vaughan was always keen on in 4 Commando. Now that he was CO of the training establishment that enthusiasm would be central to every training exercise, chance meeting and even brushing your teeth in the morning.

They discussed physical training regimes. Sonny did 100 press-ups each morning to begin his morning work-out. He also proved to be adept in jujitsu, judo and several different forms of wrestling, of which Freestyle and Cumberland and Westmorland were long-time favourites.

'Oh, and I train in using the F & S knife as well.'

'F & S?'

'Fairbairn and Sykes, they were two dotty old Englishmen about 60 years old. They had fought the terrors of the tongs in Shanghai and then came back to Blighty when the Japs invaded. They taught at Lochailort but when that was closed down, the Yanks swiped them to do training for the Office of Strategic Services. Has Colonel Vaughan mentioned about OSS?'

'Yes, and I gather we haven't got to enquire about what it does.'

'That's right Bill, otherwise I have to report you to MI5.'

It was not a joke. This man, who he liked instinctively, was actually saying that he would report him to MI5. *He was actually saying it!* There was a moment of awkwardness.

'This is a lovely place, Sonny. You wouldn't have to build too much of an obstacle course here, it is perfect, just perfect.'

The Dark Mile, the Death Slide and the Opposed Landing 147

The stately home at the centre of the complex was now the Commando Basic Training Centre Headquarters building. Around the castle, the Army had built neat rows of semi-circular Nissen huts with the obligatory military parade ground in the centre. In peacetime, it had been a glorious lawn. Now, it was covered in asphalt. Most of the Nissen huts were accommodation for trainers and trainees but three had special uses, officers' dining room, ablutions, and NAAFI. Strictly speaking, NAAFI establishments were not used by officers, but it is most likely that on remote stations such as Achnacarry, Bill would pop in to buy such essentials as Gibbs' Dentifrice tooth powder, bags of tea and soap, without raising too many conservative eyebrows. More to the point, a well-connected place such as Achnacarry might even have some small but wonderfully welcome luxuries. It was even possible that Bill Adlam might have found some of his favourite HP sauce there!

Bissell told him more about the training centre. The trainees wear denim fighting order at all times with gaiters on their boots and cap comforters. We don't do kit inspections here, the chaps who come here are really beyond the basics. They're ambitious soldiers who want to get into commandos. Did the colonel mention the funnies?'

Bill nodded.

'The funnies may look a little sloppy, actually very sloppy, but just leave them to get on in their sloppiness. We're training them to kill Germans not to look good on the parade ground. From what I hear we don't even want the funnies to look like soldiers.'

'Oh, one other question.'

'Yes?'

'Do we do any sort of propaganda training, you know, to rev the men up with anti-German fervour?'

'No, there's none of that here at all. It's all been done for us, really.'

'Were you over in France in 1940?'

'Yes, I was.'

'A lot of the lads who come through here came out of Dunkirk. Actually, most of the country has had a similar experience, what with the bombing. There is nothing we have to do to motivate people to shoot Germans. *Nothing!*'

He looked at his watch.

'I've got a class in a half hour. Be here at 1100 hours and I'll take you over and show you the Tarzan's course.'

'The what?'

'You heard, I'll show you the Tarzan's course and the death slide. We'll do them properly. So, I'll have you in denims, boots and gaiters. Oh, and with full marching order of course. No headdress, you would lose it on the Tarzan's course.'

A week later Bill was ready to take his first group of trainees over the Tarzan's course. Would he ever get used to the weather? The clouds were exactly and precisely the same shade of grey as the grim battleships that had accompanied him on the Lofoten raid. The clouds were so low it looked as though you could touch them. There was a thin mist in the air, the kind that they call Scotch mist. There was lots of it at Achnacarry. He was to learn the Scottish word *drookit*. It meant drenched.

'Right, well now, Harris, you've lost your headdress, let's be having a look at you. Everyone in denims, boots and gaiters. Have you all got a toggle rope fitted correctly around your waist? If you have not, you are probably going to die.'

The toggle rope was a piece of kit unique to commandos. It consisted of a hemp rope with a toggle at the end.

'All fitted correctly sir', announced Henshaw brightly.

Roberts, you were told to wear clean denims this morning. Your denims are bloody filthy.'

'Well, they won't stay clean for long on this thing, sir.'

'What were your orders, Roberts?'

'Clean denims, sir.'

'Alright Roberts, I'm a reasonable man. If you get through the Tarzan's course without asking for help or hesitating or grumbling, then I will choose not to notice your filthy bloody battle order. Is that fair, Roberts?'

'It's more than fair, sir.'

'And do you know how long you have got to complete the Tarzan's course?'

'Twelve minutes, sir.'

'Can you do it?'

'Yes, sir,' he said it with conviction.

'Lance Corporal Henshaw, please give each man a rifle, which he is to carry on the progression through the course. And one for me too, if you please.'

'Right, now let us just think about what we have to do. It is bloody frightening, and it is supposed to be frightening. I did it for the first time

The Dark Mile, the Death Slide and the Opposed Landing 149

last week with Sergeant Bissell and I was bloody frightened as well. But let us just think.'

He looked around for effect.

'You have all climbed up ropes and are confident in doing it?'

'Sir!'

'You have all been in precarious places and looked down and not had vertigo?'

'Yes, sir.'

'You have all been able to balance your equipment when you have been in precarious positions?'

'Yes sir.'

'Well, we have to do this in 12 minutes so all you do is to follow me. Lance Corporal Henshaw what is the time?'

'Just coming up to 0804, sir'

'Right, lads, let's go.'

He took off at the double across the parade ground and away from the castle. He led them into the avenue that led from the castle to the River Arkaig and in particular, to the beech trees which flanked it. That is where the Tarzan's course was set up. His sergeant instructors were waiting at the base of the first tree. Without any hesitation, he climbed up a vertical rope to a platform some eight metres from the ground. That was the first part of the test. He did not look back; it was his sergeant's job to see how the men were performing. His job was to set the pace and to show the trainees how it was to be done. He stretched out along the rope, trying not to look down.

He stretched out his arms in a cat crawl. The arms went out in front to grasp the rope and were used to pull him along. One leg hung down to act as a balancer. The other leg and foot gripped the rope. On the opposite bank, the sharp *cracks* of the rifles heralded the fact that he was now being shot at with live ammunition. Some bullets whistled far overhead. Some gave a distinct *crack* as they flew past his ear.

Damn! He lost his balance! The rope jerked up and down with him upon it and he had to hang on for grim death. Now he was underneath the rope and had to pull himself back on top of it. He just had to hope that the nails, which held the ropes in place, were going to hold. With a 19-kilogram pack and rifle this was no mean feat. Sergeant Bissell had fortunately showed him the technique for righting himself. He went through the drill, pulled himself forward and gradually inched along to the platform on the other side. Losing his grip had been useful. It would have showed the trainees how not to lose their confidence if it happened – and it certainly would happen – but also it would reinforce the technique of how to right himself.

The first of the trainees had started to follow him and so he was able to push on.

The next obstacle was a climbing net. It was not technically difficult but with a heavy pack and cumbersome rifle, it would drain the energy of a man who was less than fit. It would certainly soften him up for the next obstacle.

The next obstacle was a ramp of tree trunks. The tree trunks were two feet apart and the ramp was at an angle of 45 degrees. If you could get the timing right, you would be up and over it in ten seconds. The problem with it was that if you broke your rhythm or lost footing, then you would fall into the hole underneath the ramp. In that case, the best you could hope for was to redo the ramp, which would lose much valuable time or, in the worst case, break a leg.

Now came the supreme test, the death slide. Bill stood at the bottom of a huge tree on the riverbank. There was no time to pause. There were footholds cut into the tree to a level of 11 metres. He climbed his way up, his chest heaving with the weight of the pack and the awkwardness of the rifle.

Without pausing, he attained the platform at the top. Now he had to slide down a rope which would take him over the River Arkaig, which was still in flood from the melting winter snows. He hoped that no-one would fall into it because their chances of survival were 50 per cent, at best. He took off his toggle rope as fast as possible and looped it over the single rope which went from the platform down to ground level on the other side.

Two sergeants waited on the riverbank, one on each side in case of mishap. Whether they would be able to save anyone wearing a large pack in those freezing waters was very doubtful.

He grabbed the loop of the rope and pushed off with his boots. He had a good take-off and sped over the river quickly. The angry waters bubbled, snarled and roared over the rocks beneath him. As Sergeant Bissell had taught him, confidence was the vital ingredient in this type of manoeuvre. Around his ears he could hear the *thwack* as live rounds whizzed past his ears. There was no time to look for where the snipers were. He just had to hang on! In a few seconds, his boots were crashing onto terra firma, and he paused for an instant to gather his balance and breath. It was also good that the first of the trainees was now following him.

The Dark Mile, the Death Slide and the Opposed Landing 151

He now had to return back across the river by means of the toggle bridge. This consisted of two horizontal ropes strung across the river, on which the trainee was to rest his armpits. Below them was a single rope for the feet. It required a feat of strength and balance to cross. Once again, it was largely a question of confidence. For those who had the technique and the confidence, the toggle bridge was not too daunting. However, this was made up for by having simulated artillery fire, which caused huge explosions below them and drenched them with freezing cold water as they inched their way along the bridge. A few rounds of closely intruding rifle fire, naturally with live rounds, finished off the realism of the experience.

His exertions along the toggle bridge brought Bill, soaking wet, back to the original side of the river, puffing profusely. Lance Corporal Henshaw waited the return with his watch.

'Eleven minutes fifty-five, sir.'

'Sod it, I did it in 11.40 the other day. It really holds you up when you lose your grip.'

It flashed through Bill's mind that Colonel Vaughan had said to him, 'I've hand-picked you, Bill, because I know you can outperform any of the trainees on any of the courses here.'

The pressure on him was intense.

The first trainees followed him.

'Well done, McCarthy! Well done, Burnside!'

'Just under the 12 minutes, sir.'

'Good lads, I'm really pleased with you.'

Half of the trainees were still awaiting their turn for the death slide.

'That's it, Worrall.'

He hesitated.

'Come on, Worrall, you can do it. Even the officers can do it. Just let yourself go and bloody hang on! That's it! Good lad! That's excellent! Never mind the bullets.'

More trainees came in within the 12-minute mark.

After some minutes, Henshaw looked at his watch.

'Sir, there's a few left and they can't do it now in under 15.'

'Give me their names if you would.'

He turned around to the trainees who had taken off their packs and were laughing like schoolchildren in the sheer joy of achievement.

'That's a tough course, lads, you can all feel that you did very well. You're all dismissed. Go off to the NAAFI and get a cup of tea and a wad. You've got Sergeant Major Frickleton at 1030 hours for "silent killing" haven't you?'

'Yes, sir.'

'Well, if he's agreeable, I'll sit in on that one and you can all try to kill me for making you do that death slide.'

The last half-dozen stragglers began to arrive in sullen acceptance of the inevitable. Corporal Henshaw took the names.

'Well, I can only say "sorry" to all of you, but this performance is nowhere near the standards which we set here. You are all returned to unit.'

Thoughts came to him of Brigadier Laycock, who had first formed the commando units. He had survived in the North African desert behind enemy lines for 41 days without rations. The commandos needed men who could survive and only men who could survive. He hated 'RTU'ing men but there was no other remedy.

'Present yourself to Captain Gilchrist for a rail pass. If you would leave the site immediately, I would be very grateful. Don't talk to anyone on your way out, it's bad for morale. Oh, and you can't tell anyone what we do here. You can't tell anyone that you were here or even that we exist. Is that understood?'

'Yes sir,' they chorused with downcast faces.

'Good luck in the rest of the war. Dismissed.'

'Thanks, sir, sorry we let you down.'

'So am I. Goodbye.'

At this early stage, Bill doubtlessly found what all trainers find. It is the innocent questions that floor you. It is the questions which you do not see coming and which you have to answer immediately. All eyes are on you and you have to give an authoritative answer.

'What are you actually training us for, sir?' was one inevitable question.

'How do you mean, Baker?'

'Well, are you training us for single operations against the Jerries or for the invasion?'

'Who said there's going to be an invasion?' Bill would have asked.

'Well, there's this bloke from my street at home and he's in signals and he says there has been a huge upsurge in traffic in the last few months and everyone thinks the invasion is on.'

'Right, thank you, Baker, I'll pass that on to Colonel Vaughan and he can pass it on to Mr Churchill, who I'm sure doesn't know if there will be an invasion, either. Right, well seriously, we are training you for whatever operations come up. You've heard about the commandos at Dieppe, and you've heard of the raid on St Nazaire. That is what you are being trained for. I don't know if there's an invasion planned or if there ever will be an invasion.'

'Why do the Jerries hate the Jews so much, sir.'

Sometimes, even the most omniscient trainer has to come clean.

'I don't know, Norman, I really don't. How they could take their livelihoods away from them and kick them out of the country. I don't know what possesses people to behave like that .'

'Is it hard to kill a Jerry, sir?'

'Not when it's him or you, no. Don't worry, son, if you're scared enough, you'll do it and you won't feel bad about it afterwards, either. That is what war is about. It's him or you and it's better if it's him.'

15 April 1943, Commando Basic Training Centre, Achnacarry, Scotland

'Come in, Bill.'

Bill entered and gave the requisite smart salute.

'You wanted to see me, sir?'

'Yes', said Colonel Vaughan. 'Stand easy, Bill. Well, I gather from Bissell that you've settled in very well. You've been helping Captain Wallbridge out in the weapons firing?'

'I want you to spend spare time – I know there isn't much – but spend it with Frickleton and you need to spend more time on the silent killing. I know you've been helping them out but they say that some of your technique needs a bit of touching up. Let's say, a week. Then I will put you in charge of the speed marches, that will be your main focus and you will spend two-thirds of time on that. I can use you as needed on the Tarzan's course and from next week, on the silent killing as well. I like all my officers to have a main speciality but to be able to cover other areas as well.

'The first thing that you need to do is to read the new Fairbairn and Sykes' book *All-In Fighting!* It's only just come out but it's our silent killing bible. Here is a copy for you. As you can see, it's well-thumbed already. We used to have both Mr Fairbairn and Mr Sykes over at Lochailort, but they've been snaffled by someone else. Actually, I prefer Bissell's approach. Fairbairn and Sykes were very good at the theory and practice, but Bissell has a more direct approach, which involves kicking the enemy's knackers in, which is a better approach I feel.'

'Er, yes, sir.'

'Er, yes, do we give special attention to some parts rather than others? There's an awful lot here and we only spend ten per cent of our time on unarmed combat and that includes physical training and ropework. That's only giving us about two days to teach them these techniques.'

'Frickleton and Bellringer will tell you the important bits. Essentially, you need to train them in how to break an arm, break a neck, break a back and how to kill with a knife, quickly.'

'The knives that we use, sir, are they fully sharp or specially blunted?'

'They are special issue with blunt blades and no points on them.'

'There have been several casualties since I've been here, sir, how do we deal with them?'

'Well, always let the MO know when you are doing some training that could be dangerous. He can have a couple of chaps standing by. Bill, you do know that we always have fatalities here, don't you?'

'The Tarzan's course alone is going to kill people, sir.'

'We keep very quiet about it, very quiet indeed.'

'Right, well, I'll read this tonight and see Frickleton and Bellringer tomorrow.'

'Dismissed.'

'Thank you, sir.'

He had to familiarise himself with the book. He idly flicked the pages as he walked back to the castle. Bill was not one of nature's bookworms and only read if the occasion required it. This book led him to make a clear observation.

'Good grief!' he thought, 'this is a manual for murder.'

28 April 1943, Achnacarry

'It's the opposed landing tomorrow, Bill, could you give us a hand on the beaches?'

'Certainly, sir, what does it require?'

'Oh, it's relatively straightforward, when the trainees are landing out of their boats you just fire above their heads.'

'Live ammunition?'

'Yes, of course, there wouldn't be any point otherwise, would there?'

The Dark Mile, the Death Slide and the Opposed Landing 155

It was Captain Allen who spoke. He was Weapons Training Officer at Achnacarry and played the role as commanding officer of the 'enemy' forces during the exercise.

The next evening, Bill and another dozen or so of the training staff walked out away from the castle through the woods and after a kilometre or so, they stopped, and looked down on the lake.

'Now', proceeded Allen, 'I just want to know if everyone has got their marksmanship proficiency badge?'

He looked pointedly at Bill's lower left sleeve, which was dimly lit by the pale and insipid moonlight.

'Bill, I see you haven't got the marksmanship badge, I take it you can fire that thing in a reasonably efficient manner?'

'Had plenty of practice before Dunkirk, sir. I did the course at Hythe but didn't get the 85 per cent bullseyes that you need to get the badge.'

'Well, alright then but try not to hit anyone, there's a good chap, otherwise the colonel will get landed with no end of paperwork. You will find that the armourers have already set the sights to 150 yards for tonight's party.'

'Question, sir!'

'Yes, Bill?'

'Do you give an order to fire, or do we fire at will?'

'I hope everyone understands this. No-one is to fire until I give the order. Now, you are all firing live rounds. What you are required to do is to put your rounds as close to the trainees without actually hitting them. If you hit them, you will probably kill them. Now, has everyone here got their weapon ready with at least four clips and the safety catches on at this stage?'

'Yes sir,' they chorused.

Bill's position was a vantage point 50 yards above the lake, at a distance of some hundred yards. His position was masked by dense foliage, which allowed him a good view of the landing area but was sufficiently in the shadows that he could not be seen. He was also deeply enough hidden that no gun smoke would be visible to give his position away. He would have preferred a German Karabiner 98K with its smokeless powder, but you had to make do with what you had.

Experience had taught him that there was a danger that his muzzle flash might be visible to a well-trained and alert enemy. These exercises were an excellent *aide-memoire* [memory aid] for all the things you would need to remember when and if the invasion ever happened.

Out on the lake was an unremitting blackness. He waited. There was no sign of the attacking forces. This was starting to feel real, very real indeed. In the undergrowth towards the lake, something stirred. There was a footfall. Intuitions, which had no name but which he had learned in the long night at Ledringhem came clattering back. Shivers went down his spine. There it was again! There was a definite footfall. A twig broke.

'Captain Allen!' he hoarsely whispered. 'Captain Allen!'

'Yes, Bill.'

'Permission to take the safety catch off, sir? There's someone down there.'

'Denied, Adlam! It's a deer! If the bailies were to know that you shot bloody Bambi…'

'I know, sir, paperwork.'

'Well shut up or you'll give your position away.'

Still there was silence. He looked around. They were good, these other instructors. They had simply vanished. Not one was to be seen. Not one was to be heard. Out on the lake was nothing. Yet, there was something on the lake. He could not see it but he could hear it. It was the *plosh, plosh, plosh* of muffled oars.

'Safety catches off!' came the hoarse whisper.

It was Allen. In the darkness, Bill heard the metallic *ker-lunk* of the safety catches being disengaged. He began to control his breathing so that when he had to fire, he would be in total control of his body, his reflexes and his aim. Ledringhem was coming back to him. He pointed his weapon out into the blackness of the lake. Just there! Just there was a dark shadow. The muffled oars were still making the *plosh, plosh, plosh* sound.

'Can everyone see them?' came the hoarse whisper.

'Yes, sir,' whispered back a dozen voices from a dozen hidden positions.

'Wait for it, chaps!'

The boats were 50 metres from the shore now. Bill smiled. They actually thought that they had got this far without being seen. Ah! He had the first boat in his sights now. Wait! He had to fire away from the boat and not into it. He took a quick check. He could not fire over the first boat or he would hit the second boat. He would have to aim in a dark patch of lake where he would not hit anyone.

Plosh, plosh, plosh and onwards they came. Now he could see that there were four of them.

The Dark Mile, the Death Slide and the Opposed Landing 157

BANG! A vast explosion erupted some 20 metres ahead of the first boat. Allen must have had that placed there when no-one was looking.

'FIRE! FIRE! FIRE!'

The hillside opened up with green and red tracer bullets.

'Heck!' thought Bill, 'those are live rounds from a Bren gun!'

Now flares went up and slowly descended on their parachutes with daylight all around from the burning phosphorous. He hoped they would not come down in one of the boats. The burns from those things were terrible. There was no time for introspection, some total lunatic had started playing the bagpipes.

'Sir!'

'Yes, Bill?'

'Why is that lunatic playing the bagpipes?'

'That's not a lunatic, it's Sergeant Millin. One of the Scottish blokes persuaded him that the skirl of the pipes would encourage the Scots and infuriate the English. He thought it was a good idea. Now get your bloody head down!'

In the light of the flares, he could see all four boats quite clearly now. That meant that he could put his rounds just above the heads of the trainees in the last boat with the certainty of not hitting anyone.

He fired a full clip. The trainees were doing well. They were still coming. Mortar shells created explosions in the water. Again, these had clearly been placed previously by Allen in such a position that everyone in the boat would be soaked with the explosion, but no- one would be blown apart. Now, the boats were grating on the beach.

Thunderflashes curled their way from out of the bushes. These were grenades with an explosive charge but no shrapnel. They still made a convincing *bang* and if one exploded too closely to you, you could lose your hearing for life!

Now he changed his clip and fired another four rounds. The instructors in the boats were shouting, 'ON! ON! ON!' The first trainees were disembarked now and thigh deep in water. Now they ran as fast as possible over the beach.

'Good lads!' Bill thought. 'That's how we got over the beach at Varengeville!'

Not one of the trainees stopped or tried to vainly take cover on the exposed beach. Now Bill could fire his weapon to kick up sand around the trainees as they ran over the beach. This really was fun! The trainees moved like silent shadows into the darkness and past them, without seeing any of them. This reminded Bill so well of Herzeele, where the 5th Gloucesters had slipped through the sleeping Waffen SS soldiers on their way to the safety of the ships at Dunkirk.

Then he heard the dreaded sound of Stuka dive bombers. Good grief! Allen must have rigged up loudspeakers and got hold of gramophone records of real Junkers 87s. They sounded as if they were just overhead, just as it had been at Dunkirk. The sound of the Stukas faded away. He fired a couple more rounds at the trainees who were almost all ashore. Then it happened. Captain Allen had rigged up an exotic projector, which would fire 16 thunder flashes into the air. When they all exploded simultaneously, Bill ducked for cover. A memory came back to him.

On the beach at Varengeville, he had heard an unknown commando say to Colonel Lovat, 'It's not as bad as Achnacarry, sir.'

Now he knew what they had meant.

'Cease fire! Safety catches on!'

This time the order was shouted.

'Are we finished, sir?'

'Not quite, Bill, they have to run up that hill and complete their operation. Then when they pull out, we give them a bit more curry to send them on their merry way.'

Bill now heard more firing behind him. Further defenders were clearly positioned behind him and up the hill. The familiar sound of Bren guns came to his ears. It brought back memories of Grindorff and the armed reconnaissance where he had won his gong. The occasional *thwack* told him that a round had become a little misplaced and had strayed just a bit too close to him.

'Keep your bloody heads down if you don't want to get hit!' shouted Allen.

The action was now all behind them. Flares were going up. Red, then ten minutes later, yellow. Then ten minutes later, white over green.

Then he heard the sound of screaming men. It was not the sound of wounded men. It was the sound of men making a bayonet charge. This time it was at dummies. At Ledringhem, Bill had charged real Germans and caused several letters home to Germany, 'We regret to inform you…'

Now he heard the rattle of Tommy guns. He really hoped that those were blanks. Tommy guns were not accurate weapons, they were designed to splatter anyone or anything, which stood before them. Then after another ten minutes, he heard an almighty blast.

'Ah! They've made their objective,' said Allen. 'They'll be back in ten minutes. Everyone in position, wait for my order to remove safety catches.'

They were surprised that in less than five minutes, the trainees came crashing through the undergrowth. The silent surreptitious demeanour of the outward journey had now been abandoned for speed at all costs, as the trainees crashed through the shrubs and bushes making good their escape.

'Safety catches off! Wait for it!'

The trainees sprinted onto the beach.

'Fire, fire, fire!'

This time, he had to be really careful. If he fired too close to a trainee, there was a danger that another trainee might run into his line of fire. It was best to fire into the black water. That way it would make a convincing splash and he could be certain of not hitting anyone.

More explosions erupted on the beach from previously planted charges, all minus shrapnel. As the boats pulled away, he could see the flicker of small arms fire aimed vaguely at his position on the hillside.

Then, with a final mighty blast, which nearly capsized two boats, Allen announced, 'That's it, chaps, the show's over.'

Out on the lake, Bill could hear the *splosh, splosh, splosh* as the four Goatley boats disappeared into the blackness of the lake and back to Bunarkaig on the other side of the lake.

'Safety catches on, everyone.'

'Safety catches on, sir,' said a number of voices.

'Bill, we have to go back to the castle now. We have to meet the trainees and go over their performance with them. Now, can I have all of your comments, please? That third boat was a bit slow in disembarking, I thought. We could have shot the lot of them.'

'They made too much noise in coming back, sir. That could have killed the lot of them.'

'Mind you, they got back from the hill quick sharp, I thought. I was hardly ready for them when they came back.'

'After the debrief, chaps, I'll be in the mess if anyone would care to join me for a drink.'

'Rather, sir, I need to get my circulation back, I don't know about anyone else.'

Chapter 21

The Achnacarry High Period

21 May 1943, Commando Basic Training Centre, Achnacarry

Bill was getting into the swing of things now.

'Right now, gather round, you lot. This morning, we are going to start training with the F & S knife. Has anyone seen one of these before?'

'No, sir'

'Who uses Wilkinson's razor blades here?'

'I used to use them, sir, but you can't get them anymore.'

'That's because the factory has been requisitioned by the Ministry of Supply and is turning these evil little chivs out by the bucketload.'

'Right, well the point is extremely sharp. The blade is extremely sharp. This is a very, very lethal weapon. Now can I ask for a volunteer?'

'I'll volunteer if you won't kill me, sir.'

'No guarantees, Gunner McLintock, there's a war on. Right, well your name now is Gunther. OK, Gunther?'

'Ja, Mein Herr! Gunther is ready!'

The others in the group laughed.

'Right, well this is the basic technique for a frontal assault where the Jerry soldier has seen you.'

The trainees watched intently. Bill Adlam was instructing them how to kill.

'You go into a crouch and look him in the eyes. That is important. Corporal Henry, why is that important?'

'To get him unsure as to what you will do next, sir. To undermine his confidence.'

'Correct! It is the same move that a cobra makes before it strikes, only the good lord has provided you with arms and legs as well as two nasty fangs. Then we pass the knife from left to right and from right to left as you move slowly but deliberately up to him. Sergeant… oh what's your name… you from the Royal Ulster Rifles?'

'Murdoch, sir.'

'Why do we move on him slowly and deliberately?'

'To undermine his confidence, sir, and to make him hesitant as to what he will do next.'

'And what do you do, Sergeant Murdoch? Go on, you've seen the instructional film, what should I do next to Gunther?'

'You ease up to him like a snake, decide which hand you will strike with, transfer the knife to that hand, in your case, the right hand, sir, feint to the left, grab him with your left hand while the knife goes into his jugular vein on his left side; you press the point behind his voice box (the film said it would go in quite easily), press the point through his right-hand jugular vein and then pull for all you are worth. This will sever both veins and his voice box will come out quite nicely.'

'Congratulations, Sergeant Murdoch, you're really getting the hang of this! Now everyone is going to have a try at this so have you all got that?'

'Think so, sir.'

'Right, well Lance Corporal Henshaw has got some specially blunted knives because we don't want blood on the heather.'

'Sir, question?'

'Certainly, Gunner McLintock.'

'Why don't we just go in like the Indians on the films with your arm held high, giving a blood-curdling yell and killing the man with a downward blow?'

'We had a chap thought that on the last course,' Bill said in a fatherly manner. 'He tried it on another trainee and the result was that the chap got his arm broken. The Colonel RTUed him on the spot for being a bloody idiot. Now, if anyone wants to try the Hollywood Apache method, they are free to do so but let me advise you, gentlemen, that is a lousy way to fight with a knife. The only person who will thank you will be Gunther! Don't forget the Indians lost and don't forget that Spean Bridge station awaits anyone who wants to try that particular brand of blithering idiocy. Any further questions?'

'No sir.'

Saturday, 12 June 1943, Commando Basic Training Centre, Achnacarry

'Lieutenant Adlam!'

'Yes, Corp?'

'Colonel's office on the double, sir, it's urgent and he's got a civvy with him.'

He knocked on Colonel Vaughan's door, entered and saluted smartly, before removing his beret.

'Come in! Ah! Adlam, I'd like you to meet Mr Smith.'

'Pleased to meet you, sir.'

Bill sat down without being asked. Smith did a double take. So, he was an army man then. In the normal army, a junior officer would never have sat down without being asked by his commanding officer. This was commandos. Bill smiled inwardly.

'Right, Adlam,' said the colonel. 'This is a somewhat delicate meeting, and you cannot tell anyone that it ever took place.'

'Very well, sir.'

'We are to receive a batch of trainees who are not what we would call commando material.'

Bill was intrigued. The rule had been that anyone who was even of borderline quality was RTUed. They probably belonged to one of those organisations that the colonel had mentioned when he had first arrived a few weeks ago. Fortunately, he could not remember the name of any one of them.

'Now, the first thing that you will have to do is to sort out a light training course for them. This training course will make them as fit as possible, give them weapons training and unarmed combat training.'

'Certainly, sir.'

'There is one thing that you cannot do. You can't RTU them or at least, not unless it is absolutely necessary. You will need to bring any RTU case to me personally before it happens.'

Well that was interesting! Part of Bill's role, now, was to spot 'RTU' material and remove them from commandos at the first hint that they might not be commando material. These people must be the 'funnies' of whom he had heard.

'Very well, sir,' said Bill, a little apprehensively.

Mr Smith looked on impassively.

'Can I know who these chaps are, sir?'

'No, and I don't know either. This is being done on a need-to-know basis.

The colonel looked at Smith, who remained impassive.

'Now, I do have to tell you some things about one of the intake.' He looked at Smith. Smith nodded.

'The man's name is Ram—'

Smith touched the colonel's sleeve to stop him.

'Ramsay,' said Smith. 'The man's name is Ramsay. There is another trainee with him by the name of Wallace. They're both Scottish but I'm afraid we don't run to interpreters.'

Colonel Vaughan nodded.

'This man will appear in the uniform of the Royal Fusiliers. There is a minimum amount of information which I have to tell you about him. Now, because of his tendencies there is a fair to middling chance that he will engage in criminal activity. It is up to you to ensure that if there is any thieving then it is passed off as a joke.'

'Sir, if one of our trainees was caught pinching, they would be in Colchester prison before you could say "thief", what's more, we haven't had a single case since we arrived here.'

'That's right, Adlam, so would you not say it was logical that if there was any thieving then it was just a prank?'

Bill looked profoundly uncomfortable.

'Yes, sir. I assume the adjutant is going to bolt the office safe to the floor?'

'It wouldn't do any good,' said Smith with an air of weary resignation. Colonel Vaughan smiled a concealed smile and then continued.

'Bill, I want the proposed training plan for this intake by 1400 on Thursday? There are some people, with whom I need to review it. He looked at Smith who had regained his impassive stance. They will need to do unarmed combat, though not to the full extent and they need close quarters weapons training. They don't need to go out on the ranges for long-distance shooting and they don't need to train with captured weapons. They will need a lot of demolition training, so arrange that if you would.'

A half smile came over Smith's face.

Bill arose, snapped smartly to attention, saluted, stamped his foot and left in prescribed military fashion.

Thursday, 1 July 1943, Commando Basic Training Centre, Achnacarry

Bissell spoke.

'I think you had better come for a walk, Bill.'

'Oh, OK then but treat me gently. What the hell is worrying you, Sonny?'

They walked away from Achnacarry Castle with purpose. This was becoming interesting.

'Right, well this is one of those conversations that never happened, right?'

'Oh God, Sonny, I'm getting fed up with these flipping conversations that never happened.'

Bissell laughed.

'You know those two mad Scotsman? Ramsay and Wallace?'

'Yes, the Colonel won't let me RTU them, they're absolutely bloody useless and that is not a conversation that never happened!'

'Do you have any idea who they are?'

'Oh yes, I know precisely, they're terrible soldiers.'

'They're bloody Scottish criminal Royalty!'

'They're WHAT?'

'One of the trainees here is from the civil police in Glasgow. He told me about them.'

Sonny went on to explain that Johnny Ramensky, or Ramanauskas or Ramsay was Britain's leading safe-cracker. His professional standards in blowing safes and lack of violence led to his nickname of Gentleman Johnny. At one stage, he even wrote to the police advising that he had left an unexploded charge in a safe.

Ramensky was from Glasgow and was imprisoned frequently from the age of 11. His prison escapes were legendary. He progressed up the league table of prisons from Borstal through the Medieval Saughton prison in Edinburgh to the even worse Barlinnie prison in Glasgow and eventually, to the ultimate horror of Peterhead Prison in the North of Scotland. Ramensky had become the first man ever to escape from Peterhead and had escaped from there five times. This had led to him being kept in shackles and permanently chained to the floor. He was the last man in Britain to be imprisoned in that manner. During the war, a senior policeman wrote to the Secret Intelligence Service and recommended Ramsay as a potential high-value recruit.

He was let out of prison on licence and posted to the Royal Fusiliers, whose cap badge he wore at Achnacarry. He was being considered for the Special Operations Executive (SOE). He was destined to train their operatives in safe-cracking at their school at Beaulieu. He was turned down for SOE operations because of his lack of language skills.

Felix Wallace was no less of an exotic character. Unlike Ramsay, Wallace was from Edinburgh. He lived in relatively luxurious surroundings and was highly respected both by the criminal fraternity and the police as a man of the highest ethical standards. According to family legend, Wallace was entrusted as the banker for corrupt police in Edinburgh. Wallace would hold the money and allow his clientele to draw on it as they required funds. It was so much more convenient than washing money through banks where the money trail could be followed.

After training at Achnacarry, Ramsay and Wallace were to be posted to 30 Assault Unit, whose speciality was the acquisition of enemy intelligence ahead of attacks by regular forces. They were to parachute behind enemy lines to break open safes and steal military documents. The various legends say that as the Eighth Army moved across North Africa, Ramensky broke into safes ahead of the frontline, including that at Rommel's headquarters. Later, according to the same legends, it was Ramensky who opened the strongroom and safes at Goering's headquarters in the Schorfheide in Germany. Just before the fall of Rome, Ramsay apparently did blow some dozen safes in the recently abandoned German embassy. This was accomplished in half an hour.

There was one other noteworthy aspect to Ramensky's wartime career. 30 Assault Unit and its top-secret operations were founded and run by none other than Ian Fleming.

None of this was known or even suspected by Bill Adlam but he knew a 'funny' when he saw one!

Tuesday, 31 August 1943, Commando Basic Training Centre, Achnacarry

Bissell spoke again.

'Bill, are you getting lots of questions about when we will invade Europe?'

'Oh, don't you start, Sonny. I'm having to shut the buggers up every day.'

'Me too but you have to wonder, don't you?'

'You'd have to be daft not to.'

'So, all that talk of invasion is hardly surprising. I can't imagine it will happen next week, but you know the party line?'

'Yep! If one more person in my bloody hut mentions the word invasion one more bloody time, I will RTU the lot of them!'

'It is a fascinating thought, though, isn't it?'

'Innit?'

From behind them, they heard the sound of running boots.

'Lieutenant Adlam, Sergeant Bissell, the CO wants to see all training staff in the officer's mess straight away.'

'Thanks, corp, what's the trouble?'

'Don't know, sir, but he's in a filthy temper. If you see any other training staff, could you bring them with you, please?'

Trainers entered the mess hall from all directions. It was clear from the looks on faces that they had no idea why they had been summoned. Colonel Vaughan stood on the low stage at the end of the room. It was clear that he was not in a good mood. In fact, he was not in a good mood at all. Around his brow were several shades of thunder.

Regimental Sergeant Major James called the meeting to order. The training staff snapped to attention.

'At ease, everyone!' said Vaughan in a manner, which betrayed a tightly controlled but highly explosive demeanour. There were three types of explosives used by the demolition teams at Achnacarry, gun cotton, amatol and plastic 808. The Colonel looked as though he was primed with all three and it would not take much to make him explode.

'Right, gentlemen, well you will be wondering why you are here at short notice.'

He peered around the room. It was clear that it was better that no-one spoke.

'Well, this morning I was walking around the grounds with Sir Donald Cameron.'

He looked around again at the sea of blank faces. Sir Donald Cameron of Lochiel, usually referred to as Lochiel was the owner of Achnacarry Castle and was allowed to visit from time to time under the strict instruction that he saw nothing.

'As we walked around, we heard explosions coming from the river. Did anyone else hear them?'

Sonny and one or two others nodded.

'Right, well what did they sound like?'

'They sounded like Mills bombs, sir.'

'Well spotted, Bissell, because that is exactly what they were.'

There were more blank faces around the room.

'In fact, a load of trainees were throwing Mills Bombs into the river to get at Lochiel's salmon. We saw three of the buggers running through the woods with the fish, but we couldn't see who they were. It does not need me to tell you that Lochiel is nothing short of bloody livid. I can also confirm to all of you that I am also bloody livid.'

The faces now were of men using massive willpower to keep a straight face.

'I want all of you to find out who is dining on salmon tonight and report them to me. I want to know who they are, and I want to RTU them on the spot. Is that clear?'

'Sir!'

The next morning, the training staff reported back that no-one appeared to be dining on fresh salmon that night.

'Well, I've got to report back to Sir Donald that I've taken action, or he will be on to his pal Lovat and everyone up to Mr Churchill. For Christ's sake, impress on everyone that we can't have people poaching his fish.'

'Sir!'

The salmon poachers were never found, which was probably due to the excellent fieldcraft which was taught to trainees at Achnacarry.

Friday, 5 November 1943, Commando Basic Training Centre, Achnacarry

It had been a really good day. Lord Lovat, Commanding Officer of Number 4 Commando and Colonel Dunning-White, Commanding Officer of Number 9 Commando, were staying at the castle as guests of Colonel Vaughan. It had been wonderful for Bill to see Lovat again and Lovat clearly enjoyed renewing his acquaintanceship with Bill. He had had a quick chat with Lovat, but Colonel Vaughan's agenda of events was clearly too detailed and too pressing for them to spend a lot of time together.

'Give my regards to the lads in 4 Commando, sir!'

'Oh, and theirs to you as well, I can assure you!'

Bill knew that he could not ask Lovat where 4 Commando were stationed. In his heart, part of him would love to be among them. But then, tough soldiers would never admit to any of sort sentimental nature. By the same token, Lovat could not tell 4 Commando where he had met Bill.

As on most days, lights out was at 2200 and the entire camp fell into that special fitful sleep reserved for those who have expended a ridiculous amount of energy during the day.

'FIRE!'

Bill rushed outside. It was a freezing cold evening. The story is best told in Colonel Vaughan's words after it had all happened.

It happened on the fifth of November 1943, by no means an inappropriate date.

About midnight, there was a banging on my bedroom door, and I heard someone shouting: 'If you don't get out quickly, you'll be burnt alive!' As it was always raining at Achnacarry, I thought somebody was playing a practical joke. But, just in case, I got up and opened the bedroom door. The whole centre of the baronial hall was a mass of flames.

I shook Lovat and Dunning-White, and we all got dressed as fast as we could. But by this time the fire had such a hold that we couldn't get through the door of the bedroom. So we opened a window and climbed down a drainpipe.

It was pouring with rain, an 'elluva night. We had no fire appliances of any kind, and flames were shooting through the roof of the castle.

We phoned for the Inverness and Fort William fire brigades. The Inverness one took seven hours to arrive. The one from Fort William managed to get to Achnacarry in three hours. But it was a voluntary service and had only a small trailer pump, which took nearly another hour to get into operation. We turned on the first jet of water from it on to Michael Dunning-White, who was standing there wearing blue silk pyjamas and a dressing gown like a film star. The force of it bowled him over in the mud.

This was one of the few bright moments of the evening. By the time the fire had been put out, the whole centre of the castle had been gutted, and the roof burnt off completely. The officer's mess had gone – there wasn't as much as a bottle of whisky left. To make matter worse, Lochiel arrived in a furious temper.

It didn't improve when he caught sight of Lord Lovat. As you know, Lovat is Chief of the Fraser Clan. For a moment, I thought I was going to have another ruddy clan feud on my hands.

I don't mind telling you Lochiel got an 'elluva lot of compensation – I don't think he did so badly out of it in the end.

But I'm still suffering for it. This whole countryside is full of Camerons as you know. And they're all after my blood. Why when I go down to Spean Bridge post office now, they make me stand in the queue and wait my turn!

To add insult to injury, do you know what that clown in North Highland District does? He goes and repairs Lochiel's Castle with a tin roof!

Saturday, 7 January 1944, Achnacarry

'Colonel's office, sir, straight away if you would.'

When Colonel Vaughan called, it was always straight away.

'Thanks, corp.'

It was yet another of those days that the Scots call *dreecht*. It was cold, wet and miserable. Dawn had been at about 0900 and the daylight, what there was of it, would disappear before 1700. Still, they were Commandos and they got on with things cheerfully.

'Sir,' Bill snapped to attention like a commando officer.

Captain Gilchrist, the Achnacarry adjutant was with Colonel Vaughan. That was odd. Both looked serious.

'Stand easy, Bill.'

There was something not right, not right at all. Could it be something to do with another of his daughters, surely not that.

'Let me get to the point straight away, Bill,' Colonel Vaughan said with a grave face. The Cockney accent still sounded strange behind the colonel's pips.

'You've been posted.'

NO! Anything but that! Even despite the rain, Achnacarry had been his spiritual home for almost a year. He belonged there. He was good there. It was the best place for him in the universe. Another commando posting? Could he be posted to another commando unit?

'You're to join the Second Gloucesters on the 14th, that's next week. They're somewhere near Blackburn in Lancashire. I'll make the arrangements,' said Gilchrist.

It was a grim, tempestuous moment. He looked into Vaughan's eyes searching for the reason for this utter calamity.

'I know what you're thinking, Bill, is this a subtle RTU in some way?'

Bill smiled but did not speak.

'It's the opposite. You might have noticed that there's a war on. Well, you've noticed that I've lost one or two staff recently.'

'Bill Portman's gone back to 4 Commando, sir, is there no chance I could get a transfer back there as well?'

'It's not in my control, Bill. Second Gloucesters are where you're posted and that is where you have to go. But let me say this, I have lost three or four over the last month and I am going to lose some more. I also have orders to ramp this place up, to increase numbers. Last year, we changed our entire training focus. I remember you remarked on it yourself. We weren't training for 'butcher and bolt' raids anymore, we were training for support of assault units. We had a conversation, do you remember?'

'Yes, sir.'

'Let me tell you something else, Bill, Millin has been pinched from me as well. Lovat has pulled every string in the book to get him.'

Bill Millin was a bagpiper. Why would Lovat pinch a bagpiper? The penny dropped.

'Lovat wants Millin to pipe him ashore when he lands on the beach in France!'

Vaughan and Gilchrist both smiled the smiles of frustrated, thwarted men.

'I'm not privy to machinations in high places, Bill, but that's what it looks like to me. Your transfer has nothing to do with RTU, not with your record, for Christ's sake. It has an awful lot to do with invasion. You've only got to travel on the railways to see that the whole bloody country is geared up to one thing and one thing only.'

Invasion! The word was a mantra, the holy grail of the British soldier's life in those grim days of 1944. Colonel Vaughan was right, every railway journey now was punctuated with delays to allow the passage of goods trains with Sherman tanks, thousands of them. Aircraft parts, thousands also of transport vehicles with white stars painted on them, munitions trains marked 'dangerous load, do not shunt'. There were troop trains packed with American and British soldiers all heading south. The German bombing had stopped some time ago and was now almost a memory. The BBC was reporting that Russian troops were about to enter German territory. Invasion was on the cards, right enough.

'Sir, do you have any feel for where and when the invasion will happen?'

'Don't even ask that question, Bill. I have no idea when, where or even if the invasion will take place and even if I did, I couldn't tell you.'

'Of course not, sir.'

'Dismissed, Bill, thanks for all your help up here, you've done a great job. We'll organise a bit of a send-off for you.'

Chapter 22

The Road to D-Day

Tuesday, 18 January 1944, Whitewell, Lancashire

'Colonel Biddle will see you now,' said the pretty woman soldier of the Auxiliary Territorial Service.

Well, that was interesting! Could it be the same Biddle who was a major in the debacle with the 5th Gloucesters in Northern France? It was! Not only that, but with him was Brasington, the brilliant quartermaster, also from 5th Gloucesters. Quite how Brasington had kept them all fed and watered and supplied with ammunition in the dark months of May and June 1940 had long been a mystery. Well, he had been able to keep them fed most of the time!

'Good lord, sir, you're the CO of this lot!' Bill said snapping to attention. 'Captain Brasington as well!'

He looked at the crown on Brasington's epaulette and the maroon and white ribbon on his uniform.

'No, Major Brasington! Congratulations to both of you!'

'At ease, Bill, and welcome to the madhouse.'

'I see Major Brasington has the MC as well! There were rumours about that before I left Kington in 1940!'

'And congratulations to you, Lieutenant Adlam MM. In fact, congratulations First Lieutenant Adlam MM.'

'I'm second lieutenant, sir, not first lieutenant.'

'No, Bill, I'm promoting you, as of right now. Your record is excellent, and I have to use my men to the best of their and my ability. Right, well I suppose you are wondering what you are doing here?'

'To be totally honest, sir, I didn't understand the posting at all. But I'm sure there's a reason behind it.'

Colonel Biddle looked at Major Brasington and a knowing smile passed between the two of them.

'Right, Bill, well there is a problem. I wanted you and one or two other chaps for the battalion because you can help us out of it,' Colonel Biddle carried on.

'Monty came back to England last week to set up 21st Army Group. The 7th Armoured Division are back as well and that is not in the papers and not to be talked about. 21st Army Group are a brigade short.

'There is a show due to start called Exercise Eagle. It will take place in the North Yorkshire Moors, which are even colder at this time of year than this God-forgotten place. Within that exercise, we will fight alongside the 2nd South Wales Borderers and the 2nd Essex. If we all perform well, we will form into a brigade with them and be in the invasion.'

'Well, sir, I suppose it all comes down to a case of how much we want to be in the invasion. Personally, I do.'

'We all do, Bill. The whole country wants payback for Dunkirk, and we need good officers to get us there', said Brasington. 'And that is why we have pinched you from wherever you were.'

It was making sense. It was making a lot of sense. In a backhanded way, it was flattering.

Sunday, 20 February 1944, Middlesbrough, Yorkshire

Oh God! It was cold! Exercise Eagle has an innocuous sound about it but in reality, it was as close as British troops came to the conditions on the dreaded Eastern Front where Germans and Russians clawed each other to death in the ice and snow. The lucky ones lived in tents. The unlucky ones lived in foxholes in temperatures of minus ten degrees Celsius. Looking on the bright side, Bill was away from the ceaseless rain of Achnacarry.

Bill was to show that his leadership skills in adverse conditions were of the highest value. Colonel Biddle did not need officers who would bully conscripted men that would rather be at home with their Gloucestershire families in Stroud or Dursley. He needed officers who knew when to shout, when to cajole and when to put an arm around a man's shoulder. Above all else, Biddle wanted men who would lead from the front. Commando training, plus real battle experience from the Dunkirk debacle, meant that Bill knew how to do that. Biddle did not know of Bill's war exploits at Lofoten and Dieppe.

During the all-too-brief periods of thaw, the moors melted from hard ice to a very unpleasant, mucous-like, primordial slush. The engineers were in daily action recovering bogged vehicles. According to legend, there is a still a Bren carrier left up there, which fell into a slough and could not be extricated despite the rigorous efforts.

To make Exercise Eagle more realistic, live rounds were used in some areas. Inevitably there were casualties. Equally and inevitably, these were airbrushed out of official reports. Spitfires and Hurricanes swooped and attacked, mercifully without live rounds. One survivor of Exercise Eagle commented that he had never seen so much armour in one place at one time. Eagle was not for fun. It was totally dedicated to the central decision as to which battalions would take part in the invasion and which would not. Other than combat experience, this was the most important and decisive exercise in which Bill Adlam had taken part. He had always trained well but this was a new form of training, there was a direct reward for success. If the lashed-together brigade on the moors was successful, their reward was to wet their boots in the brine of northern France in the invasion.

And so, Bill Adlam waited to hear the result. Would he be in the invasion or not? If he were not to be in the invasion, would the colonel sanction a transfer elsewhere? He knew that he would be in demand. The notion of sitting around in England, while the culmination of the war played out in continental Europe, was a source of constant and irretrievable frustration.

'All officers to the CO's tent!'

It was the adjutant, Captain Nash.

The tent was too small to assemble all the officers inside. Colonel Biddle stood with the senior officers outside. The tension was very similar to that before opening fire in an engagement with the enemy.

'Gentlemen, I have a communication from General Montgomery at 21st Army group. The second Gloucesters are to form the 56th Independent Infantry brigade together with the 2nd South Wales Borderers and the 2nd Essex. The new brigade will remain unattached. It will not be part of a division; it will be independent in its operations and will attach to different divisions as the invasion progresses.'

'Did you say "invasion", sir?'

'I did, indeed say "invasion", Major Brasington.' If ever Bill Adlam had felt that he was put on earth for a reason, then it was in that moment. There was indeed to be an invasion of Nazi Europe. He was to be right in the middle of it.

Training began for the landing straight away,

Thursday, 16 March 1944, Clacton, Essex

The previously theoretical brigade of Operation Eagle was now a real brigade. Brigadier Pepper had arrived at Clacton on 4 March, two days after Bill and the other battalions.

'We are the 56th Independent Infantry Brigade,' he announced breezily to an assembly of officers.

Pepper's first task was to learn the correct nomenclature. The South Wales Borderers were always referred to as the 24th, the Essex as the 44th and the Gloucesters as the 61st. These were the regimental numbers which went back 90 years to the time of the Crimean war. British army units adhered to the use of the traditional names with great enthusiasm. Brigadier Pepper's next task was to order some senior officers to find a suitable house for his brigade headquarters. They walked around the town until they found just the property, a large, detached house, just off the sea-front at Harold Road in Frinton on Sea. Such was the power of wartime requisitions that a day later, he had set-up his brigade headquarters there. The civvies had been moved out, more or less politely but very quickly. Where they had gone was not the concern of the 56th Independent Infantry Brigade.

New weapons arrived. Lee Enfield rifles, Bren guns, Sten guns, grenades and ammo, lots of it.

It was like Xmas that wondrous week. A troop carrier had turned up on 9 March, then another and another, until 18 of them had arrived. Then a Bren gun carrier and another and another, until 17 had arrived. Then two three-ton trucks arrived and then two jeeps. With some 40 vehicles, the 56th Independent Infantry Brigade was going to ride to battle, not march to battle as in 1940, as if they were still fighting for the Duke of Wellington.

For First Lieutenant Adlam, this was starting to feel like the real thing!

Thursday, 9 March 1944, Clacton

'Stand easy, Bill' Colonel Biddle had said.

'Sir!'

'Right, well I've decided on your role in the battalion. You will be in support troop in charge of the pioneer section. The main job of your team will be dismantling mines and booby traps. It will put you where you want to be, right up front. As you know, under the standard battalion structure, you will also be in charge of the tradesmen, masons, bricklayers and so on, who will be responsible for construction work as we push forward.'

'Very good. Thank you, sir.'

'Now with a section like that, you will not want any Tom, Dick or whoever. You will need men you can rely on. You will need to rely on their hands when they are taking mines apart. You will need men who will not crack when their mates are blown to bits in front of their eyes. You will need men who can go without sleep under intense psychological pressure, snipers and all the rest of it. You will need to pick your own men.'

'Right, sir, I've got some ideas. Well, you'd better get your list complete by tomorrow because you are all due to join the 235 Field Park Company, Royal Engineers for a two-day training course. I have no idea at all where the course is but the adjutant has the details, and the railway passes and so forth. You're off on Sunday so sharp's the word!'

Bill was to learn the joys of dismantling the S mine. This was a mine which lay dormant below the ground. When weight was applied to it, it would jump a metre in the air, explode and shower steel balls in all directions. Because of its jumping characteristic, it was known by the grimly jocular name, the debollocker. They were deadly to anyone within a four-metre radius.

Teller mines were much bigger devices. They required 158 kilograms of pressure to trigger them. Their half-kilo of TNT was intended to blow the tracks off tanks or the wheels off other vehicles.

The shoe mine was an altogether different challenge. It contained explosives in a compact 15 cm x 15 cm box. It was not designed to kill but to mutilate anyone stepping on it by removing the victim's foot. The injured man would then require two or three other men to carry him and more to transport him to a medical facility. Because of the wooden construction, mine detectors would not find them. Another variant of the shoe mine, cased in glass, was equally difficult to detect.

The Germans had also perfected a flamethrower mine, which triggered a stream of burning petrol some four-metres wide and 20-metres long.

The bar mine was perhaps the worst. It consisted of a long, thin rectangle, some 80 cm in length and filled with explosive. It could be fitted with anti-handling devices. The slightest disturbance could trigger an explosive.

'There's just two things I have to say, Bill' said Colonel Biddle on Bill's return from training. 'Firstly, I order you directly not to dismantle any bombs yourself. Your job is to organise the team, not be a bloody hero. Secondly, and it's not an order just don't get too close to anyone in the unit. With your job you do not want to make any pals. You are going to see men blown sky high. You're going to take casualties and a lot of them. Right, dismissed.'

Thursday, 30 March 1944, Inveraray, Scotland

The front of the landing craft dropped with a loud crunch.

'Right, move split-arse across the beach, don't stop!' shouted Bill. 'No-one is to stop for any reason.'

The platoon ran forward. Live bullets cracked over their heads. Three men, who had been briefed beforehand, fell down and writhed as if hit by bullets. Two men stopped to help them. Two others were digging holes in the beach. Bill gave a signal to an umpire who blew a whistle and raised a flag. The shooting stopped.

'What on earth do you two think you are doing?'

'That's me mate, sir, and he's been hit. I've got to help him!'

'What was the last order when the landing craft beached?'

'Don't stop, sir,' said the hapless man in a crestfallen manner.

'Right, well, everybody gather around. I'll go through this as many times as it takes because if you do not understand it, you will die.'

The platoon gathered around. There was an air of scepticism.

Bill proceeded.

'When you come onto that beach, Jerry will be firing at you. Have any of you been under fire from a German MG34 or a MG42?'

A chorus of 'no, sir' mumbled its way around the group.

'Well, I have been under fire from both. They have twice the rate of fire of a Bren, and they will not only wound you, I have seen men chopped in half by them. If you stop on the beach for any reason whatsoever, you are almost certainly going to die.'

'Right, sir.'

'You two who were digging holes, can you please explain to the rest of us what you were doing?'

'Well with all these live rounds coming, in sir, we thought we'd better go to ground and dig in, like. You know, sir, self-preservation and that.'

'Ok, lads, and how long will it take you to dig a hole deep enough to take cover in?'

'Oh, only a minute or two, sir.'

'And how long will it take Jerry with his MG42 to splatter you across the sand?'

'It'll take about two bloody seconds, you daft bugger,' said one of the platoon members.

'Right, well he's said it, so I don't have to.'

The platoon grinned and nodded.

'Now, we'll go again and this time no-one stops for anything. If your best mate is hurt in the invasion, there are medical orderlies coming after us. Now, you are not trained to give medical assistance unless you are a nursing sister Civvy Street. So, you blokes who stopped, were you nursing sisters in your former life?'

'No, sir.'

'Well in that case, you are not qualified to do anything more than put an Elastoplast on a blister. For that matter, neither am I and neither is Colonel Biddle. Is this getting through to you all?'

'Yes, sir.'

'Well, when we advance over the beach, you will see men drop because they are hit. Behind us, there are medical orderlies. These are highly trained and very experienced individuals and Mr Churchill has spent an awful lot of money in developing their expertise. They are equipped to take care of the wounded. They have the skill to do so. Your job is to get across that beach, to get into those low hills and to get to the rendezvous place where I will give you further orders.'

'Right, sir.'

Inveraray! Bill had been there on the *Glengyle* in his own initial training in 4 Commando. He had trained there for the Lofoten raid. It brought back memories of Sir Roger Keyes, of Lovat, of 'Jumbo' Morris and all those wonderful soldiers. Some had not made it back from Varengeville. If only he could be with that brilliant bunch of men, now! No! There was no point in thinking like that. He was going to be in the invasion and that was something to be happy about, not to mention the second pip which he was given on his latest promotion. His experience in commandos would prove useful to this battalion and his natural bent as a trainer was very useful to the colonel.

From the early days at Inveraray, when the landings were an undignified shambles, to the later days a transformation was to occur. In that first week of April, the men could file into Landing Ships Infantry (LSIs) in the dark, in full kit, and find their exact position without a mistake. They could tranship into the smaller Landing Ships Assault (LSA) with a minimum of mishap. They had trained firstly in companies, then as a battalion, then together with the 2nd Essex and 2nd South Wales Borderers as a brigade.

Going into battle with the South Wales Borderers resonated within Bill. He was fighting with men who were the military descendants of those who had distinguished themselves at Rorke's Drift in the Zulu Wars and won 11 Victoria Crosses in one evening. He was touching the hem of history. Now they were not fighting spear-wielding Zulus but fighting Nazis with the finest fighting equipment known to man. He needed to focus on that to the exclusion of all else. The immediate issue was that every one of his men had to know where they would be situated in the landing craft and where they would be in relation to everyone else.

At last, Colonel Biddle asked the vital question of his officers.

'Is this battalion fully trained for operations in landing craft, to cross a beach under fire and to reach a forming up place as required by Brigadier Pepper's orders?'

'We're ready, sir.'

'Lieutenant Adlam?'

'We're getting it right, sir, but it is still not smooth. With more practice, I think we can knock four minutes off the landing.'

A four-minute saving off the landing time could save a lot of lives.

Friday, 7 April 1944, Ossemsley Manor, Hampshire

Major Brasington was not amused.

'Lieutenant Adlam! Where the hell is Lieutenant Adlam?'

'Yes, sir.'

'At ease, Bill, glad you've made it at last, do you know what the previous load of buggers who were billeted here have done?'

'I really don't, sir, I've just arrived.'

'Well, they've booby trapped the whole place.'

'WHAT?'

'Half of the tents in the camp have got booby traps in them. I need your pioneer platoon to go in and dismantle them and do it now.'

'Right, sir, what unit was it who was here, sir?'

'You don't need to worry about that but there's going to be some sodding court martials, I can tell you.'

He drove off in his jeep to report to Colonel Biddle.

An hour later, Bill reported to the colonel.

'It's all clear, sir. They weren't well hidden; they weren't concealed at all. It was easy to sort them out and quite good practice for the lads.'

'Thanks, Bill, so we can take possession of the camp, can we?'

'All clear, sir, it's a nice camp as well. Can I ask that my Pioneer Platoon have first choice of the accommodation, sir, seeing as we made it safe for everyone? I see there are one or two Nissen Huts, sir.'

'You're far too late, Bill, the Nissen huts were bagged long before we got here.'

Bill, like all the other officers, addressed his Pioneer Platoon.

'Right, lads, there are one or two changes about to happen. There are signs around the camp, DO NOT LOITER. CIVILIANS MUST NOT TALK TO MILITARY PERSONNEL. Have you seen those?'

'Yes, sir.'

'I have to inform you that talking to civvies is now a court-martial offence.'

'Bloody hell.'

'There is a change in writing letters home. I have to read all of them. My orders are that if there is anything in a letter that is sensitive, then the letter will not be sent. I am NOT to reveal to you that the letter has not been sent.'

He waited as the members of the platoon looked at each other in blank incomprehension.

'I am to tell you what material is sensitive. You cannot reveal your whereabouts to your family. You cannot tell them that you think the invasion is imminent. You cannot tell them about the unbelievable amounts of military equipment that you have seen on the roads and railways. You cannot reveal anything which refers to the invasion at all.

'You can say that you are well, that you hope the Rover the dog has got over his worms and you can say that you played a good game of cricket. I have also been briefed about those clever codes that people use in their letters. Don't do it. If you disobey these orders, you will enter a world of trouble which will be worse than anything that Jerry can devise for you, I can assure you of that.

'Now, when you are writing to your girlfriends, please make them as sexy as possible because I have to read the whole lot and I really do need the entertainment, which I am sure you will give me.'

'How is it possible that we don't talk to civvies when we go on leave, sir?'

'Leave is cancelled forthwith, that is the other thing I have to tell you. There is now no more leave. Dismissed.'

The platoon was silent. Matters were becoming serious.

Thursday, 25 May 1944, New Forest, Hampshire

'Right! Listen to me, everyone. At 1330, lorries will arrive, and we will pass on to a new destination.'

The new destination was a sealed camp. The camp itself was called B7 and was situated at Pennerley Lodge near Beaulieu in the picturesque New Forest area. The camp was surrounded by rows of concertinaed barbed wire. Exit was only possible under orders and under military police escort. Entry to the sealed camp was possible only for those in uniform and with the requisite official passes. There was no order not to talk to civilians now, it just was not possible to see them, let alone talk to them. The charm and picturesque quality of the scene was lost on the Gloucesters.

'Christ! This is a bloody prison camp!'

This observation was accurate. Other ranks were only allowed out for specific reasons. Bren gunners, for instance, were taken out under supervision into the surrounding woods for target practice and to zero their sights. At the end, they were all brought back under close supervision. The two main aspects of the stay at Pennerley were to be boredom and rain. There was to be lots of both.

There was, however, one really popular aspect to camp B7. It was run by Americans. As compared to the spartan British tents which were narrow and cramped, the US Army tents were huge and commodious. It was possible to stand up in them! Each man had a camp bed with a mattress. A mattress! There were blankets and a bolster to rest your head on. This was luxury beyond belief, but there was more. There was a canteen where free coffee was available all day. American cigarettes such as Camel and Lucky Strike were available in packets of 50 for a shilling (£0.05p). There were glossy, colourful, and fascinating American magazines to read and lots of them.

There were so many cigarettes that it occurred to the men that if they could smuggle these outside, they could make a fortune selling them to the civvy population, except of course, there was no way out.

The crowning glory, however, shone at mealtimes. The Gloucesters were given American-size rations.

'What the bloody hell do you think you're playing at?' the quartermaster Major Brasington had thundered at the American cooks. 'You've just dished out a week's bloody rations in one bloody morning. Where do you think we're going to get rations for the rest of the bloody time here?'

This led to full and frank exchanges behind locked doors in the CO's hut!

By some mysterious means, additional rations were found. This was not the end of the affair. The Americans were at least as unhappy with Major Brasington, as Major Brasington was with the Americans.

It was clear now that the invasion day was coming closer and closer. As a platoon leader, Bill had to leave the camp to attend meetings at the Brigadier's headquarters at the Pennerley Lodge main building. Driving the Jeep even a couple of kilometres was becoming difficult. The road was clogged with tank transporters, three-ton trucks and huge low loaders carrying 25-pounder artillery pieces. 'Queen Mary's' were everywhere: the huge transport vehicles which carried parts of Typhoon fighters, Tempest fighters and some unrecognised American planes, which Bill had never seen before. They held up the traffic for kilometre upon kilometre. The whole vast circus was presided over by red-capped and officious military police. There were thousands of them to direct traffic, manage the eternal traffic jams and noticeably put an end to any chat between service personnel and civilians. Many civilians offered the troops cups of tea or cigarettes. Some were successful. In many other cases, the redcaps would stop the conversation with a stern warning, 'Oy! You with the red hair! No talking with civvies!'

At one edge of the camp, there was a Nissen Hut. It was even more closely guarded than usual by redcaps. This was interesting. It was even more so when those on guard duty reported back that the Nissen hut was guarded for 24 hours a day. It had not been possible for the patrolling soldiers to strike up a chat with the military police, who issued a blunt warning that they were not to talk to anyone.

A stern notice told all ranks to keep away, unless specifically ordered to approach the hut by an officer. During the day, all ranks had seen senior officers go into and out of the hut. Something was afoot, but what?

Saturday, 27 May 1944, Camp B7, Pennerley Lodge, Hampshire

On Thursday, Colonel Biddle had declared Camp B7 completely sealed. Now, no-one was allowed in. No-one was allowed out. On that Saturday morning, the colonel ordered all officers to report to the mysterious hut.

'At ease, everyone, please be seated,' said Colonel Biddle. 'Right, gentlemen. Well, I have to tell you that this is it. The moment for which we have all been training is almost upon us.'

He gave a nod to two sergeants who removed the cloth from the table. Bill's initial impression was that this looked like another exercise. A three-dimensional table map showed a beach and a seashore. The topography appeared to be that of the approaches to Wareham in Dorset, where they had trained to do landings. At least it *almost* looked like the topography at Wareham. The same German defences were present, the same German troop deployments were present, and the same beach obstacles were there. Most remarkable of all, the villages and landmarks all had the same fake names, which they had used for the exercises in the Wareham area. There was one aspect that he picked up on immediately. The pattern of roads was different.

This was not Wareham! This map showed where the real landing was going to be! It was somewhere in France. The realisation hit him with the force of a well-aimed cricket ball. British army intelligence had the precise German deployments and had recreated them in Dorset. Every detail was perfect, or at least as far as he could remember from the exercises. The minutely detailed and utterly pedantic planning of Operation Overlord, for so it was called, had led to it being nicknamed, Operation Overboard. He could see why.

What he was looking at was one of the greatest military secrets of World War II, the landing ground for the invasion. It contained the answer to the question, which had been asked 10,000,000 times over the last year.

Where was the invasion to take place?

Colonel Biddle spoke. 'The purpose of this morning's meeting is to appraise you as to your part in the invasion of Europe. Please note that I am not, repeat not, authorised to reveal where the landing is to be. I will communicate that to you when we are on the invasion barges. We move on Saturday to Lymington and will take our places in the invasion barges there. Over on that wall, you will find a list which gives you the number of the invasion barge on which your unit will be travelling. Before you leave here, please note the number and communicate it to your NCOs.'

He waited for the impact to filter through.

'D-Day has been set for a week on Monday, 5 June. The 231st Brigade and ourselves will attach to the 50th Northumbrian Division. The 231st will land at 0700 hours on a beach which is called Gold Beach. We are due to follow the 231st at 0720 hours. We will land at this point, near this village. We will land, exit the beach as quickly as possible and form up at this village. Our orders are to proceed to this town and take it on the first day.'

'The Nottinghamshire Yeomanry are attached to 231st Brigade and their DD tanks will have cleared the beach of any mines. The mine-free area will be marked clearly with white tape. Please impress on all of your men that no-one is to go outside the white tape. That is vital to the success of the enterprise.'

'Are we to know what DD tanks are, sir?'

'Well, seeing as how we are locked in, I can tell you. They are 'duplex drive' tanks which means they can operate on land or in the sea. In essence, they are swimming tanks. They will swim ashore. They have flail contraptions on the front, and they will use these flails to explode any mines, thus driving a safe path up the beach.'

This brought a chorus of understated wolf-whistles.

'We do not talk about DD tanks outside this room. The other ranks will see them soon enough when we land.'

Colonel Biddle waited while several officers made notes.

For Bill Adlam, this meant that he would take his two assault Pioneer sections, but the tradesmen's section would follow later. His mine-clearing detachment would not be needed on the beach so the orders stood, 'get off the beach as fast as you can!'.

'You will notice from the map that the German deployment, pillboxes and so forth, are exactly in the positions that you have trained for. Are there any more questions?'

'As far as we know, are there any Waffen SS units in the area, sir?'

'We believe not.'

'Thank God for that,' said a voice.

'Er, no, that man! It is not, 'thank God'. The 61st will take on all comers including the Waffen SS and any other so-called elite units that Mr Hitler can throw at us. Oh, and we intend to beat them as well. When we have taken this town, we will detach from 50th Northumbrian Division and attach ourselves to the Seventh Armoured Division.'

Bill smiled and thought, 'We're going to fight with the Desert Rats!'

This was partly good and partly bad. The Desert Rats had defeated Rommel and were famous for their wonderful esprit de corps. On the other hand, they were also famous for obnoxious behaviour, especially regarding other units of the army.

'Well, that is all I have to say for the moment,' said Colonel Biddle. 'Sergeant Major, dismiss the men if you would. Please familiarise yourselves with the schedule on the wall.'

Bill gave the orders to his sections as ordered by Colonel Biddle.

'Now, as you know, the camp is completely sealed. No further letters are to be written home. You are each to write a farewell letter to your family and give that letter to me. I will pass the letter on to the appropriate channels. Your letters will only be sent if you are reported as killed in action. If you are not killed, then the letter will not be sent.'

'What's it like fighting Jerry, sir?'

'They're good soldiers, they're well motivated, well trained and they have good weapons. Their better units are bloody aggressive as well. But with the training and the leadership in this brigade, we have the beating of them. I'll tell you a trick as well.'

'What's that, sir?'

'Well, when we land, try and get hold of a German Schmeisser machine gun if you can. They're streets better than these bloody Sten guns, they're better made and they're more reliable. They use the same 9-mm ammo as a Sten as well. If you can pick them up, I can train you in how to look after them and how to fire them.'

'Right, sir.'

'Just one thing, though, I get the first one!'

In the intervening days, before leaving camp B7 and embarking onto their landing craft, a new word was being used and being used several thousand times a day.

The word was D-Day.

Chapter 23

Embarkation for D-Day

Sunday, 4 June 1944, Camp B7, Pennerley Lodge, Hampshire

The air sparkled and crackled with the electricity of men on the move. Men were busy making vehicles waterproof; loading vehicles; undertaking last-minute vehicle servicing; checking equipment; sharpening bayonets; cleaning weapons; drawing compo rations to take in their kitbags. Compo rations were Rations – Composite. There were variations on the theme but essentially, they consisted of a variety of foods such as canned meat, M & V (meat and vegetables), cans of beans, cans of soup, malt tablets, biscuits, chocolate, cigarettes and toilet tissue. Conversation was limited to those communications, which were necessary for the work at hand. Good-natured banter had all but disappeared. Every man felt as though he had a heavy stone in his stomach. Bill knew that feeling from Dunkirk, the Lofotens and Dieppe. It was the feeling that said, 'this is becoming serious.'

Bill's role was to ensure that his men's equipment was in working order, that their personal weapons were in working order and that their morale remained high. That was the hardest part. This was where his reputation came in very handy. The MM ribbon on his tunic, the commando mystique and his known penchant from leading from the front gave him a huge advantage. If he was calm, professional, and methodical, then his men would follow suit.

During the day, several of the battalion had remarked on a singular happening. All day – and for some days now – they had seen squadrons of British Lancaster and Halifax Bombers and American B17s and Liberators flying overhead, clearly destined for northern France. They had seen numbers of Typhoon and Tempest fighters with their rockets at the ready heading in the same direction. On the radio, there was no mention of this. It was as if all this ordnance was heading southwards to the French coast as part of a parallel universe, but it had to be going somewhere.

'Right, you lot, gather round. I have to pass operational order number one on to you. There are a number of things that we have not got to do when we get over there.'

The men appeared grateful that their attention was being demanded. It took their mind off their nerves.

'Right, well first off, there are some properties we have to try not to destroy if we can avoid it. These include hospitals, post offices, reservoirs, churches, or any government buildings. If we have to occupy them, then we will have to but try and avoid if possible. Now there is somewhere else to avoid. There are legal brothels in France, and they are to be avoided at all costs.'

'Oh sir, have a heart, won't we have earned ourselves a bit of a treat for liberating the frogs? I mean it's only fair.'

'No, it is not fair. There were some of those places over on the Maginot Line in 1940 and we had a lot of chaps – a lot mind – got some very nasty diseases out of them. So, we keep out, is that clear? I do not want to see eyes rolling to the heavens, either!'

'Yes, sir.'

'Lieutenant McConnell, the medical officer, has given out a warning about some things that each and every man has to look out for. For Christ's sake, be careful what you eat over there, there is a lot of dysentery around. There is polio, smallpox, typhus, and hepatitis, so if you feel a bit off colour, I advise every man to see the medical officer without any delay. No, that's not advice, it's an order. Oh, and apparently, the German soldiers have brought an awful lot of venereal disease with them, so be warned. I also have an address to read out from the CO.'

> From Lt Col Biddle to All Ranks: the 61st are about to re-enter France. The task before us will be hard, but we have a debt to pay off towards those of this battalion who defended Cassel towards the end of May 1940. We shall now have the opportunity of demonstrating the fruits of four years waiting and preparation. As the commanding officer of the 5th Battalion said at Ledringhem, 'up Gloucesters and at 'em.'

'Well Major Biddle was there when Colonel Buxton said those words and so was I. We behaved like British soldiers at Ledringhem, and I expect every man in this platoon to behave like that in the coming days. Parade is at 1200 and I want every man looking like a soldier, and a British soldier as well, is that understood?'

'Yes, sir.'

Everyone present that day recalled that lunch that the American cooks provided was wonderful. With the rationing of the last four years, they had not seen some of those wonderful meats, puddings and fruit and had almost forgotten of their existence. At the appointed hour, the Gloucesters mounted into their three-ton trucks, Bren carriers and, for Bill Adlam, his personal jeep with driver. The gates of the sealed camp duly opened, and they were out into the outside world again, but it was a changed world. The scenery around Lymington in Hampshire is classical 'England's green and pleasant land' territory. However, in the run-up to the invasion every 100 metres or so stood a red-capped military policeman or a green-capped field security policeman. The civil police had cleared the roads and sealed them off. There was no other traffic. As they passed through villages, the locals would wave from the streets, windows and doorways.

'Good luck, lads!'

'All the best, you bloody heroes!'

'Give Adolf one on the nose for me.'

The support from the British people was hovering on the 100 per-cent level. They never thought it would be anything else. It made going into battle worthwhile.

At the end of that short sortie, there was a field outside of Lymington where the vehicles lined up to embark on their landing craft. At last, it was the Gloucesters' turn. A military policeman on a motorbike took them to the harbour. There were the three landing crafts (infantry): LCIs 2906, 2907 and 2908 with LCI 255 for Brigadier Pepper and his staff. More people cheered, waved Union Jacks and gave thumbs-up signs. Considering that the invasion was supposed to be top secret, there seemed to be a huge number of civilians who knew precisely what was going on.

This was not a time for introspection. The weather was worsening.

The Gloucesters were eventually all packed in and stowed on their landing craft and waiting for the order to cast off. In the intense training for 'Operation Overboard' they had practised it so many times that they could have done the entire operation without orders and if necessary in their sleep.

'Right!' said Bill, 'Everyone has been issued with a Mae West. You are to wear them at all times on the vessel. There is no excuse for anyone to be found without a Mae West. Is that clear?'

'Yes, sir.'

'Major Brasington has also organised rubber waders for all of you, you will be issued with them but don't put them on until we transfer to the Landing Craft Mechanised. Everyone got that?'

'Yes, sir.'

Brigadier Pepper ordered all officers to his landing craft LCI255. He gave a short address and showed them the map. They were to land near the village of Le Hamel, make their way overland and form up at a village called Buhot and then proceed to Bayeux. Bill's platoon would have the job of clearing mines and booby traps. They would be in the very front. Behind him would be the khaki of the British and Canadian forces. In front of him would be the grey of the German Army. It might not be the commandos, but it was where he wanted to be.

This really was it, the landing was to be in Normandy!

As he walked back through the drenching rain to his own landing craft 2907, there were three things that struck him. Even in the darkness, he could see that Lymington harbour was absolutely stuffed with landing craft, support craft, motor torpedo boats and other grey, menacing, miscellaneous naval boats whose job was to sink, shoot down or lacerate as many German craft as humanly possible. Then there was the security. He was in possession of the secret, where the landing would be. The quayside was lined with redcaps, green caps and civil police. There was no possibility for anyone to escape to the outside world. The third thing that he noticed was the singing. Singing? Why the bloody hell was there singing?

'Of course,' he thought, 'it's the Taffs.'

The South Wales Borderers – the 24th – were on landing craft adjacent to those of the Gloucesters. The singing was beautiful, haunting but uplifting at the same time. Did he stop to listen? Did all of them walking along that dark, blacked-out dockside? Up on the deck of their landing craft, the lead tenor sang the melody.

> *Mae d'eisiau di bob awr,*
> *Fy Arglwydd Dduw,*
> *Daw hedd o'th dyner lais*
> *O nefol ryw.*

From the dark inside of the craft came the chorus.

> *Mae d'eisiau, O mae d'eisiau,*
> *Bob awr mae arnaf d'eisiau,*
> *Bendithia fi, fy Ngheidwad,*
> *Bendithia nawr.*

Goodness only knew what it meant, but it sounded wonderful!

Of the D-Day survivors, no-one who heard that singing was ever to forget it. That was a four-part chorus! Who actually taught them to sing like that? He had not cried at Ledringhem or other nameless places in Northern France, but he could have cried now.

Back on the landing craft, he gathered the platoon together.

'Right, lads, this is the situation. We move in the landing craft to Southampton docks now and we move into the channel at 0400. We will follow the 231st Brigade onto the beach. The place is called Le Hamel. When you arrive at Le Hamel, you will find unit landing officers, they will be equipped with flags and blackboards and will point the way to Buhot. Buhot is where we form up into a unit.'

'Are we landing at Dunkirk, sir?'

'The invasion will take place in Normandy.'

This led to a hubbub of surprise, victory, defeat, amazement, 'told you so', 'no you never', 'Thompson, you tosser, you owe me five quid.'

'QUIET! I do not care who owes who five quid. This is it. This is the bloody invasion. Now this is what will happen.'

He pointed to the map.

'We land at this point here. We form up at Buhot and proceed to this point, a mile and a half [two kilometres] north-east of Bayeux.'

There was silence in the craft.

'We then proceed to capture the high ground above Bayeux. We are in reserve to the 2nd South Wales Borderers and the 2nd Essex. They will call on us, as and when they need us. If we are not called upon, we are ordered to pass through the centre of Bayeux and form the southern and western edge of the battlefield.'

He looked around to make sure that everyone was taking it in.

'You will notice that we land at Gold Beach, just like in the training. We land on Jig sector, green sector, just like in training except that we don't take Wareham, we take Bayeux.'

'Isn't there a famous tapestry there, sir? Are there any special orders about that?'

'Just keep shooting Germans and the tapestry will have to look after itself. The 231st Brigade are due on the beach at 0700 hours. We follow the 231st at 0725. The beach will be marked with white tape. This will show you where the mines have been cleared. It is just like the practice landings.

Outside the white tape, there are mines. If you stray out there, neither I nor anyone else will come and get you. Is that clear? If you are stuck in a minefield, I cannot spare men or risk equipment to get you out. You will be treated as lost, unless you are lucky enough to find your own way out. Now, is all of this clear?'

'Yes, sir.'

'When you come off the landing craft and feel the sand beneath your boots, come on, I want to hear what you have to do.'

'We run split-arse across the beach, sir.'

'If your best mate is hit, what do you do?'

'We keep on running, sir.'

'Why do you keep on running?'

'Because the medical orderlies will look after him, sir.'

'If you stop on the beach to dig in, what will happen?'

'You will personally bloody shoot us, sir.'

'Will a court martial convict me?'

'Not a chance, sir.'

'When you get over the beach what do you do?'

'We take cover in the *bocage*, sir, until the NCOs and yourself come to get us.'

The word *bocage* was now becoming current in the everyday language which they used. Curiously it is not even a French word. It is a Norman dialect word. It refers to countryside with high hedgerows, small fields with small dense forests and a mixture of woodland and pasture. It sounds like a rustic idyll. They would find that the *bocage* was good for the German defenders and awful for the British and Canadian attackers.

'Right, there will be hedgerows to hide under and farmhouses to grab as defensive points.'

'Where is all our transport, sir? Do we have to walk to Berlin?'

'If you look out for a landing craft LST519, you will see there are a load of vehicles on it. Those are ours. They will join us at Buhot. I had to walk all the bloody way from the Maginot Line to Dunkirk four years ago and I do not intend to do a repeat performance. We are motorised infantry now, just like Jerry.'

'Are there any 88s, sir?'

This referred to the dreaded German 88-mm artillery.

'There are to the west but too far away to trouble us. Some other bugger will get the benefit of them. Intelligence tells us there are no tank brigades in the immediate area. The RSM will be setting up a cage for the prisoners, so if there are any German prisoners take them along there and turn them in.'

'What if the prisoners give us any trouble, sir?'

'This is an invasion, Evans, you just shoot them, there won't be any comebacks.'

If the reality of an invasion had not hit the men before, it certainly did now. The uppermost question of the last two years had been, 'where will the invasion take place?'. Now the uppermost questions were, 'will I survive the beach?', 'will I let my mates down' and 'if I have trouble with a German prisoner, will I be able to shoot him?'

'Alright, everyone, we're very cramped on here. Get whatever sleep you can. If anyone has to go to the loo just do it over the side, eh? There is only one loo and it's impossible to get to.'

The engines started up, a throb went through the small, cramped craft and the boat wallowed under its heavy load.

'Listen! Can everybody listen? Have I got everyone's last letter home? That is really important if you don't make it back?'

'Yes, sir,' chorused the replies.

It seemed only a minute later, he must have dozed off, it was already half-light.

'Lieutenant Adlam, sir?' A corporal who he did not know spoke.

'Yes.'

'Message from Brigadier Pepper, sir, it's postponed. The invasion is postponed.'

'What?'

'Apparently, there is a hell of a storm blowing up the channel, so it's postponed.'

Bill retired to his berth below the LCI conning tower. His natural inclination was to be in with the men, but the British Army kept its officers and men separate. Instead of spending the night in the bowels of the ship, he would have his own bunk. Space was tight but at least, he had more than a two-foot-wide space to sleep in and – wonder of wonders – he even had a porthole to look out and to see the unfolding drama. That postponement was going to be bad for morale. He needed to do something to counter any bellyaching and negative attitudes. Sleep overtook him.

Chapter 24

A Trip across the Channel – Operation Neptune

Monday, 5 June 1944, Southampton Water

The rain hammered on the small craft like a punishing and malevolent God. The naval personnel were chatting to officers and said they would even stop cross-channel ferries on days like this.

'Christ only knows when it will stop,' said one of them.

It didn't stop and clearly had no intention of stopping. The rain battered down. The men played cards and told tall stories about their conquests and the joys of different beers and the joys of watching Aston Villa play and debated whether Tommy Handley was a better comedian than Gert and Daisy.

'Keeping the men busy, Bill?' Colonel Biddle had asked.

'Certainly, sir!'

Commandos (or ex-commandos) routinely met challenges, even difficult ones, with good humour and positivity.

'I'm afraid there's no let-up in the weather.'

'Oh God, sir, any idea when we'll get off?'

'None whatsoever. At least the Luftwaffe can't pop across and have a look at us. The cloud cover is at about 20 feet above the sea as far as I can see.'

The day was to have its compensations, however. At Southampton, they could see several large concrete structures squatting on their spindly legs on the water.

'What on earth are those, sir?'

'Apparently, it's called Mulberry, Bill, and it's a portable harbour. There are two of them and they come over just after us. One will be landed at Arromanche near where we land, and the other is for the Americans' use somewhere further west.'

'A portable harbour, sir?'

'Yes, the planners didn't think we could risk another Dieppe debacle, so this time, we're taking our own harbours with us.'

'And what is that contraption over there?'

'Bill, let me introduce you to PLUTO.'

'What on earth is that?'

'Did you ever wonder how we would get our petrol supplies in northern France?'

'Yes, sir, with 40 odd vehicles in the battalion, it went through my mind a lot.'

'Well, PLUTO is a pipeline under the ocean. We just pump the stuff through and at least in theory, we have all the petrol we need, which is more than can be said for the Germans.'

Colonel Biddle moved on. The dead hand of the dead hours descended once more.

The loudspeaker crackled into action.

'All ranks to leave the vessel. Leave all kit and personal weapons where they are. You are to proceed to the customs shed where tea and sandwiches are waiting.'

It turned out that there was an air show as well. It was not just entertainment; it was to show the troops what the different allied planes looked like. They cheered the British and American Spitfires, Hurricanes, Tempests, Typhoons, Mustangs and Lockheed Lightnings. Then they booed the fly past of captured German planes, Messerschmitt 109s and 110s; Focke Wulf 190s; Junkers 87s (the infamous Stukas) and 88s. The loudspeaker on the wharf gave the title of each plane and extra detail of the German planes to allow identification.

Tension was beginning to show now. Some men found the noise from the aircraft too much. Firing in the frontline against the enemy was now only hours away. Nerves frayed. Men began to quarrel over trifles. The tension mounted.

Fortunately, there was a NAAFI on the wharf where they could buy newspapers, sandwiches, cigarettes, write more letters if they so wished and drink even more tea. Alcohol was noticeable by its absence. They were constantly aware of the menacing cordon of military and civil police. They knew that even to attempt to talk to a civilian was now a serious court-martial offence. They were quarantined for the glory to come, if that is what it was to be.

The loudspeaker crackled into action again.

'Stand by for an important announcement.'

Is this it? Are we to embark for France?

'The War Office has issued a communiqué, which states as follows. "As of this morning, United States troops have entered Rome. German personnel have vacated the city, which has fallen without hostilities. The Pope has spoken to cheering crowds from the balcony of the Basilica of St Peter in the Vatican City."'

The fall of Rome was a major landmark. The allies were winning the war and the Germans were losing it. That was a very heartening message for men about to embark for the beachheads of northern France.

In the middle of the afternoon, the quayside loudspeaker ordered all ranks back on board. There was little to do but go back to sleep.

He awoke with a start. Somewhere a warship was playing 'A Hunting We Will Go!' over the loudspeaker. At the end, the troops all cheered. Then, from a French warship came the stirring sounds of 'La Marseillaise'.

Allons enfants de la Patrie, [Forward, children of the Fatherland]

Le jour de gloire est arrivé! [The day of glory has arrived]

Would it be glory? Would it be another debacle like Dieppe? Would it be another successful massacre like Varengeville? Would it be… whatever? He dozed off again.

There was a definite feeling of movement and energy around the harbour. You could almost touch it. Did this mean that they were off to France?

The engines throbbed. He awoke. A sense of motion. It was 1915 hours. The craft pitched a little. Once, twice then it pitched quite a lot. He stood up and looked over the gunwale. The craft was moving. Sailors on nearby ships were lining the deck rails, high above them. The sailors waved, just as the civvies had done on the long drive from camp B7.

'Good luck, lads!'

'Bayonet a Jerry for me.'

The individual cries gave way to a general roar around the harbour. Their landing craft was on its way. Now, for the first time, he could see the full majestic scope, size and magnificence of the invasion. His wartime career had already seen him take part in history. Nothing had prepared him for this. No-one in world history had taken part in anything this big. If he was still tired, the burst of adrenaline made him forget it immediately.

His own landing craft cleared the harbour at Southampton. One moment, the craft moved smoothly, then without warning, the craft pitched robustly into the sea. They were in the Channel and heading for France. The landing craft came into formation with the other dozen or so landing craft of the brigade. Then the landing craft with the vehicles joined them. Then further dozens of landing craft carrying the units which would land on Gold Beach King sector. These included the 79th Armoured Division with 69th Brigade followed by 151st Brigade. Then there were the armoured units from the 4th/7th Royal Dragoon Guards. It was too complex, too huge and too utterly overwhelming to comprehend. Their dozens of landing craft came into formation with dozens of other land craft to form this vast armada, the like of which the world had never seen in all history. Around the landing craft were escort vessels, cruisers, destroyers, corvettes, frigates, every type of ship imaginable. Each ship knew where it had to be, what speed it had to travel, how far it should be from the other ships around it.

He could not count the ships but would not have been surprised to learn that there were 5000 of them. Five thousand! Someone had actually planned all of this. It was difficult to find words to describe it but 'breathtaking' and 'genius' would be two of them.

Bill's landing craft was forming up into the convoy known as G3, which comprised some 24 landing craft together with its escorts HMS *Hind*, a sloop, plus several destroyers.

As the convoy formed up, Bill made a visit to his troops.

'Alright, lads, best get some shut-eye if you can. We'll be transferring into the smaller craft at about 0630 for our landing at 0725. Get whatever sleep you can, and I'll see you in the morning.'

'Will you come and tuck us in, sir?'

'No, that's the Regimental Sergeant Major's job, from what I remember.'

This was a reference to the popular song 'Kiss Me Goodnight, Sergeant Major.'

'There is just one more thing, lads. I don't want any of you keeping anything in your gasmasks. Jerry hasn't used gas yet in this war but when he sees this lot on his doorstep, I wouldn't put it past him. Carruthers, I know you've got an apple in there. I do not want that apple in your gasmask when we are running up that beach. Do we have an agreement?'

'Alright then, sir.'

'Lawson's got a dirty magazine in his gasmask, sir.'

'I bloody have not.'

'Alright, lads, let's get some shut-eye.'

'Best of luck tomorrow, sir!'

'Best of luck to all of you, lads, now get some sleep.'

As he returned to his berth, he looked up. Through the few breaks in the clouds, he would see the dark shapes of squadron after squadron of Typhoons and Tempests, of Lancasters and B17s, Lockheed Lightnings and Mustangs, as they rumbled south to deal death and destruction to the enemy. He was deeply aware that he had no words to describe this. None of them ever would.

He was also deeply aware that this small vessel held over 200 men. It felt as light and insubstantial in the rolling swell and that if it was hit by a mine or even a burst of cannon shells, then none of them were likely to survive.

It was time to turn in, even though it was still quite light. He awoke with a start, the landing craft was pitching and heaving and bucking. It was dark. He must have dozed off for a moment, but a chink of light allowed him to see his watch, it was 0200.

Chapter 25

Adolf Hitler Responds to the Normandy Invasion

Early on the morning of the Normandy invasion, 6 June 1944, Hitler was with his entourage in his private residence at the Berghof in the breathtaking mountains of Bavaria. He had been watching films on his home projector, together with Eva Braun, Doctor Goebbels and his wife Magda. Blondi, Hitler's German Shepherd dog was in attendance. At 0200 hours, Goebbels' private train was ordered to be ready, and the main lines cleared across Germany for him and Mrs Goebbels to return to Berlin.

At 0730 hours, Hitler was wakened by his valet Günsche and ushered with all respectful haste into a meeting with the military high command including Jodl and Field Marshall Keitel. They advised that American and British landings were taking place in Normandy. At first, these were thought to be diversionary attacks or possibly armed reconnaissances similar to the shambles at Dieppe. Now it was clear that more and more troops were landing. Offshore, Royal Navy cruisers and at least two battleships were pounding the shore batteries. Bombing raids had been taking place all night.

The supreme commander in the west, Field Marshall von Rundstedt had taken the initiative to order the 12th SS and 21st armoured divisions forward and also two available infantry divisions: the 352nd and 716th static infantry division. The first of these was a seasoned combat unit; the latter was a division of older soldiers and various ethnic volunteers picked up on the eastern front. Hitler approved this initiative which had been taken without his express orders.

Hitler ordered that Goebbels' train be located and stopped. He would order Goebbels to make a rousing broadcast to the German people to the effect that Germany welcomed the attack and would throw the invaders back into the sea.

Hitler was also aware that Field Marshal Rommel had advised that if the invasion came and the invaders got a foothold for 24 hours, then it was unlikely that German forces would be able to stop them.

Matters were becoming critical indeed.

Chapter 26

D Day: Bill Adlam Wades Ashore

Tuesday, 6 June 1944, Off Gold Beach, Normandy

He came to with a start. It was a grim, grey morning. What was that bloody noise? *WHOOSH – WHOOSH – WHOOSH.* There it was again. He looked through the streaky thick glass of the porthole. Rocket ships out in the murk were firing salvoes of 1100 five-inch rockets. Hundreds, thousands, tens of thousands of these red-tailed demons sped towards the French coast at supernatural speed. The direction at least told him which way France lay.

The landing craft was pitching and rolling and yawing and pitching again and rolling and what was that smell? It was sour, it was all-pervading, it was inescapable. He knew it from the Lofoten raid. It was the smell of sick. He looked at his watch. It was 0830 hours. He had actually been to sleep. They were supposed to have landed over an hour ago. Was something going wrong?

The large G3 convoy, which he had watched the previous night, had now been joined by others. This was not a matter of a few others. There were dozens of convoys, hundreds upon hundreds of ship. Overhead, the Typhoon and Tempest fighter planes continued to surge ahead toward France with their rockets and cannon fire which could equal the broadside of a destroyer. Somewhere above them, he heard the droning of the Lancasters and Halifaxes. He could not see them because of the low cloud. Enough of this daydreaming, he had better see what his platoon were doing.

Below the gunwale of the main deck, he was met by the sight of 200 heavily armed men, without their rifles, gasmasks or, in some cases, regulation uniform blouses, who were all bringing back yesterday evening's meal. The landing craft was flat bottomed, flat fronted and of shallow draft. The angry sea threw the craft around as it wanted, with no let up or escape. The men were vomiting into the sick bags; vomiting into rolled up newspapers which they had brought back from the NAAFI; vomiting into their helmets; vomiting into their gasmask holders and some, with faces as green as the sea in the early morning light, were just vomiting uncontrollably onto the deck of the landing craft.

All he could do was to leave them to it and seek out Colonel Biddle.

'Morning, sir, I wish this darned wind would drop a bit. we've got a couple of hundred very sick men down there.'

'The weather boffins tell us it is not going to get any better, Bill, please tell your lads that they'll have to pull themselves together. There's no other option.'

'The landing is very late, sir, is everything going OK?'

'The wallahs who went in before us at 0700 are having a bad time of it. We are being held back until the beaches are clear. You can let them break out their rations, those that want to, any time you like.'

'Very good, sir, but still no sign of Jerry?'

'Not a sausage.'

They both looked over the gunwale. It was impossible not to be utterly impressed by the vast armada of hundreds of landing craft, the escort destroyers busying around their charges, the Royal Air Force and US Air Force aircraft droning endlessly overhead.

'What do you think has happened to the Luftwaffe, sir. We had a bad enough time with the buggers at Dunkirk. I'm just astonished that we haven't seen anything of them.'

'I could only hazard a guess that they've run out of petrol' said Colonel Biddle. 'They're being bled white on the Russian front from what we hear. Until today, they thought that was where they had to put their effort. And of course, things are going badly for them in Italy, you heard that Rome has fallen, have you, Bill?'

'Yes, sir, it really makes you wonder why the silly sods don't throw in the towel.'

'Would you, Bill, with only "unconditional surrender" terms on offer?'

Bill reflected on the difficulty of the immediate task at hand. The transfer of men from the larger to the smaller landing craft. Too many men had drowned in training to allow a direct landing from the larger craft on this beach. Now the landing craft was circling offshore. That meant that instead of merely running into the waves, the waves were crashing into the vessel from one side and then the other. The vessel was pitched up into the air and then dropping rapidly down into a deep vale of despair, as the waves came and went and came and went.

Men were still vomiting. Most were dry retching. Few remained unaffected. Those who had tried to eat their rations had seen their breakfast come back with speed. Bill must have been quite fascinated to recall that phenomenon, which he had first noticed on the Lofoten raid. It is actually possible for a seasick man to turn green. He was not feeling too well himself but the responsibility for 20 men told him that he could not allow that nausea, that awful inescapable nausea, to get the better of him.

They were now severely behind schedule. On the land, he could see the puffs of smoke from artillery, he could not see if that was from ours or theirs. The vessel pitched and rolled, and the seasickness proceeded unabated. Out in the mist, the cruisers HMS *Ajax* and HMS *Belfast* were firing their heavy armament onto land-based targets. The massive battle wagon HMS *Rodney* was firing its 10-ton broadsides. Further away, the old but venerable battleships HMS *Ramillies*, HMS *Frobisher*, HMS *Arethusa*, HMS *Mauritius*, HMS *Dragon* and HMS *Warspite* and the monitor HMS *Roberts* were hammering away with shells, which weighed as much as the average family car. The sharp blasts drowned out the sounds of moaning men, time and time again. The vessel was shrouded in intermittent mists of dark grey-brown acrid smoke from the aftermath of those endless barrages. Was this ever going to end?

The morning was becoming brighter. The French coast was clearly visible ahead. Somewhere behind the beaches, palls of dark smoke reached to the sky and beyond. Some Air Force activity was paying dividends at least. Again, he heard a salvo. The first artillery support units were firing their weapons from inside their landing craft before they beached. The chances of hitting anything meaningful from a bucking, dancing, weaving gun platform were negligible. The effect on morale, however, was positive.

The word now spread. The 69th and 231st Brigades were ashore and pressing inland.

Bill stood with the other Gloucestershire Regiment officers on the bridge. A naval rating brought some steaming mugs of cocoa. Colonel Biddle joined the group.

'Oh lord, everyone, I hope you don't catch my cold. It's an absolute stinker.'

Major Good vomited his cocoa into a bucket placed on the bridge for that purpose.

Through his field glasses, Bill could see some burned-out tanks and one or two bodies on the beach.

'It's not as bad as we might have expected, sir,' he said to Colonel Biddle.

'This an absolute joy ride after Dunkirk, eh, Bill? ATCHOO!'

At 1100, an announcement came on the landing craft's loudspeaker.

'This is your captain speaking. All officers please make sure that everyone on the craft can hear this announcement. General Graham in the headquarters ship HMS *Bulolo* ordered the 151st and 56th Brigades to land. Good luck to you all! God save the King!'

In different circumstances, a cheer might have gone up but to the hundreds of seasick men, the relief of escaping the seas was more important than anything the might of Hitler's *Wehrmacht* might do to them. The loudspeaker announcement proceeded.

'All officers to report to Colonel Biddle in the wardroom.'

'Gentlemen,' began Colonel Biddle, 'I have a late order from the naval commander on HMS *Albrighton*. Jig beach green is proving to have too many obstacles for us to pass through it. It is also being enfiladed by a strong enemy position at Le Hamel. We are being diverted to Jig beach red. That is only a couple of hundred yards to the east but do be aware that we will not be landing exactly where we expect. You will probably come up across a lot of Canadians. If you do so, please keep them on your left-hand side. Let me repeat, if you have Canadians on your right, then you are going astray.

'My advice is that the expected transhipment into smaller craft for the final landing will not take place. In short, the sea is too rough. We will land directly from this landing craft.'

The change of beach was something that could be managed but not to tranship into the smaller craft was extremely worrying. It made the landing a lottery. The larger craft would not be able to pull as far up the beach as the smaller ones. They would have to wade through the sea for some distance. If the sea had unseen potholes or depressions under the surf, then dozens or hundreds of men would be pulled under by the weight of the equipment they carried and would drown in front of his eyes.

'Come on, you lot, shake a leg.'

This was Bill's cue to take charge and play his officer's role.

'Right, I want everyone in full battle order. Anyone with sick in their helmets, get them cleaned out with seawater or any other means. I want you all in proper order for the...'

WHOOSH – WHOOSH – WHOOSH. Several thousand more rockets headed for a demolition task on Hitler's defensive wall.

'… landing.'

'If we aren't going to transfer into the smaller craft, do we have to put the waders on, sir?'

'No, if you put those things on and they fill with water, you'll fall over and drown. OK, has everyone got that? Throw those bloody waders away, no-one is to wear them. I don't care what the bloody orders are.'

The training was paying off. Each man was rapidly in position, in proper order and knew what to do next. Some had taped field dressings, cigarette packets, emergency rations and spare ammunition pouches to their helmets, to keep them dry during the landing.

'Good luck, Snudger.'

'All the best, Pete.'

'Mine's a pint of best in the Black Dog if we make it back.'

'Course you'll make it back, Jerry couldn't kill a tough old bugger like you.'

They both knew that was not true, but it was good to hear it.

The French coast was nearer now. The sand, the low dunes and the grass waving in the breeze was clearly visible. Somewhere on shore, a German MG42 was chattering its streams of death at them, but the gunner must have been inexperienced and was not finding the range.

The beach of Le Habel de Hurtot was only a hundred yards away now. He heard a grating sound beneath him, another grating, a prolonged grating and then a long rasp on the flat metal bottom of the landing craft.

'Steady, boys! Hang on to something! This is it!'

The landing craft bucked, graunched against the sandy, stony seafloor, and came to a swift halt. Men were thrown off their feet. Some fell in piles of humanity, interconnected with khaki webbing, Sten guns and bulging back packs. This was not a time for capers, it was a time to get upright again as quickly as possible.

Bill's role as an officer was to keep the men alert, sharp and above all moving quickly over the beach.

'Come on, you lot! Stand on your feet. You know the drills and do what you have been trained to do. Make sure all of your ammo and your compo rations and your field dressings will land dry. I do not want to see anyone stop for any reason on this beach.'

'Captain speaking!' came over the loudspeaker.

Again, a salvo of huge sea guns roared out from one of the mighty battleships a several kilometres away.

'I'll say it again. All army personnel, ready to land. All sea personnel, in places for landing procedures. Gunners, fire at will at anything that looks suspicious. Drop anchors. Ready, boys, when I give the order.'

Over to the west, he could hear the sounds of a major battle. He saw clouds of opaque brown-grey smoke and saw squadrons of fighters attacking German positions, which were out of sight to him around the headland.

'God, the Yanks are having a bad bloody time!'

Their landing ground was Omaha Beach. Its name would become synonymous with 'bloodbath': a landing against prepared defences on a clifftop. There was no time to worry about slaughtered Yanks. They had to arrange how they, themselves, would not be slaughtered.

The heavy machine guns on the landing craft were manned and ready but yet, there was no obvious target to aim at and they remained silent. Shells and mortar fire were hitting the beach, but the Germans must have been somewhere behind a range of low hills and were not visible. The shelling gave the impression of being tentative and hopeful rather than accurate and murderous. That told Bill that the first wave had dealt with the German artillery observers. That was good!

Over the loudspeaker, he heard the command that he had heard so many times in training, 'Drop your landing gates!'

The gates went down with a splash. This was not Wareham. They were coming ashore in France. After four years of waiting, he was back!

'Drop your landing stairways!'

The movable stairways on the front of the landing craft were dropped.

'All army personnel disembark as fast as possible.'

'Victoria Station,' said an amiable seaman. 'This is as far as we go. A 52 bus will take you up to Harrods.'

The landing craft of the 56th Brigade landed in perfect formation, line abreast and exactly as in training, within five seconds of each other at 1159 precisely. It was some four hours late, but they had made it.

'Right, you lot! I want you over that beach as fast as you can. No-one stops for anything!'

Bill looked at the naked, empty beach with horror. There was no cover of any kind from enemy fire. There were just sand dunes, patches of soggy clay and a few clumps of seaweed. Fortunately, the enemy fire was sparse and inaccurate on this beach.

Men were dropping into the water now, some up their waists, some up to their chests. One or two went under, but friendly hands pulled them up gasping and spitting out seawater. Now it was his turn. He worked his way awkwardly down the stairway with his mass of equipment, arrived at the last step and jumped. He was in it to his chest. Yes! He was alright. The sea was surging around him, but he was in control.

'Come on, you bloody lot! The water's lovely!'

He worked his way gingerly for the ten or so metres to dry land. The rest of his platoon were behind him. Where were the paths across the beachhead? There they were with their white markers.

'Come on, lads, between those white ribbons. No-one stops on that beach, has everybody got that?'

'Yes, sir.'

Shells continued to rain down but lacked accuracy. On the beach, he saw two burned out tanks from the Sherwood Rangers' landing. They were still smouldering and giving off a revolting oily stench. There were one or two bodies. There was no doubt about it, it was not as bad as Bill or anyone else had expected.

'Come on, lads, after me, we'll take cover under that hedgerow.'

They had made it. *They had actually made it*! He was back on French soil for the third time in the war.

Chapter 27

The Road to Bayeux

Tuesday, 6 June 1944, Le Hable de Hurtot, Normandy, France

'Good, everyone is here. Right, lads, first things first! Throw away your Mae Wests, you won't need them anymore. Now, has everyone got their gear in perfect working order?'

This was replied to by a few desultory 'yes, sirs'.

'No come on, I want to know properly. Is there anyone whose weapon or rations or field dressings or anything else have been spoiled by seawater?'

'No, sir!' came a more positive chorus.

'Evans's cigarettes got soaked sir, he left them in his trousers.'

'Well silly blighter him. Now everyone, pay attention.'

A salvo of rockets whooshed off from a launch craft just offshore. He waited until the sound had passed over them. Over to the west and around a headland, they could hear the sounds of a major battle as the Americans on Omaha Beach were being savaged by the Germans from the high cliffs. There was no time to worry about any of that.

'As you know, we have landed at red beach, not green beach. We are about a quarter of a mile [half a kilometre] east of where we should be. We still have to get to Buhot, which is that way.'

He looked back at the rest of the brigade who were dropping off their landing craft and running over the beach. He could not see any casualties at all. None!

'Lads, I am ordered to find signs from the unit landing officer if you see them shout out and make sure I hear you, has everyone got that?'

On farmhouse walls, the doors of dairies and even on country cafes, the men pointed out large white letters.

'56 this way.'

That's what he was looking for! The unit landing officer and his men were doing a good job.

'There are signs over here, sir.'

'Thanks, Thompson, this way, lads.'

Out at sea, the battleships, cruisers and monitor were firing salvoes again. Even as Bill's pioneer platoon moved inland, they could sense the blast from several kilometres away. Several ducked instinctively as the mighty shells breezed over their heads.

Bill edged the platoon forward, ordering them to keep heads down.

'Remember, lads, do not make any shape against the skyline! Keep as close to hedgerows and buildings as you can. So far, they had not encountered a machine-gun nest or the dreaded Spandau machine guns, which he knew only too well. He was grateful that there were as yet no mines for his Pioneer Platoon to take up. He knew – they all did – that this easy ride was only for a short time. It was not going to last.

They found a narrow track, some three metres wide, to the east of Le Habel de Hurtot. As they moved along, they passed three soldiers from the Devons, who were wounded and were huddled together under a ground sheet. One man stopped – or almost stopped – to give a wounded man a cigarette.

'Come on, we can't hang about, keep bloody moving.'

They proceeded up a sandy hill.

'There's not much shooting from Jerry, sir, I thought it would be worse than this.'

Before Bill could answer a voice said, 'Oh my Christ!'

Before them, they found a tree full of German soldiers, all dead, not one had a mark on them. Someone started firing a Sten gun at them.

'Cease fire,' shouted a voice of authority. 'They've all gone for a Burton, you silly bugger.'

'Sorry, sir, I thought they were snipers.'

Naval gunfire had accurately wiped-out a nearby German pillbox. The inhabitants had been killed, and probably, so had these men from the effect of the blast from the huge naval shells.

Now, the detritus of war was becoming increasingly evident. They saw many dead horses and cattle. Afterwards, a lot of the men said the sight of the dead animals affected them more than dead soldiers. The animals were the ultimate non-combatants. They came across a German *Kübelwagen*, similar to a jeep. Inside, four officers were dead.

'Oy, get away from that bloody vehicle!'

'I just wanted an Iron Cross as a souvenir, sir!'

'I'll give you a bloody souvenir with my boot, you silly sod! How do you know some Jerry gunner hasn't got you in his sights? How do you know the bloody thing is not booby trapped? Use your bloody brains!'

'Sorry, sir!'

Further along, some civilians came out of a farmhouse. They were jumping up and down for joy. They were offering drinks, beer, Calvados apple brandy, wine.

'Get away from them, we have a job to do. Once we stop, we're sitting ducks for Jerry.'

In a field further along, there were several more dead Germans, blown into chunks of meat.

Bill sent the closest man to report on the uniform badges of the prisoners.

'The badge says 352nd Division, sir.'

'Thanks!'

This was bad. Briefings from the intelligence officers at Pennerley Lodge had told him to expect an under-strength 716th division, but these men were not them. What on earth was the 352nd? No-one in the intelligence hierarchy had mentioned them or apparently, even knew about them. Somewhere over the hill, they could hear disciplined and well-ordered shooting. They were up against a determined enemy.

The Pioneer Platoon passed through a field with high grass.

They heard a shell whiz its way towards them. They all fell to the ground, a second before the shell hit the ground and exploded. Thick red smoke came out of the place where it had exploded.

'That first one was a smoke marker. When you see those, you always, always hit the deck without me telling you or you will lose your head, do you understand? Right now, everybody stay down, there are going to be incoming shells in about ten seconds' time. Several artillery rounds whistled overhead and exploded some hundred metres away. One of the shells had hit a Bren carrier. They heard the scream of the crew. Whether the occupants of the Bren carrier survived was not clear. It was not their job to find out or do anything about it. The job of the Pioneer Platoon was to keep moving forward.

An explosion ripped the air, shrapnel ripped its way into a nearby hedge. More explosions came, a dozen of them. There was no screaming and no calls of 'medical orderly'.

'Everybody OK?' There were only a few mumbled answers. Pioneer Platoon, I asked if everyone was OK!'

'Yes, sir!'

'Right come on, let's get moving.'

No-one had been hit this time but who knew what would happen next time? The shells and mortaring were becoming thicker and heavier now but were passing over them and aiming towards the beaches further away.

'Lieutenant Adlam!'

Major Goode rode up in his jeep.

'Sir?'

'Which way is Le Hamel? Can you get a fix on it?'

'If we keep going south-west, we should get there OK, sir. This lot are the 352nd Division, have you ever heard of them?'

Captain Goode shook his head.

'Oh Christ! Look at that!'

They were coming further into an area of German defences now, which had been heavily pounded by naval gunfire. Out of one house window, a pair of German boots was hanging limply in the air. The legs of the owner were still in them. A German officer had been climbing out, presumably to escape the fire within. The roof had caved in and crushed him. There was little to say.

Right, well, Bill, you'd better get your lads under cover, there are some of their blighters in that hedge 150 yards ahead over there and we can't even see them, let alone fire at them.'

Bill ordered his men to take cover behind a farm wall.

'Just bloody stay there until I tell you to move forward.'

Colonel Biddle joined them.

'How's the cold, sir?' Goode asked him.

'Bloody miserable but not as miserable as those Jerries are going to be.'

The firing from the hedge was increasing now.

'You know, the trouble with bloody *Spandaus* [the British name for the German MG34 and MG42 machine guns] is that they fire smokeless ammunition, and you can't even see where the buggers are.'

'Well, never mind about that, Adlam. I want one Bren firing forward and everyone else take cover. I want every man to change into dry clothes and then keep low so that those bastards can't hit us. Do it now!'

'Sir!'

Major Goode did the same. The firing from the hedge carried on apace, but only one Bren was firing forward. Bill wondered what was going to happen now.

A mighty *WHOOSH* went over Bill's head, it seemed only a few yards above him. Then another *WHOOSH* and another *WHOOSH*.

This was followed by a deafening roar as three Typhoon ground attack aircraft followed them. The hedgerow exploded in sheet of orange flame shot through with yellow.

Experience had told Bill what to do next.

'Keep those bloody heads down.'

Pieces of charred tree stump, hedgerow, German military equipment including gas-masks and webbing floated down from the sky. A few charred remains appeared to be body parts although precisely how they would have fitted onto a typical human body was uncertain. The firing from the hedge had stopped. The hedge no longer existed. Where the hedge had stood 30 seconds ago, there was now only a black crater, a mini-Vesuvius. Of the defenders, there was no sign. The Typhoons circled round and flew over them waggling its wings. One man stood up and gave a thumbs-up sign to the pilot.

'Hey, Harrison, do you want to be on a charge? I told you to keep your flippin' head down.'

'The RAF blokes have knocked the Jerries out, sir.'

'Listen, you daft bugger, the RAF blokes cannot tell from up there if you are a Jerry, a Tommy or Vera bloody Lynn and if they see something move, they are going to fire at it! Do you understand?'

'Yes, sir.'

He checked to make sure all the men had their heads down and reflected that it had been so much easier in commandos with the calibre of soldier there.

'Right, you four, go and pick up any prisoners.'

They returned five minutes later.

'Sir, there aren't any prisoners, we can't even find any bodies.'

Colonel Biddle spoke, 'It should have been like this at Ledringhem, Bill.'

'How true, sir, how very true.'

The Gloucesters pressed on towards Buhot and the planned forming up place. They were finding prisoners now but there was something very odd about them.

'These blokes are old enough to be our dads, sir. What are we going to do with them?'

These were not the Teutonic superheros that Bill had encountered before Dunkirk. Their uniform badges proclaimed them to be from the 716th division. This was the unit, which they had been expecting. They were overweight, over-age and overawed by what was happening around them. Their weapons had been abandoned in a ditch somewhere and there was no fight left in them. They appeared very happy to surrender and immediately brought out photos of their wives and children in an attempt to ingratiate themselves with their captors. There were jokes that some of them even had photos of what appeared to be their grandchildren.

'Point them towards the POW cage and tell them to get a move on. Come on, lads. Let's see if they've left any Schmeissers for us. The first one is mine and no-one is to fire one of these until I've shown you how they work.'

The prisoners appeared grateful for the chance to surrender. They checked the details of how to find the cage in a manner similar to a tourist asking the way to a local place of interest and cheerfully proceeded in that direction.

Another group caused a lot of interest among the troops, they were taken to be Japanese. They were clearly Asiatic. Spoke little or no German and, as with the over-age soldiers, were very happy to survive the morning without tempting fate by firing their weapons. These proved to be Soviet citizens of Central Asian origin who had joined the German Army, apparently to fight against Stalin.

They passed through the village of Meuvaines on their way to their destination at Buhot. Smouldering houses and dead horses gave witness to a substantial firefight here a couple of hours ago, but now that the fighting had subsided, there was possible danger from a residual sniper but no more than that.

'There's still no sign of mines or booby traps on the roads, Bill, but keep your lads' eyes peeled.'

Colonel Biddle was making one of his lightning visits in his jeep across the battalion to see that all was well.

'Any casualties on landing, sir?'

'None reported to me, Bill. I think we have actually got ashore without a single one.'

'Would you have put money on that, sir? I wouldn't. By the way, sir, what's that big fire over on the horizon?'

'Oh, that is – or was – a Jerry radar station at a place called Pouligny. Jerry has pulled out apparently and set the place on fire. I suppose he doesn't want us to know how his radar works.'

Buhot was much more difficult to take than expected. The Gloucesters were concentrated at 1600 hours in the woods between the village of Ryes and Buhot itself. Brigadier Pepper ordered The Gloucesters into the front line at Buhot to back up the Dorsets and Number 47 Marine Commandos. They duly took the village and flew the Union Jack over it. This opened the way for all of the motor transport to move forward and for the two brigades, 151st and 56th, to form up into full battle formation. The Royal Army Medical Corps established its field ambulances and field hospitals into a semblance of order. Brigadier Pepper established his brigade headquarters in a truck.

The radio operator relayed orders to Bill from Colonel Biddle.

'Lieutenant Adlam, sir, colonel's orders are to stop at the next village called Magny en Bessin. We've got to dig in there and await orders to advance at first light.'

'Thanks, Sparks. Alright you lot. Get your kit together, we're pushing along the road to a place called Magny en Bessin.'

The first of the Gloucesters arrived at Magny en Bessin at 1940 hours. The hoped-for lull in the action was not to be.

'Sir! Lieutenant Adlam!'

'Yes, Sparks, what's up?'

'C Company have flushed some 20 Germans out of a farmhouse and they're coming this way. Colonel's orders are to challenge, take prisoners or shoot them.'

Bill took the Pioneer Platoon in the direction where the Germans were heading.

'Right, lads, no heroics, just take them prisoners if they'll come in.'

Small-arms firing erupted all around them.

'Fire at will at anything that moves.'

'They're running for it, sir!'

'Sergeant Davies, take ten men and get after the blighters. They get one chance to surrender, if they don't just shoot the bloody lot of them.'

'Very good, sir!'

Five minutes later, the sounds of automatic weapons firing were to be heard beyond a small rise. Sergeant Davies and his men returned.

'They didn't surrender, sir. A few of them went down and we've got the rest of them prisoner.'

'Who got the first one?'

'Got him myself, sir.'

'Good lad, well when we've got sorted out in Magny en Bessin, I want you to report to me and look as smart as you can under the circumstances.'

'Certainly, sir. What's that for, sir, if I might ask?'

'You'll see, lad, you'll see.'

And so, on the evening of 6 June 1944, Bill Adlam found himself in the hamlet of Magny en Bessin. He had arrived in France as part of the biggest invasion in history and had survived it. The Germans were on the run, for the moment. He and his Pioneer Platoon were dry and had something to eat.

Davies reported to him as ordered. Bill took him into the church to see Colonel Biddle.

'Yes, Bill?'

'Sir, has anyone claimed the five-pound prize for the first in the battalion to shoot a German?'

'No, they haven't actually, I was rather expecting a queue to have formed by now, have you got someone in mind?'

'Sergeant Davies, who's one of my lads, sir. He shot one in that skirmish an hour ago. I think he might be the winner.'

'I rather think he might.'

And so, Sergeant Davies of 2nd Gloucesters' Pioneer Platoon created battalion history by being the first member of the battalion to shoot one of the enemy during the invasion.

'Well done, Davies, keep up the good work!' said Colonel Biddle. 'Carry on! Dismissed!'

'Thank you, sir,' Davies stamped his foot in the prescribed manner and marched smartly out of the church.

'There's a couple of things, Bill, while you're here. For Christ's sake, make sure he doesn't spend all that money taking his mates to one of those French knocking shops. The MO says they're riddled with some very nasty diseases. If I remember France in 1940 correctly, those tarts are more deadly than a bloody German tank.'

As Bill was an officer, it fell to his batman to blow up his mattress and make him a comfortable place to sleep. It was the batman's job to find a quiet corner of the church and to prepare some food for both of them. In the context of Magny en Bessine, this either meant iron rations (emergency rations of spam, biscuits and cheese) or self-heating cans of soup.

As Bill's platoon slept overnight, Brigadier Pepper had sent out a fighting reconnaissance patrol which had captured several troops of Germans.

These were equipped with some very impressive and lethal 105-mm artillery pieces.

Lieutenant Tucker of B company, 2nd Gloucesters, was to figure in not one but two tragi-comic episodes, which were to end his involvement in the war. Firstly, in the darkness around the church in Magny, he saw a dark figure and engaged it in conversation. His blood ran cold as he realised the figure was, to his horror, a German soldier. Not only that but there were several of them. He raised his pistol and shot at the figures. Simultaneously, they fired back. The entire platoon was now woken from sleep and fired their weapons towards the low bank where the dark German shapes were now disappearing.

'Cease fire!' Sergeant Frank Clarke screamed.

The panic in the ranks had caused one set of British soldiers to fire over the heads of other British soldiers. This caused more danger to their own men than the German fire. The Germans got away and disappeared into the night. By the time Colonel Biddle ran over to find out what was happening, the show was over. He did, however, have a job for Lieutenant Tucker.

'Tucker, go over that hill and find a village called Vaux sur Aure. I want you to confirm that the 2nd South Wales Borderers are there. It's a mile and a half [two kilometres] due west. Just take two blokes, find a bike and pop over there. For God's sake, try not to get into any more trouble.'

Tucker dutifully found an untended bike and headed west through the pitch-black lanes between the high hedges and thick *bocage*.

On approaching Vaux, they heard a voice in the darkness. Whether they did not hear the challenge correctly or there was some other misunderstanding, a hand grenade was thrown in their direction. All three were injured and for them, the war was over.

Frank Clarke was made up to platoon commander but kept his rank of sergeant. He was the first battlefield promotion in the battalion. He was not destined to be the last.

Tuesday, 7 June 1944, Magny en Bessin, Normandy

All battalion officers were assembled in the church at Magny. Colonel Biddle spoke.

'Right, chaps, Division have ordered us forward into Bayeux.'

In the grey half-light of dawn, the church was dark and gloomy but to men who might have been killed yesterday, being alive felt good.

'We move into the town centre and occupy the *mairie*, that is, the town hall. The South Wales Borderers will be on our right and the Essex will be on the left. Our orders are to move in and take it by 1200.'

'Any sign of Jerry, sir?'

'We have a report from the Brylcreem Boys. They've run patrols all night. The German strength is about half a division, and they're dug in some six miles [ten kilometres] south of Bayeux. As far as we know, it's an infantry outfit, probably this lot that we ran into yesterday. Also, as far as we know, there aren't any tanks.'

'Now, there's another thing. Brigade inform me that there are bloody dozens if not hundreds of Germans swanning about behind our lines. They're turning themselves in quite happily and none of them seem interested in fighting. They're old enough to be your dads. But you never know. Tell your blokes to pick up whatever prisoners they can and send them to the Regimental Sergeant Major in the rear. There is a perfectly good cage for them. Any questions?'

'What are our casualties from yesterday, sir?'

'One officer and four other ranks wounded. We've taken 31 prisoners.'

'Who's missing? Is that Tucker, sir? Did the Jerries get him?'

'No, the South Wales Borderers got him actually. He was wounded by a grenade but is on his way back to Blighty. He'll live. Honestly, the Taffs are more dangerous than the Hun! Good singers, though! Now where is Adlam?'

'Here, sir!'

'Right, well you're the key man this morning, Bill. We have a mile and a half [two kilometres] to cover to get into the centre of Bayeux. Now we do know that Jerry has had some time to pull back so there will be mines and booby traps. Your lads will be up front. You will need to work fast but work accurately. I don't want to lose any men or equipment as we move in. Is that clear?'

'Yes, sir, my lads are waiting for the "off" sir.'

'Dismissed, everyone and good luck!'

'How's the cold, sir?'

'Bloody awful!'

Chapter 28

Bayeux

Wednesday, 7 June 1944, Bayeux, Normandy

To Major Goode, the early morning was not at all unpleasant. At least it started that way. He had a rather luxuriant wash and shave in a horse trough, the crisp morning air was very energising. A conveniently placed outhouse afforded him the luxury of a loo.

BRRRRRRP! Everyone knew that sound, a German MG42 *Spandau* machine gun.

Bullets flew around Major Goode, who dived behind a wall.

'Where is the bastard?'

'He's up there in the church tower, sir.'

'I thought we'd knocked off all the buggers!'

'Well that one seems to have rather evaded us, sir.'

Major Goode got his sergeant major to open up with a Bren gun, aiming at the narrow slits at the top of the church tower where the sniper sat concealed. Others opened up with rifles, a PIAT anti-tank projectile and an anti-tank gun.

'Will you lot bloody stop that firing?' shouted a desperate English voice from inside the tower.

'Who the bloody hell is that?'

'This is Sergeant Walker, you bloody lot, you're supposed to be on our side...'

Then they heard him shout, 'RUN FOR IT!'.

Sergeant Walker of C company had led a detachment of men into the tower. Inside the tower, the German sniper had started dropping stick grenades down inside the tower.

Two muffled explosions were heard from inside the thick medieval walls.

The sniper of Magny did not do any damage. The MG42 is an excellent machine gun but given the narrow medieval loophole, its traverse was severely limited.

'Stupid bloody place for a sniper!' muttered Colonel Biddle. 'If an officer of mine put a sniper in a ridiculous bloody place like that, he'd be court-martialled for incompetence.'

Then the reality struck home. This man was not a sniper as such. Real snipers used single-shot Karabiner rifles with smokeless charges, whose position could be hidden. You couldn't hide a machine gun up a church tower. In fact, there were far too many soldiers engaged in sniping actions for them all to be snipers. They were German soldiers acting on their own initiative to keep fighting in a hopeless situation. This was an odd situation. The determination of these lone and self-motivated snipers contrasted against the dozens or hundreds of Germans swanning around behind the lines trying to give themselves up.

At 0830, Brigadier Pepper ordered the 2nd Gloucesters to move forward and occupy the town centre of Bayeux. Matters were becoming more serious. Bill's Pioneer Platoon was at the front of the advance. They were now finding and clearing mines, cutting tripwires and dismantling booby traps.

Over on the horizon, Bill could already see the towers of Bayeux Cathedral. It looked medieval, wonderful, and very impressive. It had been there for hundreds of years. He hoped it would still be there by this evening.

The Pioneer Platoon cleared sector by sector. This was slow painstaking work. They had to proceed with mine detectors, dig out the mine with bayonets or some similar tools and render it harmless. As they moved forward, 100 metres at a time they would declare the sector clear and the rest of the Gloucesters would move up behind them.

Bill's Pioneer Platoon worked its way gingerly forward. They found a few tripwires, an assortment of teller mines and two forms of evil anti-personnel mines.

After a couple of hours, the Pioneer Platoon had reached the cobbled streets, which marked the entry to Bayeux. There was no possibility that he would have gloried in the ancient, cobbled streets, the wonderful houses from the middle ages or the photogenic ambience. He was too busy setting up Bren gun positions to guard his men against snipers as they searched for tripwires and booby traps.

'Christ! What was that?'

A sharp blast split the morning air from some two or 300 metres east. It was one of the 2nd Essex vehicles.

'Right, lads, I want you to listen to what I have to say. That bang was a Teller mine going off. I don't need to tell you but those are designed to blow the tracks off a tank. Someone has gone over one of those and they would have to be very lucky indeed to still be breathing. Be bloody careful because there are going to be bloody dozens of them ahead.'

Because the Pioneer Platoon had to proceed before all other troops, Bill's platoon was the first into the town centre. At 1130, he was able to report to Colonel Biddle, 'She's all clear, sir, we can move forward.'

The troops moved in quickly but quietly. They used doorways for cover, hid behind walls and looked for places where a sniper might be lurking in order to consign them to instant oblivion. The streets were quiet. Neither terrified French civilian nor German rear-guard were game to venture outside. Neither had they encountered any snipers as they entered the town. You just never knew. From second to second, you just never knew.

A few civilians appeared in the street.

'Get back in your bloody houses!' shouted a South Midlands accent.

The civilians disappeared rapidly but more came out.

'Get off the bloody street, you silly sods, you could get shot!'

Men came out of doorways, women came out of doorways, children came out of doorways. Smelly 2nd Gloucester troops, some still damp from yesterday's seawater, were being kissed by local girls, having their hands shook by local men and embraced by local women. Within very few minutes, all caution was thrown to the winds.

'If schoolboy French serves, sir, they say the *Boche* left yesterday, and they're all gone.'

Flags appeared out of windows: French flags, Canadian flags, British flags, American flags. One group sang 'La Marseillaise', another danced for absolute joy, and still others plied the troops with bread, with beer, with wine, with cider. '*Vive les anglais*' was to be heard from young, old, male, female, fat, thin and medium sized. The local population were overjoyed. Men and women in the street stood and applauded in frantic approval of the greatest moment of their lives. Schoolboys in berets and short trousers applauded. Local gendarmes in smart *kepis* [military caps] and capes saluted and applauded.

'Sir, we're conquering heroes. We're conquering bloody heroes!'

'What the bloody hell is that firewater?' asked Bill Adlam.

'*Ces't Calvados, Monsieur L' Officier.*'

'Jesus, it tastes like the Domestos we clean our lav with at home.'
'Monsieur l'Officier, encore du Calvados?'

Actually, the second one did not taste too bad. It was like a mixture of brandy and the sort of petrol that powered a Hawker Hurricane.

In the midst of the singing, the dancing, the renditions of 'La Marseillaise' and the libations of fighter-fuel a group of earnest men ran into the square shouting, *'Boches! Boches!'*

Sergeant Clarke was nearest and took his platoon to investigate a house near the cathedral where some townspeople had seen some grey uniforms. The house was quiet. Nothing moved. It was hidden behind a high wall.

'Oy, you and you,' said Clarke, give me a leg up onto this wall. They rather overdid this and shot the hapless Clarke flying over the top of the wall. His fall was fortunately broken by some dense rhododendron bushes. He waited for firing to begin. Still there was silence. A flash of reflected sunlight showed him the barrel of a gun. It was a Spandau. It could do a lot of damage. It was poking out of a window situated just above ground level. It must be a cellar. Around the window were sandbags. Possibly, the sandbags had obscured his inopportune arrival over the wall.

He carefully opened a gate and beckoned several of his platoon forward. A single slip, a single movement or a single noisy footfall would alert the machine gunners and the Spandau would kill all of them within seconds. They tiptoed around the back of the house and did a room-by-room search. There was no sign of Germans. Clarke then beckoned a Bren gunner forward and led him to a room just above the cellar.

'Fire!' he shouted.

The Bren gunner started at one end of the room and began to fire downwards into the floorboards, the bullets flying into the cellar below. After firing one short burst, he then began to move slowly forward, firing downwards in the same manner.

From underneath came shouting and screaming. They did not understand German, but the general gist appeared to be that the Germans in the cellar would rather like to give themselves up. At that moment, others of Clarke's platoon burst into the cellar and covered the Germans with their weapons.

'Right, you lot, out here!'

The Germans did not understand a word of English, but the meaning was clear enough. There were ten of them. They lined up with hands in the air against the garden wall. The garden gate burst open, and several townspeople burst in. There was anger on their faces, a deep primeval anger which knew no hint of humanity. Their agenda was clear. Murder. They were rushing up to the disarmed Germans with a look in their eye which said that killing was about to be done. In the absence of weapons, the locals were perfectly happy to kick them to death, strangle them, and beat them with garden stones or anything else at hand.

Sergeant Clarke ordered his men to cock their weapons and point them at the townspeople.

The townspeople, who spoke no more English than the Germans, backed off.

'Alright, lads, get the Herrenvolk off to the MPs, nice and slowly.'

The look on the faces of the townspeople showed clearly the scores which they wanted settled. As the Gloucesters brought the Germans out, the crowd surged forward. This resulted in a few black eyes. Kicks and punches landed but nothing to trouble the medical officer.

Outside in the square, the party was in full swing.

Reports came to Colonel Biddle that locals were looking for collaborators.

'Good lord, we haven't got the orders, time or inclination to sort out the locals' problems. Tell you what, if they start setting up guillotines in the main square, you might mention it to the military police in due course but otherwise, leave well alone.'

Revenge, unfortunately, had already started. Several townspeople had placed chairs in the city square. They were pulling forward girls to have their hair shorn off.

'Must be the girlfriends of the *Boche*. Apparently, they're being accused of horizontal collaboration whatever that might be. The locals don't seem to be doing anything nastier. Just let them get on with it, we have orders from division to move forward.'

A company found a German post, which consisted of ten men. They were showered with Bren gunfire and rapidly put up the white flag. One of their soldiers disgraced Adolf Hitler by screaming for his mamma. He was 17.

Colonel Biddle put his battalion headquarters in a school. He took over a large garage as shelter for A company. This was wonderful! Many of the spare parts fitted his own trucks. He was also able to sequester two further vehicles. D company was billeted on the main square, grimly situated beside an undertaker's establishment. Many of the others including Bill's platoon were billeted with local families.

Overall, the families appear to have been happy with this arrangement. Standing orders were that any house so occupied should be turned into a fortress. This brought back memories of Ledringhem where they demolished walls between rooms to improve access. It would have involved smashing out glass from all windows. It would have involved barricading front doors. As compared with Ledringhem, this proved much harder with the smiling French families looking on benignly.

At night, with an outer perimeter set up and patrols organised, it was left to Bayeux to celebrate being the first town in France to be liberated. The few detailed accounts, which exist, suggest that this was a boozy affair, which went on most of the night.

The next morning, a wireless van screeched into the town square. It played 'La Marseillaise'. The townspeople joined in fervently despite the hangovers and lack of sleep. Local people began to erect a platform in the town square.

'Christ!' said Colonel Biddle, 'are they setting up a guillotine?'

Enquiries ascertained that it was merely to allow some local dignitaries to make speeches. The colonel breathed a sigh of relief.

Chapter 29

The Road to Tilly – Operation Perch

Saturday, 10 June 1944, Bayeux

To his considerable amusement, Bill Adlam awoke this morning to discover that he was a Desert Rat. This proud title was bestowed on the Seventh Armoured Division after their legendary feats in North Africa. On the previous day, Brigadier Pepper had returned from a staff meeting to announce that the 56th Brigade had been detached from the 50th Northumbrian Division. The 131st Queens Brigade had been held up in landings due to appalling weather in the channel. Field Marshall Montgomery had moved 56th Brigade in their place.

Colonel Biddle called the officers to an early morning meeting.

'We will support the 7th Armoured in their push on this village here.'

The Colonel indicated a straight road on the map leading in a south-easterly direction

'It is called Tilly-sur-Seulles and then we push on here,' he indicated a hamlet '… to Juvigny. It is ten miles [15 kilometres] and we are ordered to be there by tonight to take and hold this crossroad. Our role is to guard the flanks, clear out any snipers, make sure that any of those buggers with the Panzerfaust things are taken out and that all mines are cleared.'

'What do we know of Jerry activity, sir?'

'Jerry has been moving large numbers of troops forwards. Intelligence says that we are likely to run into the German 130 division. We don't seem to know an awful lot about them, except that they have a lot of tanks. They are also known as Panzer Lehr, which means the Panzer Training Division. They certainly have Mark IV tanks, they appear to have a number of Mark V Panther tanks and there are reports of Mark VI Tiger tanks, but they are in small numbers. Adlam! Where is Lieutenant Adlam?'

'Here, sir.'

'Bill, your lads are going to be up in the front in the vanguard. You are to advance to contact and clear what mines you may find. We don't think that Jerry has had time to put down many mines before we approach Tilly, but we still need your mine-clearing expertise in the front to be sure. Don't forget Bill, you're the officer, your lads have got to do the work. I can stand casualties among your men, I cannot stand it if you are a casualty yourself. As you get into the village itself, I would imagine there will be mines and booby traps all over the place. I need your radio chappie to report back to me every quarter mile [half a kilometre] or so that the way is cleared.'

'Right, sir, I've got that.'

The purpose of the operation called 'Perch' was simple enough: move forward and occupy Tilly on the way to outflanking the large German concentration in Caen, some 15 kilometres to the east.

Had his war ended at this point, Bill might afterwards have spoken of it in a reasonably cheerful manner.

At 0830 hours, his small column of vehicles stood with engines running by the railway level crossing on the Rue de Tilly just to the south of Bayeux. The radio crackled in the cool morning air.

'Colonel Biddle's orders, sir, the order is "Pioneer Platoon to advance with caution".'

'Thanks, Sparks!'

He stood up on his jeep and waved his vehicles forward. They moved forward at walking pace looking for trip-wires, any suspicious mounds of earth and any places where the roadside had been disturbed. At each successive bridge over the River Aure, he gave a wave to the 2nd South Wales Borderers who stood at grim action stations with PIATS anti-tank guns at the ready. The Welshmen had just fought a vicious stonk at the Chateau of Sully, two days previously and had done well, *very well*. It was good to have them standing guard.

Behind his vehicles came the Gloucesters' rifle companies, looking for snipers or, indeed any enemy activity.

Almost immediately, they heard the *brrrrp* of German MG42 Spandau machine guns. It was impossible to locate their positions, they were in well-dug-in positions. Further back on the horizon, he saw the ominous dark shapes of the Mark IV and Panther tanks of Panzer Lehr. Bill reported to Colonel Biddle the furthest point that he could guarantee was mine-free. Several dozen 7th Armoured Division Churchill tanks revved their engines and trundled forwards over the level crossing and down the road to Tilly.

This was where it began to be difficult.

The Road to Tilly – Operation Perch

The *bocage* country around Bayeux is perfect for a defending army. It is nightmarish for an attacking army. The *bocage* was perfect for the defending Germans to hide their tanks. It was extremely difficult for the British and Canadians to move their tanks forwards. The *bocage* was wonderful to hide snipers and machine-gun positions. It was difficult to approach because Bill's Pioneer Platoon – and the rest of the invading armies – never knew what was lurking in the green and pleasant leaves or underneath the fields of half-ripe corn.

The Norman stone farmhouses offered ready-made pillboxes to the Germans and were very difficult for the British to knock out. The small stone-built villages offered ready-made strong points.

Having left the level crossing at 0830, Bill in the vanguard of the 7th Armoured Division had only progressed one and a half kilometres down the road by 1100 hours.

What they were about to discover was that the German 130th (Panzer Lehr) Division was one of the best-trained, best-organised and best-equipped armoured divisions of World War II. As of this morning the Panzer Lehr strength was 14,699 men heavily armed with 237 tanks and assault guns, of which 89 were Mark IV Panther and eight were Mark V Tiger tanks. Its men were carried in a fleet of 650 armoured half-track vehicles. This was a more formidable force than the 20th Panzergrenadiers, against whom Bill had fought at Ledringhem. Despite this challenge, this time, the British Army was equipped and organised for hard-fought success rather than ignominious defeat.

The division pressed slowly on. Bill's pioneer platoon pressed on, hour after hour. They swept the ground with mine detectors. They dug out the mines that they could find. As an officer, he knew that if he hurried them up then he was consigning them to a short sharp death. The infantry who followed up sorted out the snipers and machine-gun posts. The tanks behind them moved forward to clear the remaining infantry and to engage and destroy the German tanks.

Three kilometres to the west, he could hear the Essex as they assaulted the Monastery of Juaye Mondaye, which the Germans had turned into a fortress. The British Artillery were pouring 25-pounder and 5.5-inch shells relentlessly into the monastery. He was happy not to be inside it but had little feeling for those that were. Then his platoon reported to him a new and deadly German tactic. Their German opposite numbers would place a

Teller mine, designed to blow a track off a tank in the roadway. The normal method of dealing with such a mine was to take cover in a roadside ditch while the Pioneers carried out a controlled explosion. However, in the ditch beside the Teller mines the Germans were now placing shoe mines, designed to blow the lower leg off any member of the pioneer platoon unwise enough to dive into the ditch without taking careful precautions first.

By 1910 hours, the Gloucesters were still mopping up Germans by the hundred. By now they had reached woods on the outskirts of the Village of Jerusalem, which was clearly so strongly held that infantry could not assault it. Brigadier Pepper called in the armour. High-explosive and armour-piercing shells poured into the village until it was pounded to rubble. The assault battalions were exhausted at this stage and settled for the night. They had moved forwards only seven kilometres all day. Every metre had to be fought over.

The Gloucesters fought through the next morning and by 1300 had taken the village of Buceels. It was heartening that this was now only two kilometres from the centre of Tilly-sur-Suelles. However, the German positions were dug in even more so than previously. The tanks that they were now encountering were almost entirely the Mark IVs and the Panthers. The casualties on the British side were increasing dramatically. Goodness only knew what casualties the Germans were suffering under the constant artillery bombardments and rocket fire from the Royal Air Force Typhoons and Tempests, but they were not giving up. *This was Ledringhem in reverse!*

To make matters worse, the tanks churning up the dry unmade roads had created dust storms. The British khaki uniforms were now grey. To the untrained eye, the British and Canadian khaki were difficult to tell from the *Steingrau* [stone-grey] of the German army uniforms.

German machine guns opened up without warning from behind innocuous-looking hedgerows. Men were being spattered with machine-gun bullets without warning. The stretcher bearers were doing wonderful work. It seemed that every half hour infantry would duck into a ditch to escape the murderous fire and call tanks forward to kill the German machine-gun crews. Nevertheless, the weight of British armour was forcing the Germans inexorably back. In over a day of fighting, there had never been a point where the Germans were strong enough to counterattack.

Still, there were more mines. They found *Teller* [plate] mines, anti-personnel mines and also *Topf* [pottery] mines. These were designed, like

Teller mines, to cripple vehicles but the outer casing was made of ceramic or glass so that a mine detector would never find them.

At one point, a platoon of Gloucesters advanced in open order across a farmer's field. In one corner, a bull stood with blood pouring out of multiple shrapnel wounds. Some of the Gloucesters were about to run before the bull charged at them. The officer raked the poor creature with Sten gunfire and killed it. The platoon pushed forward towards the outskirts of Tilly. They all hit the ground as an artillery shell whistled towards them and exploded in the field. One man saw a severed hand thump into the ground beside him and promptly threw up his lunch.

'Oh, for Christ's sake, man! Pull yourself together!' shouted a voice from behind him.

'Very good, sir.'

The advance proceeded.

The 7th Armoured Division was now able to run patrols into Tilly-Sur-Suelles. Panzer Lehr drove them back with fanatical gunfire, discipline and fighting élan. At the end of 11 June, the situation was grinding down into a frustrating stalemate. Nevertheless, there were lighter moments on the battlefield. At one point, three British tanks were being threatened by one of Panzer Lehr's 88-millimetre guns. These were viewed by many, including allied personnel, as the most effective artillery piece of the war. They were deadly as anti-aircraft weapons, free standing artillery or later in the war, as the tank gun on a Tiger tank. A single shell could easily knock out a British tank and cause it to 'brew up'. This apparently innocuous expression referred to what happened when a tank burst suddenly into flame killing everyone inside. Major Goode called Brigade headquarters and asked for artillery fire. He was in the middle of enjoying his cuppa when he found a naval lieutenant crawling along a ditch. With him were two naval ratings carrying a huge radio.

'Good morning,' said Major Goode, in typically British fashion, 'who are you?'

The officer explained that he was a Forward Officer Bombardment from HMS *Rodney*, the huge battleship, which was lying in the English Channel, some 20 kilometres to the north. Bill knew this enormous battleship, which had been the escort for the Lofoten raid, three long years ago.

'What do you want?', asked the major. 'Oh, and would you care for some tea?'

'Well, thank you very much, Could I just see where the target is, sir?'

On seeing how close the farm was, the lieutenant said, 'Christ! That is close! Get your men to dig in deep and do it bloody quickly.' He made a short radio message to the ship.

It seemed only seconds later that they heard a noise like an underground train entering a station at speed.

'Everybody get down for God's sake,' shouted the lieutenant.

The first shell exploded with a mighty bang only 100 metres from them. The second flew over the farm. The third was a direct hit. Major Goode reported that 'there was no more trouble from that 88!'

Wednesday, 14 June 1944, Lingevres, Normandy

Day after day passed. Tilly had still not fallen, casualties were mounting, and blood was flowing freely. The initial timetable to take Normandy was already slipping considerably, only one week after the first landings. The 131st (Queens) Brigade had at last made it to the battlefield. General Montgomery brought them into the 7th Armoured Division and placed the Gloucesters under the Command of 151st Brigade. They were learning very clearly that the Anglo-American Sherman tanks were just not a match for the German Mark IVs or Panthers or the huge and terrifying Tigers with which the Germans were equipped. Bill was to learn something sombre in addition.

'Sir, have a look through the field glasses. Can you see those Jerries up on that ridge there? What sort of uniforms are those? I've never seen anything like that before. They're sort of mottled green and brown, like camouflage.'

'I've not seen those either, but I have an idea what they are. I think they're a Waffen SS unit. If so, they are absolute bastards, and we will have our work cut out.'

Fighting at the village of Cristot, a few days previously, a tank crew had been taken prisoner by a unit from the 12th Waffen SS *Hitlerjugend* Division. They had been murdered and at least one had been tortured to death.

'The bastards were doing their massacres of prisoners before Dunkirk and they're doing it now, they just do not get any better.'

The *Hitlerjugend* Division was made up of some of the keener alumni of Hitler Youth. They had been indoctrinated into Nazism from childhood and were true believers in the cult of Adolf Hitler. There is no question that they were excellent and brave soldiers. Their fighting élan meant that they would attack with vigour and were quite happy to take casualties. They were also ruthless and were capable of pretending surrender only to pull out a stick grenade and murder their would-be captors.

The word was informally but effectively passing through the battlefield, 'Don't take SS prisoners.'

The Gloucesters edged forward, accompanied by Sherman tanks from the 4/7th Dragoon Guards but were getting the worst of it. The German tank guns, their superior armour and the penetrative power of the German 88 meant that progress towards Lingèvres was perilous at best and suicidal at worst.

On this morning, the stalemate was again becoming established. Moving forward was blocked by German tanks and artillery. Without warning, three Typhoons flew over them at a low altitude making everyone duck. They fired their rockets right into the German tanks, exploding them into a plume of flame. The Gloucesters cheered as if they were at a football match. More Typhoons flew over firing rockets into the village, where the bulk of the German troops from Panzer Lehr were situated.

At that point, two German soldiers appeared out of one of the thick hedgerows and offering to surrender. Moreover, to show what good blokes they were, they were supporting two wounded members of the Durham Light Infantry. The surrender was accepted, whereupon a further 40 Germans emerged from the hedgerow with their hands up, looking apprehensive.

'Any SS among them?'

'No, these are grey uniforms, the SS are in those green camouflage uniforms. Looking at their shoulder patches, this is the 130 Division, German Army.'

The deadly process went on. Roads were cleared of mines. German tanks were shot one after another. If they stood and fought, RAF Typhoons would appear flying almost at ground level and neutralise them with rocket fire.

As the Gloucesters entered Lingèvres, the Germans were on the point of surrounding the Durhams, but the arrival of a superior force swung the balance. Bill's Pioneer Platoon had first to enter the town and ensure that any mines and booby traps were defused.

The Gloucesters were taken out of the line and replaced by the 131 (Queen's Brigade). Tilly-sur-Seulles did not fall until 1400 hours on 20 June, ten days after the order to take it 'that day'. The local war cemetery contains 945, some six times more were wounded.

The British Army had moved forward 12 kilometres in ten days.

Thursday, 15 June 1944, Lingèvres

At last, the fighting had died down and he could snatch some kip in his tent.

'Sir! Sir! Wake up! Come and look at this!'

'Oh, bloody hell, what time is it?'

'It's 0600, sir, but come quickly.'

Then he saw them. In the almost-dark sky, there were strange aircraft flying north.

'What the bloody hell are those? They're not any kind of German fighter that I've ever seen. They're too small for German bombers and what is that light coming out of the back of them. There are loads of them. But they aren't heading this way, they're heading for the coast. Are they going to England? Hey, Sparks! Get on the radio to the colonel and tell him to look to the eastern horizon and tell him to be sharp about it before they disappear.'

None of them had ever seen anything like it before. They were aircraft but smaller than any German fighter such as *Messerschmitt* 109 or *Focke Wulf* 190. The oddest thing of all was that they were not powered by conventional propellers but by some sort of rocket device.

He could see the glow of flames coming from the back. What on earth could they be? There was no time for introspection, he had a platoon to feed.

Chapter 30

The Road to Caen – Operations Bluecoat and Charnwood

Sunday, 18 June 1944, Ellon, Normandy

The realities he had now encountered were considerably worse than any of his previous experience of war. Twelve days in the field without sleep, under permanent hostile fire and with the hourly expectation of death, had reduced the horizons of his human experience to a very few but very important questions. 'What do I want my men to do?' 'Will I be alive in an hour's time?' 'Where will I sleep or eat?' Otherwise, the rich tapestry of life on planet earth held no great interest. The one exception to that was 'What do I have to do to stop the bloody lice biting?'

The battle within himself was more insidious, more intense and more indefatigable than the war against the Germans. He had seen dead Germans, dead Canadians and dead Englishmen. He had seen his own men blown up by mines and killed outright. Death had ceased to disgust him. It was merely a part of everyday life like shaving, drinking tea or checking his weapons.

He was aware that people around him were developing the 1000-yard stare. That vacant expression, which presaged the man sinking into apathy. That death was expected. That hope was going. He had to get a grip! Twenty men – or their remnants – depended on him for inspiration and leadership out of this particular brand of hell.

Perhaps worst of all was the fact that he had known these blokes personally. If he ever made it back to Gloucester, he would bump into their families in Eastgate Street or Brunswick Road. 'He never felt a thing', he would say. 'It was very quick, and he would never have known what hit him.' You could not tell a family that he had seen their dad lying in his own mess for two days with his entrails hanging out screaming for his mother. If fortune said that he did not make it back to Gloucester, at least he would be spared that.

The sight of rotten bodies with maggots wriggling out of eye holes had become an everyday occurrence. It was curious. The first time you saw one you wanted to look away and throw up. After you had seen your twentieth, it was merely a part of the landscape. Some were British or Canadian, some were German. Interestingly, many of the men became so used to it that picking souvenirs such as regimental badges or Iron Crosses from bodies became as common a hobby as schoolboys collecting stamps. He had to curtail this practice among the platoons because of the German practice of booby-trapping bodies.

Perhaps the screams were the worst of it. It was even worse than the sights. The screams were primeval, beyond control or reason, coming from the deepest reserve of human misery. Good strong men had screamed for someone to shoot them or give them a weapon to do it themselves. At least there had been morphine to put them to sleep.

He had heard the screams of men trapped in burning tanks. Rumours said that sometimes officers had gone forward and dropped a hand grenade into the tank turret to put the burning crew out of their misery. Bill knew about that. If he were called upon to do it himself, would he be able? Yes, he would be able because that is what you did in wartime. There was a war on, and this is the sort of thing you had to do.

The Gloucesters' war diary shows that at this stage three officers and 71 other ranks were either dead or wounded. He did not want to be the fourth officer to push up the daisies, not yet anyway.

Some engaged in a macabre form of mathematics. Given the level of casualties, how long could you expect to live? One member of the Gloucesters calculated six weeks. Perhaps it was significant that a similar calculation by one of the 2nd Essex came to the same conclusion. So, if you lasted into the first week of August, you were doing well. After that, you were on borrowed time. It was up to him as an officer to stop that kind of talk before the colonel got to hear of it and gave them all a bollocking.

He would also have heard of the feat at Lingevres. Sergeant Harris D.C.M. with his gunner I D Mackillop, knocked out five Panther tanks with five shots. He would also have heard of an even greater feat down the road at Villers Bocage, two days previously. A single German tank had ambushed 14 Cromwell tanks and destroyed the lot of them one after the other.

Bill would have heard about something else that day. He would have found out what the strange aircraft were that he had seen two nights previously. The Germans had started to aim pilotless bombs into the UK. That is what they had seen. They would soon know them as V1s. They flew as fast as a

Spitfire and there was little that could be done to stop them. *The bastards!* They would stop at bloody nothing. The only thing that a man could do was to shoot as many of them as possible until they bloody gave up or were dead.

More news was circulating.

The 12th Waffen SS *Hitlerjugend* Division had murdered 134 Canadian prisoners of war at Fontenay-le-Pesnel. This was only four kilometres away from where he was placed outside Tilly-sur-Seulles. There was another factor which would have made his blood run even colder, had he known it. The German officer who allegedly ordered the massacre was *Standartenführer* [Colonel] Wilhelm Möhnke: the same officer who had ordered the Wormhoudt massacre in 1940, where 80 soldiers were murdered in a barn across some fields well within Bill's earshot.

There was still more. He was to hear from French locals that the same unit, the 12th Waffen SS *Hitlerjugend*, had murdered 92 civilians near Ascq, near Lille, in late March.

It was difficult to find words to describe feelings about these. He did, however, have a Sten gun or a German Schmeisser by now and was fortunately in a position to do something about these atrocities.

We could only wonder what his feelings were when he discovered that Canadians had cut German soldiers' throats at Courselle and that some British tank drivers were tying German officers to the front of tanks to act as human shields and of alleged murders of eight staff officers of Panzer-Artillerie-Regiment 130. The latter were part of Panzer Lehr. Presumably, they had been killed in an attempt to elicit information from them.

The battlefront was becoming very, very nasty.

Friday, 19 June 1944, Ellon

Colonel Biddle ordered all officers to take their men from the camp at Ellon into Bayeux for rest and relaxation. This was not merely a matter of good psychology; it was freedom from the incessant German shelling and the eternal irritation of lice. There were now cases of malaria. There were also rumours of 100 civilian cases of typhoid. Mobile bath units were operating. The military authorities were working with the *Mairie* [town hall] to utilise the town public baths to clean up the troops as well.

A trip back to Bayeux also meant that radios were available. Bill could listen to songs by Vera Lynn, the comedy of The Huggets and Tommy Handley and the BBC news. After the BBC news, there came the inevitable.

Jarmany calling, Jarmany calling. This is Jarmany calling from Reichsender Hambursh and stations Bremen and DXB on the 31-metre band.
'Oh my God! Is Lord Haw-Haw still going? Has the RAF bombing not killed that sod yet? We took Hamburg off the map last year, surely to goodness a friendly bomb could have sorted him out?'
I'm afraid that the Jarman government does rather need to point out some salient facts to the British public who are being duped by the official BBC.

The war in Normandy is not going particularly well for the British and their partners in crime, the Americans and Canadians. Nearly a month has gone by and Caen has not yet fallen. The Somersets, the Dorsets, the Hampshires and the Duke of Cornwall's Light Infantry are all taking terrible casualties.

The British population also needs to consider whether it really does want to continue to receive the flying bombs, which are hitting London day after day. The Jarman government has no wish to continue with this but, in essence, the British government and Mr Churchill in particular leaves them with no other alternative. If many British people were to complain to their members of parliament about the needless and avoidable suffering, which they are receiving, it would not be surprising in the slightest.
'Oh, turn it off! Why was that rubbish on the radio?'
'Oh, he's a good laugh sir!'
'That man would be a good laugh if I ever got my hands on him.'
'You'd have a couple of million in the queue before you, sir. There's just one thing, though. What was that that Haw-Haw said about flying bombs? Could those be the things we saw heading north towards England a few days ago?'
'I don't know, I suppose they might be.'
They were.

Friday, 7 July 1944, La Butte

'Ah! Colonel Biddle, you sent for me, sir?'
'Yes, Adlam, I've got a task for your chappies. I'm getting bloody tired of our lack of progress in the *bocage*. The hedgerows and embankments are a nightmare for tanks and personnel carriers. I want you to experiment with

Bangalore torpedoes to see if they can be used to blow holes in these bloody endless obstacles.'

'Very good, sir, I'll report back at 1800.'

Bill was not an explosives expert, but he would have access to plenty that were. A Bangalore is an explosive charge placed inside a hollow tube which may be one or up to two metres long. They are used for clearing mines, booby traps and wire entanglements. Bill had seen them in use in storming the beach at Varengeville and also in exploding mines in Normandy.

The experiment failed. The charge was not strong enough to clear a hole wide enough and deep enough to let a tank pass through the hedgerow. Sod it!

He would remember that evening as one of the most memorable in his life.

As dusk settled, a flight of planes was to be seen from the north.

'Are those ours, Bill?' Colonel Biddle asked.

'I think so, sir, Mosquitoes if I'm not mistaken, they do look a bit like Junkers bombers though.'

The *crump* of the German 88s began. Flashes of exploding shells lit up the sky, the clouds and the first wave of bombers.

'They're ours, sir.'

Red, white and green tracers began to ascend now, snaking into the darkening sky.

'They're heading towards Caen, sir, but it's not a very big force.'

'I would imagine those are the Pathfinders, Bill. Their job is to mark the place where the main force will aim.'

The Mosquitoes now let their loads go. These were not bombs but, brilliantly coloured, red, yellow and green fireworks which floated gently down. They were strangely beautiful.

'They're like Christmas trees, sir! What the heck is that noise?'

A low roar was starting to be heard. The twilight was dying now, and the cause of the roar could not be seen. The German aerial barrage increased in intensity. From the light of the bursting shells, they could now see the main force start to arrive: the lumbering four-engine heavy bombers.

'Looks like they're sending in the Lancasters and the Halifaxes, Bill, I would not want to be underneath that lot.'

Somewhere, high above them, they heard the Mosquitoes as they flew overhead changing from a southerly to a northerly direction and heading back to their Royal Air Force station in Cambridgeshire.

'Lucky buggers! They'll be going out for a pint of wallop tonight!'

'And sleeping in a nice warm bed, Bill.'

'What exactly is a nice warm bed, sir? I don't think I can remember what one of those is.'

The droning was becoming louder and louder. The whole of the north-eastern sector of their little world was now full pyrotechnic extravaganza of anti-aircraft guns, tracer shells and searchlights.

'What is that violet-coloured searchlight for, sir?'

'That's the master searchlight, Bill, if he catches one of our lads, just see what happens.'

Just at that moment, the violet searchlight caught a Halifax bomber in its eerie grip. Immediately a dozen other searchlights locked on to it. Shells were bursting all around it now. Could the plane get out of the dance of death?

'Oh dive, dive, you silly bugger!'

The pilot corkscrewed his plane into a tight circling dive. They saw it for a moment as it flew with its wings at right angles to the ground and then disappeared out of the cone of searchlights.

'Well done, RAF! Bloody well done! God, sir, we must be making Halifax bombers bloody well, I would have thought that dive would have torn it to bits.'

'Good British workmanship that, Bill, have you been up in one of those?'

'Never been up in a plane, sir. Oh look!'

The first explosions were starting in Caen. Fires started immediately.

'They're hitting them with incendiaries, Bill. Nasty things, they're made of phosphorus.'

Then the high-explosive bombs began to explode, spreading the fires.

As he watched the horror of the firestorm descending from the clouds, he could only repeat himself. 'God! I would not want to be under that lot.'

More bombs burst and more bombs. The ground began to shake.

'God, sir, we're ten miles [15 kilometres] away and you can still feel it, what must it be like in Caen?'

'Poor buggers!'

'Well, the Germans came to Gloucester dropping their bombs and now the jackboot is on the other foot! I must say, I do hope the French civvies got out of town, though. I don't feel sorry for the Germans after what they did in Warsaw and Rotterdam, not to mention Coventry.'

From the fires in Caen, they could now see that wave after wave of bombers were flying in loose formation over the town dropping bombs at will. The earthquake went on and on and on.

'How many bloody bombers are there, sir?'

'Hundreds, Bill, absolutely hundreds of them.'

As Caen burned, they could see the Lancaster and Halifax bombers as they looped around overhead. The Englishmen returned to Nottinghamshire, Lincolnshire and Suffolk, the Canadians to Yorkshire.

Still the ground shook, the livid barrage from Caen still fired colourfully, noisily and impotently at squadron after squadron, who carried on in their calm determined procession to drop death and destruction onto the German Army in and around Caen.

'Oh Christ, sir, they've hit a Lancaster!'

Flames shot out of the back of the hapless plane. It had been hit by flak. It quickly lost control and began to lose height. Then it began to corkscrew out of control.

'Can you see any parachutes, Bill?'

'Not from this distance, sir. They'd be lucky to get out of that.'

The plane was vertical now and heading in freefall with flames pouring out of the petrol tanks in its wounded wings. The plane went out of sight. The flash of a huge explosion lit up the countryside.

'Rest in peace, Brylcreem Boys! Sir, have you noticed that there's one plane flying above all the others? It looks as though he's the master of ceremonies.'

'That's the master bomber, Bill, he circles around the target and tells the others when to come in and bomb.'

'You know, sir, when you come to think about it, this war is getting bloody sophisticated.'

The earthquake still kept on, more and more heavy bombers were over Caen now. There was more and more shooting, but no more planes appeared to be hit. More and more planes flew over them, banked over and headed north back to England.

The earthquake subsided. The last of the planes went home. Caen burned. The anti-aircraft fire subsided. All night, the light from the burning of Caen lit the sky.

'God sir, I hope it was worth it!'

A day or so later, it proved not to be worth it. The bombing had ruined the town completely but had hit very few German military positions. Moreover, the wrecked town now made a perfect defensive position for the Germans to fight in. They fought house by house and room by room. This, however, was not the Gloucesters' fight. The 56th Brigade was tasked with moving south of Caen to outflank it.

Saturday, 29 July 1944

The fighting was becoming more and more bitter, if such a thing were possible. The Germans were using portable rocket launchers called *Nebelwerfers* [fog throwers], which fired multiple high explosive rockets. To be hit by a salvo of those was a terrifying experience for anyone who lived to tell the tale. From the British side, they were using more Crocodile tanks. These were Churchill tanks whose main gun had been replaced by a high-powered flamethrower. These did not shoot shells at German positions, they drenched them with burning petrol and incinerated them. Bill would have watched as German soldiers burned to death, screaming like wild animals caught in a forest fire.

After a small action at Launay and Anctonville, Bill's Pioneer section was extremely busy and cleared no less than 300 mines of all kinds plus eight booby traps.

Early August 1944, somewhere in France

The time away from the battlefield gave Bill time to think. Almost half of the lads who had landed were now gone. Casualties were mounting. In June, the battalion had been losing perhaps 15 a week. In July, the casualties rose to 30 a week, then to 56 a week. In August, this had doubled to over 100. Well over 100. Given that the battalion establishment was 794 it meant that every one of them was now on borrowed time. Statistically, Bill Adlam should have been killed or wounded about now.

Then there was the other element to life, the one that he tried to suppress. It was now probable that he would not go home in one piece. He had to think about what that meant. The immediate thought was that if or when he would go down, then he would go down fighting. He hoped that when it came, he would not scream or let himself or his men down.

There were other noises. There was the never-ending sound of the incoming rockets from the German *Nebelwerfers*. There was the sound of the shells from the German 88-millimetre artillery. There was the *b-r-r-rp* of the MG42s. He had seen how each sound could be followed by decapitation, amputation and splatters of blood. He had seen body parts hanging in trees where the birds fought and squabbled over some poor sod's liver. He had seen the flies, bloody millions of them, which fed obscenely in the pools of blood, excrement and rotten flesh.

He had seen dead animals, cows, horses, dogs. Their bodies had been pitted with bullets or they had been blown to pieces stepping on a mine. Why did they have to die? They were innocent of any of the political idiocy, which had created the disaster of this obscene war.

There was little time for introspection, thought or philosophising. If there was any such time, then a very relevant question was, 'If I ever get out of this, what sort of person will I be? No-one here will remain unchanged.'

He would also have wondered how he would ever tell people back in Gloucester what it had been like. No! He would not tell them. It was better that civilised people did not know of such things as this. Anyway, if he ever got back home, he just wanted the whole bloody lot of it out of his mind altogether.

Chapter 31

The Road to La Mailleraye and Endgame

Wednesday, 9 August 1944, approaching Thury Harcourt

Brigadier Elkins, who had replaced Brigadier Pepper as battalion commander, ordered the Gloucesters forward and across the River Orne at 1500 but as expected, they ran into German resistance. This faded away and the battalion entered Brieux at 1730. They joined up with the 2nd Essex to push forward to contact. This led to a strange state of affairs. The armoured support and anti-tank platoons had not caught up with them. There were now 1000 men gingerly moving forward. They had no idea where the enemy were. They had no idea where minefields might be. The Pioneer Platoon did not appear to be called on to search for mines.

They crossed a narrow bridge at 2200 and pushed on into enemy territory under the moonlight. There was no resistance on the bridge. There appeared to be no mines. Were the Germans starting to fall apart? It would be a brave man who would make such a dangerous assumption.

They passed through a burning village but there was no sign of life. At Courmeron, they found several sleeping Germans and took them prisoner. There were no sentries to contend with. The Germans had not been like this last week. It was beyond comprehension, 1000 men in heavy hobnailed boots had clattered into their territory and taken them by surprise.

They pressed on to La Forge a Cambro. Once again, the Germans appeared to have no idea that the British force was approaching. The Gloucesters and the Essex deployed for the attack and waited for tanks to catch up with them. Out in the woods, there were the sounds of skirmishes but nothing too onerous.

From his position on the frontline, Bill would have seen something that he would never have believed possible. Two men of the 2nd Essex brought in 120 prisoners, all of whom appeared to be very grateful for the chance to surrender.

This was not time to count chickens before they hatched. At the next village of Esson, the Germans were still making suicidal counterattacks with automatic weapons and only tank fire and heavy artillery was driving them back. The sight of a British motorcycle despatch rider hanging in a tree caught the eye. He had been thrown there, killed outright by an artillery shell.

'Right, you lot, you've seen it all before, it's someone else's job to get him down. Come on, keep moving.'

Thury Hurcourt was coming into sight now. Brigade headquarters moved up into a field. Divisional intelligence said that the Germans had left Thury Hurcourt.

Then it happened!

Heavy artillery fire rained down on the Brigade headquarters vehicle. The Germans had not left, and they still had plenty of fight. Everyone dived for cover, several were hit.

A Gloucesters patrol had pushed forward to the outskirts of the town. They found that German resistance was stiff. For Bill Adlam, there was a task to do. They were finding hundreds of Teller mines that the retreating Germans had left behind them. They also found roofing slate strewn over a crossroads. These did not look too threatening but a jeep which passed over them touched off a Teller mine. The men in the jeep were killed outright. He saw at very close quarters what a Teller mine could do to occupants of a jeep. The remains looked more like something from a butcher's shop than the soldiers who they had been, just four minutes ago.

It was the task of Bill's platoon to remove the slates, dig out the mines and neutralise them. One snag was that the crossroads was covered by German machine-gun fire. How they accomplished this is not recorded.

On that same afternoon, Colonel Biddle was badly wounded in the head by a German mortar round. He was taken to a local farmhouse which was being used as a makeshift field hospital. His brains were exposed although he was still conscious and still talking. Such was the nature of warfare that Major Lance took over the battalion until Colonel Butterworth could take up the role a week later.

Friday, 11 August 1944, Thury Harcourt

At 1400 hours, a massive Allied artillery bombardment from behind the Gloucesters' positions rained down on the village. The Pioneer Platoon kept their heads down, but the firing was accurate enough and was clear of their positions. There was little reply from the German forces. The Gloucesters were ordered forward at 1430 to occupy the town. For a half hour, all remained quiet. At 1500, a considerable amount of small-arms fire, machine guns, mortars and snipers commenced. A company was stranded on a cliff outside the village. The stretcher bearers had to climb down the cliffs and climb back up again with wounded men on their backs.

The German unit which they now faced was the 271st *Volksgrenadier* Division. Although under strength, this division was composed of battle-hardened veterans from the Russian front who had been in action for two years. They were stiffened by *Kampfgruppe* [battlegroup] Wűnsche. This unit was very interesting to the British army. It was made up of the remnants of the 12th SS *Hitlerjugend* division. When Bill had encountered elements of the 12th SS Panzer Division near Tilly-sur-Suelles in June, it had numbered 20,000 men and 150 tanks. Now, eight weeks later at Thury Harcourt, it had 300 men and ten tanks. Such was the fighting in the pleasant *bocage* of Normandy.

On this afternoon, D company of the Gloucesters was pinned down in a shallow depression. The murderous fire from a German MG42 position kept them hunkered down. Any attempt to return fire with a Bren gun was mown down mercilessly by the rapid rate of the German machine-gun's fire. A radio message told the stranded Gloucesters to keep their heads down until a relieving force could get to them. They were protected from the line of fire, so some of them took their pack of cards out and started a game. No relieving force came. Eventually, one of the Bren gunners lost his patience. He picked up his gun without orders and charged the German position, firing from the hip and spraying bullets before him. The German position was silent. He had killed all of them. He went back to his mates. The card game continued. The man did not get a medal and his name does not appear to be recorded anywhere. He was not mentioned in despatches. By this stage of the war, the man was probably not interested in that sort of irrelevancy. He was still alive. That was all that mattered.

As against this display of sangfroid, some men were going bomb happy, and their entire nervous systems had shut down. This led to trembling, screaming, strange laughter and other neurotic symptoms. They were taken behind the lines immediately.

Unlike in World War I, they were not shot for cowardice.

Saturday, 19 August 1944, Les Loges Saulces

The 56th Brigade now made its final structural move. The 56th Brigade now came under 49th (West Riding) Division. The 49th Division had fought with singular ferocity against the Germans, who called them the Polar Bear Butchers. This was a reference to vicious Polar Bear emblem which the division wore as a shoulder flash.

The Gloucesters approached Thury Hurcourt and were ordered to stop. Other troops joined them and together they took the town and the high ground around it. No-one noticed or cared who these new troops were. The Gloucesters were ordered to St Remy to rest. Even here, there was no rest for Bill. The Germans had left thousands of mines. Vehicles were being blown up. Civilians were being blown up. Farm animals were being blown up. At least the French people appreciated that they had been liberated! The days after the slaughter of Thury Harcourt were spent alternately in rest and in fighting patrols against German infantry. On this day, however, the Gloucesters were ordered into their trucks to join their new division at Airan.

On the way, they passed through Falaise.

Every house in the town of Falaise was burning. There were dead Germans strewn around. There were dead civilians. There were dead farm animals. The entire town was ruined. It seemed that nothing of the normal, healthy world that they had all known was left. If hell was worse than this, then it would be bad indeed. For Bill Adlam, and everyone who saw the destruction at Falaise, this would be something that they would never forget. They might want to forget it. They might try to forget it, alcohol was a possible method. They might try to wipe it out of their memory. They never could, and they never would.

Aside from the endless human tragedy, the Battle of the Falaise Pocket was one of the most significant military victories of the Normandy campaign. It was the tipping point where the British, American and Canadian Armies broke the back of the German Army in Normandy. Bill had played his role in fighting from Tilly to Thury Harcourt; had he known the totality of the operation, he would have been amazed to the depths of his being. Like almost every soldier in the Normandy campaign, he had known what was happening in his field. All that mattered now was, 'Am I alive or am I dead?'

Within the Falaise Pocket, some 80,000 to 100,000 German troops had been encircled. Some 15,000 were dead. Some 50,000 were prisoners. Some 35,000 had escaped and were now on the run. Despite the excellent staff work and first-rate military discipline, the German Army was now starting to unravel. They had lost some 355 tanks, 2500 trucks, 250 field guns. The 56th Brigade was now tasked with pushing on 100 kilometres to the Seine.

Thursday, 24 August, Cormeilles

The Gloucesters were moving forward now at the unprecedented rate of ten kilometres a day. From time to time, they met a German rear-guard but all it could do was hopefully halt the inevitable by some few hours. They were on the heights outside of Cormeilles at 0300 and prepared for a fight such as the one at Thury Harcourt. The Germans had gone. There were doubtless mines to clear up but the Gloucesters and the Essex were able to enter without difficulty. As there had been less fighting in the towns in the past few days, there were more townspeople to wave and welcome them.

'*Vive les anglais*! *Vive Churchill*!'

Friday, 25 August 1944, Epaigne

Epaigne proved to be a tougher nut. Three armoured cars from the Reconnaissance platoon were knocked out by Germans who were well dug in. Local people were keen to give information on the deployment and the strength of the Germans. The local French Resistance appeared and gave even better intelligence. It turned out that there were probably two companies of Germans in the town, around 300 men.

The skirmish involved the entire 2nd Gloucester battalion and turned into a 'real roughhouse' as one survivor described it. It began at 0930 hours. The fighting went on house by house and room by room until the superior British numbers told. Much of it was close-quarters fighting where each side saw the whites of the eyes of the others. The Gloucesters lost 14 dead and had 40 wounded, the Germans lost 48 and had five taken prisoner. The fighting did not end until 2230. Why on earth were they fighting like this when the end was inevitable? A memorial in the town commemorates the names of the Gloucesters who died there.

Sunday, 29 August 1944, Foret de Brotonne

The 56th Brigade was now tasked with taking the Foret de Brotonne, a heavily forested area just before the River Seine. They were then to take

Le Mailleraye on the Seine itself. The probability was that the fighting would be tougher now. The remnants of the German Army had their back to the Seine. It was now difficult for them to retreat. This proved to be the case and several vicious firefights took place on the outskirts of the woods. Clearly, the Germans were holding their positions to the end, to allow them to pull back whatever men and materiel they could across the wide expanse of the Seine with a view to regrouping. The Gloucesters and South Wales Borderers together pushed forward. From behind them rocket-firing Typhoons appeared. That silenced the German guns. They pressed on in their vehicles into the forest, firing automatic weapons blindly into the dense forest land and meeting little resistance. Few muzzle flashes returned their fire.

Then, what they found utterly amazed them. Under the cover of the canopy of trees, there were hundreds upon hundreds of German Army vehicles. There were trucks, guns, *Kübelwagens* [German jeeps], and almost every kind of known German Army vehicle. The Germans had assembled this vast vehicle fleet to move it across the Seine. The British and Canadian advance had been too fast. The haul of vehicles was the remains of the transport of the German 7th Army. Without their vehicles, it would be difficult for the retreating Germans to stay ahead of the rapidly advancing Allied army. The Gloucesters did not know it but the officer in command of the seventh army, Colonel General Friedrich Dollmann had died of a heart attack.

Bill was called to the colonel's tent.

'Morning, Bill, there's no time to beat about the bush, you're promoted to captain. As you know, we've been taking casualties and I need a good man as captain. The adjutant will tell you your duties. He will give you your pips, you are to wear them immediately.'

Bill had been promoted as captain to the support company. He had not trained with the infantry companies and such a move would have been difficult. He did know the work of the support company. He had the support of his own platoon and was well known to the officers and men of the other companies in the support platoon.

'Thank you, sir.'

In the normal course of events, the highest aspiration for an 'other rank' and a reservist to boot was regimental sergeant major. He had attained the rank of captain. It would have been a moment of supreme pride. There was, however, no time for congratulation. He had orders to move his formation forward. He had to get around and make sure that all of his new subordinates knew that he was in charge. He had to find out what the issues were and the things that needed attention. There may have been the odd 'congratulations, Bill', but there was a war on and too much to worry about.

Monday, 30 August 1944, Foret de Brotonne

Having spent the night in the forest with minimal German harassment, the Gloucesters drove on through the forest. They could see Le Mailleraye on the other side of the Seine. It was burnt out and looking very desolate.

Others of the brigade had occupied La Mailleraye the previous day. Even despite the destruction visited on their village, the French civilians were coming out to wave at the British soldiers and give them whatever food and drink could be spared. It fell to the Gloucesters to take possession of any of the useful booty left by the Germans in the forest.

The Gloucesters forward patrols were pushing German soldiers into La Mailleraye and straight into captivity at the hands of the South Wales Borderers. Many Germans appeared to be quite content with this arrangement.

The windfall of vehicles proved to be beyond belief! Bill's first job as captain was to stop as many men as possible from jumping into the German vehicles and driving around in them.

'Oy! Get out of that bloody *Kübelwagen* it might be booby trapped. And you, do NOT drive any further down that track, it might be mined!'

Curiously enough, the vehicles were not booby trapped. That was a mark of the haste and disarray of the Germans as they withdrew across the River Seine.

Bill never arrived at La Mailleraye. He was never to take his place as a captain. His jeep struck a mine on one of the tracks in the Foret de Brotonne. There was a flash and a sickening thud. The jeep flew through the air. Seat belts were unheard of. Bill was driving and appears to have been saved by the fact that he was following standing orders, he had a sandbag below the driver's seat. His batman who was in the jeep with him was killed instantly. His record shows that despite the explosion, the injuries and the massive shock to his nervous system, Bill stayed at his post.

'Stretcher bearers! Hey! We need some stretcher bearers over here! Captain Adlam's in a bad way.'

'What's his batman looking like?'

'No, he's bought it. Better get him out of here, he's a hell of a bloody mess and I mean that literally.'

Captain Adlam lay on the ground in shock. No bones were broken but the daze from the blast left him bereft of faculties. The muscle on his left chest was ripped apart, possibly from landing on a tree stump. He would not have known where he was or possibly even who he was. The sky would have looked wonderfully blue. Inside he would have known a heavenly calm. His battledress was covered in gouts of blood from the heavy wound on his chest. It didn't hurt. Did he laugh at that? There was this bloody big hole in his chest, and it didn't hurt.

He knew that the adrenaline rush was acting as a temporary anaesthetic and that soon he would be in agony.

Hands fumbled in his battledress trouser pocket to find the morphine syrette. A hand plunged the spike through his battledress trousers and into a muscle. The sharp little prick seemed a long way away.

'There you are, sir, that'll fix you up for the next couple of hours.'

Gentle hands picked him up. It was all hazy now. He looked up and saw that wonderfully blue sky. It was all quiet there was no shooting now. He was in a vehicle, there were other wounded men around him.

'Right, that's us full, next stop Bayeux.'

It occurred to him that he was in an ambulance. One man had his face covered. Bill would have hoped that it was no-one he knew. He drifted in and out of sleep. The stench of blood, vomit and excrement made him want to be sick. Instead, he drifted into sleep. His men, what about the support company? He was captain now. He drifted back into sleep.

'Well, Captain Adlam, you're in a mess.'

He could smell antiseptic hospital smells now. There were doctors, nurses and other people in clean clothes. He noticed there was no smell of sweat, death, cordite or excrement. There was no sound of gunfire. How many weeks was it since he had not heard gunfire every day?

'Doctor, what about my batman, do you know if he's alive?'

'Sorry, Captain, I don't even know what battalion you are from or even where you were wounded. The ambulances just bring people in, and we patch them up.'

'Can I go back, Doctor?'

'You're in a bad way, captain. It looks as though you've been blown up by something pretty big. You haven't got any fresh shrapnel in you, which is good. There is some shrapnel in your legs, but it has been there for some time. There are no broken bones, which is also good. The tissue damage to that wound in your chest is a mess. No, I cannot release you in that condition.'

'You've been sending men back to the front with worse than that wrong with them!'

'No, Captain, we haven't. You are in a state of severe shock. In cases like yours, it can be months or even years before you are yourself again. What's more if that chest wound is not cleaned up very quickly, it is going to turn very nasty indeed. I'm sorry, I cannot take part in a discussion with you, I have other men to see to.'

In the next days, men were brought into the ward and were patched up and despatched to the front. A few were from the 2nd Gloucesters. He would have heard the gossip about who had been wounded, who had been killed. Did he have any news on Charlie or Jimmy? They'd gone out on patrol and never come back. No, he hadn't heard that and had no idea what happened to them.'

Friday, 3 September 1944, Hospital in Bayeux

Other men were still coming in and returning to the front.

'Doc, for Christ's sake, what is the bloody matter? Other people are going out of here, why can't I?'

'Captain Adlam, that wound in your chest is developing a very nasty septic poisoning. In the last war, you would already be dead and in this one, if you walk out of here, you will not last two days. I will not release you. If this is not treated, it will turn to gangrene, and you will die.'

'Christ al-bloody-mighty!'

The idea of being dead in two days' time was amusing. Last week, he would not have believed that he would still be alive once the moon came up that evening.

Later that day, the wound was becoming more infected.

'Right, Captain Adlam, well, it's a good job we didn't let you go. Your wound has turned to gangrene. I shall need to operate immediately.'

He came to with a burning pain in his chest.

'Ah! Captain Adlam, you've woken up. Well, the good news is that I believe we got all of it. It was rather like scooping out the innards from a very rotten banana and we had to take out a bit of good flesh just to make sure that the infection would not come back. You will regain physical fitness in time, but I'm afraid the explosion has really knocked you about a bit. There is no question of you going back to the front. As soon as you are strong enough to be moved, we'll send you back to Blighty.'

It was now five years to the day since Neville Chamberlain had declared war on Germany. Bill had survived. The question, however, was 'is it enough?' and the answer was 'no, not until it was finished'. Even at this late stage, there were still millions of bullets to be fired.

Medical orderlies loaded Bill onto a hospital ship on 9 September and sent him back to England for recuperation. His physical condition at this time was D, the fourth level of fitness. By 25 November, he was back to category A, which meant that physically he was eligible for further active service. He was awarded this category despite having major hearing loss and breathing difficulties from the explosion. He was posted to a holding battalion on 25 November. The record shows that he was attached to the 4th Royal Berkshire Regiment with 'view to employment as an instructor'. This was unsuccessful. The explosive shock to his nervous system was still with him. The attachment was annulled, and he was back to the holding battalion. Clearly the A fitness category had been granted prematurely. He was posted back to 21st Army Group in March 1945. This was also unsuccessful. The massive impact of the blast had impaired the function of his nervous system more than had been apparent.

Sunday, 30 April 1945, Location Unknown

'Jarmany calling, Jarmany calling.'

'Is that silly bugger still spouting over the airwaves?'

'He's a star, Captain Adlam, he really is.'

'Well, I could do with a good laugh, leave it on and let's hear what he has to say.'

Haw-Haw remained defiant. The would-be upper-class drawl still talked down to the rest of the world. The arrogance was still there. There was a difference. He was completely drunk. He was not only drunk, he was plastered, sozzled, smashed.

'This evening, I am talking to you about… Sharmany. (Heavy breath) That is a concept that… many of you may have… failed to understand. Let me tell you that in Sharmany… there still remains the spirit of unity… and the shpirit of shtrength. Let me tell you… here we have a UNITED people… who are modesht in their wishes… they are not imperialists… they don't want to take what doesn't belong to them.'

This was a cue for laughter which could be heard the length of the British Isles.

'All they want is to live their own simple lives… undisturbed by outshide influenshes.'

Germany had invaded Czechoslovakia, Poland, Norway, Denmark, Belgium, Holland, France, Hungary, Croatia, Serbia, Greece, Tunisia, Algeria, Cyrenaica, Egypt, the Soviet Union and the Channel Islands. Germany had pulled Slovakia, Hungary, Rumania, Bulgaria, Italy and Spain into a war. Haw-Haw's credibility had plunged to the point of high comedy to rank with Tommy Handley at his best.

Whether anyone heard the rest of the broadcast is not known. It is more likely that the staid, brave citizens of the United Kingdom fell about laughing until their sides ached. At the same time that Lord Haw-Haw made his final comedic broadcast, Adolf Hitler and his wife, Eva Braun died in a suicide pact. Bill was not recovering from the effects of the blast. He was sent back to the holding battalion in May. His injuries had clearly left him unable to carry on even as an average soldier. It would have been in character that he would have requested to return to the battlefront, demanded and even begged for it.

There is some evidence that he did make it back to the battlefront. In conversations with son-in-law Peter Nash, Bill talked of having gone back to the front and having landed in a glider. His most likely landing by glider would have been in Operation Varsity. This was on 24 March 1945 when the 6th Airborne Division was ordered to capture the villages of Hamminkeln and Wesel and thus establish a foothold on the east bank of the River Rhine.

However, his record for this period merely says he went from No 15 Holding Battalion to 21 Army Group and back to the Holding Battalion. As 21 Army Group comprised over a million men it is uncertain what may have befallen him.

At any rate, the injuries won in the end. The medical staff were not clearing him for active service. In the terms of the day, he was a nervous wreck. In the first week of August, it was confirmed that he was no longer physically fit enough to carry on in the army. He was given a rail pass home, told that he could pick up his demob suit and his army career ceased abruptly and irrevocably. He arrived back in Gloucester to find that his marriage was ended. His daughters Gladys (Poppy) and Pamela (Pauline) were living with his parents in Hailes Road in the Coney Hill area of Gloucester. It was now his job to look after them with whatever employment he was able to undertake in post-war Britain. Employment was scarce; he was no longer a Captain in the Gloucestershire Regiment. He was a man out of work who used to work in a factory making matches. His standard of living dropped so sharply that he sold the Military Medal. He regretted it instantly and spent the rest of his life nursing that regret.

On 15 August 1945, he walked down Hailes Road in Gloucester. He bumped into a lass who was riding a bike along the street. She was called Moreen.

'Fancy going to the pictures?'

'Alright.'

And with that, a new day and a new era dawned.

Bill and Moreen went on to marry and have a daughter, Linda, in 1952. She is co-author of this book. He moved to Australia in 1964 on medical advice that the climate would be kinder to the wounds that he had incurred in the war.

As for what happened in the war, he rarely mentioned it. For him, the war was over. His only souvenirs were the crimson regimental sash, the officer's swagger stick, the Commando's Green Beret and a tendency to dive into a corner if someone turned a light on without warning.

The people he knew, the places to which he travelled, the operations in which he took part, the glory, the guts and the grime all remained unspoken. He just wanted it out of his head. The rest was silence.

Linda, however, wanted to know what had happened and commissioned this book. And that is the end of the story, except that fate decreed there was to be a sequel.

Epilogue

Seven decades had passed since the end of World War II. Bill had died in 1980. Now it was 2014.

Jeff Steel had researched the story and written it. Now I, his daughter, knew what had befallen my father and also understood why he had wanted to forget the whole heroic, bloody and catastrophic mess.

Neither I nor Jeff had realised it, but the story was not yet at an end. What happened as a postscript to the story could only be written in a work of non-fiction. In fiction, it would be laughably implausible.

The miracle arose suddenly and with a resemblance to a shell bursting without warning on a D-Day beach.

In February 2015, an email came out of the blue from my Uncle Colin: Bill's brother-in-law. He and the Rotary Club of Gloucester had visited The Soldiers of Gloucester Museum. What happened next bordered on the incredible. A staff member remembered that Colin had a connection to my father.

What he said to Colin was a bombshell beyond belief. Bill's Military Medal, which he had won for gallantry was up for auction in London.

I mobilised my sons, Tim and Chris Nash.

'Get it at any cost,' was the order. An observer might see this as the commando gene popping out in the next generation.

Tim appointed an agent to bid at the auction on his behalf. Tim followed the auction minute by minute on the internet. The tension was at a similar height to that on the night before D-Day, up to a point.

In true commando fashion, we achieved the objective, and the medal was secured. My family now have it in secure storage. It will not be sold again.

My dad would have liked that, *he really would!*

Linda Adlam Nash
May 2017

Acknowledgements

Writing this book was honestly straightforward. There was so much source material readily available that my acknowledgements are largely to those who, over eight decades, have provided a rich source of archival information for me to work on.

I must firstly acknowledge my co-writer Linda Nash, Bill's daughter. Linda initially requested the project, provided photographs and details of her father's life and carefully vetted the developing drafts. She was a joy to work with throughout.

I particularly wish to acknowledge the United Kingdom National Archives at Kew for the now-declassified records relating to all aspects of British Army operations in World War II.

I also gratefully acknowledge the United Kingdom Ministry of Defence. They provided Bill's army personnel record to Linda, and this gave us the road map to follow for all subsequent research.

I would especially like to acknowledge D.C. Thompson publications of Dundee, Scotland for their permission to reproduce a 'Victor' comic from 1971 which told Bill's story of winning the medal.

I would also like to acknowledge the other authors who have written about Dunkirk, the Lofoten raid, the Dieppe raid, the Achnacarry Training Centre and the Normandy landings. There are too many to cite in their entirety, but I would like specially to mention Jimmy Dunning, two of whose books provided vital information on 4 Commando. I contacted Jimmy shortly before he died, he remembered Bill at Achnacarry and provided additional detail.

I must pay tribute to Allison Paterson of Big Sky Publishing for her enthusiasm, encouragement and belief in the project and her managerial skill in turning the project into a book.

Finally, I wish to pay tribute to the Allied military personnel, their determination, their modest courage and their acceptance that their own life may have to be given to rid the world of an appalling evil. Many of the stories are lost.

Not this one!

Jeff Steel
Melbourne, Australia,
March 2022.

Select Bibliography

Books

Beevor, A. 2009, *D-Day the Battle for Normandy*, Viking Press
Bellamy, C. 2009, *Absolute War*, Pan Military Classics
Daniell, D.S. 1951, *Cap of Honour The Story of the Gloucestershire Regiment*, Harrap
Dear, I.C.B. and Foot M.R.D. 1995, *The Oxford Companion to the Second World War*, Oxford University Press
Dildy, D.C. 2010, *Dunkirk 1940 - Operation Dynamo*, Osprey Press
Dunning, J. 2003, *The Fighting Fourth: No 4 Commando at War 1940 – 1945*, Sutton Publishing
Dunning J. 2007, *The British Commandos*, Paladin Press
Fowler, W. 2002, *The Commandos at Dieppe*, Harper Collins
Hastings, M. 1984, *Overlord: D Day and the Battle for Normandy*, Michael Joseph
Holborn, A. 2010, *The 56th Infantry Brigade and D-Day*, Continuum Books
Lewis J.E. (editor) 2010, *D Day: The Normany Landings in the Words of Those Who Took Part*, Magpie Books
Lovat, Lord. 1978, *March Past*, Weidenfelt and Nicholson
Macintyre, B. 2010, *Operation Mincemeat*, Bloomsbury Publishing
Mitcham, S.W. 2007, *German Order of Battle (volumes one two and three)* Stackpole Books
Meyer, H. 2005, *The Twelfth SS*, Stackpole Books
Meyer, H. 1996, *Kriegsgechichte der 12ten SS Panzerdivision 'Hitlerjugend'*, Nation Europa Verlag
(War History of the 12th SS Panzer Division 'Hitler Youth')
Neillands, R. 2005, *The Dieppe Raid*, Indiana University Press.
Rankin, N. 2011, *Ian Fleming's Commandos – the Story of 30 Assault Group in WWII*, Faber & Faber
Sebag-Montefiore, H. 2004, *Enigma – The Battle for the Code*, Cassell
Sebag-Montefiore, H. 2006, *Dunkirk: Fight to the Last Man*, Harvard
Westwell I. and Dunstan S, 2007, *Allied Special Forces*, Compendium Publishing

Journals
Victor Comics, issue number 545 July 31, 1971, D.C. Thomson

UK National Archives
Military record of 5183147 William George Henry Adlam MM.

Selected Websites

Commando Veterans Archive
https://www.commandoveterans.org/WilliamAdlam4Commando

Britannica: Dunkirk Evacuation World War Two
https://www.britannica.com/event/Dunkirk-evacuation

Imperial War Museum: what you need to know about the Dunkirk Evacuations
https://www.iwm.org.uk/history/what-you-need-to-know-about-the-dunkirk-evacuations

National Army Museum: the commandos
https://www.nam.ac.uk/explore/commandos-WW2

Youtube: No 4 Commando Lofoten Raid (24 minutes film)
https://www.youtube.com/watch?v=zQhD8H0W9B8

National World War Two Museum (USA): The Raid at Dieppe
https://www.nationalww2museum.org/war/articles/operation-jubilee-dieppe-raid-1942

Youtube: The Raid on Dieppe WW2 (67 minutes film)
https://www.youtube.com/watch?v=TqXoENpS-Zc

Youtube: No 4 Commando Achnacarry (Commando training centre) from Scottish Television (23 minutes film)
https://www.youtube.com/watch?v=7E1vMzzIm8E

Imperial War Museum: 10 things you need to know about D-day.
https://www.iwm.org.uk/history/the-10-things-you-need-to-know-about-d-day

Youtube: D-day, Gold Beach. (14 minutes film)
https://www.youtube.com/watch?v=Je34i0auNTE

D-Day Overlord: Operation Perch
https://www.dday-overlord.com/en/battle-of-normandy/allied-operations/perch

About the Authors

Jeff Steel

My interest in Hitler's war started dramatically. At age seven, I emerged from Euston Station in London with my parents. The immediate area resembled a smoke-blackened Pompeii. 'There was a terrible war,' my parents told me. Their house in Coventry had been bombed, their sole remaining possession was a large mirror. The world had gone mad. This triggered a strong desire to understand the craziness.

The result of this seminal event was a lifetime of intense curiosity on all aspects of the war. As a student, I had worked in Germany on the site of the Battle of the Bulge. I found many artefacts, fortunately, none of them exploded. During my professional life in Information Technology, I visited many World War II sites. These range from Pearl Harbour and Dresden to the Burma Railway. I also met and got the stories from men who had fought for the Allied side but also veterans of Stalingrad and the Siege of Leningrad.

Over time, one paramount feature distilled its way to prominence.

In the crucible of war, ordinary men do extraordinary things.

My breakthrough in writing was to ghostwrite *No Heil Hitler* for my friend Paul Cieslar. It has won a literary prize and is now published in four countries.

This success led to other assignments. *Bombs and Barbed Wire*, the story of Bill's brother and *Best of Times Worst of Times* found publication via Big Sky Publishing. And so it is with *Dunkirk to D-Day*. For the Adlam family, their father had survived the war but died relatively early in life. He was an ordinary, decent, undramatic man. The key to the secret of his extraordinary wartime adventures had lain out of sight – but strongly suspected -- for seven decades. The family had often thought about it... then his daughter wanted to know the story.

Linda Adlam Nash

I was born Linda Adlam, the only child of William (Bill) and Moreen Adlam, his second wife. I live in Melbourne, Victoria, Australia. As mentioned in the book, as a result of his active service, Dad had health issues which demanded a warmer climate. We arrived in Australia in 1964.

Growing up in Gloucester, England, I knew that Dad had been a soldier in World War II. He mentioned that he had been a commando, whatever that was. I was intrigued by an old newspaper cutting which talked about Dad having been the first Territorial (reserve) soldier to receive the Military Medal. I always noticed that other people in Gloucester would excitedly wave when they saw him and appeared to hold him in high regard. I did not understand all of that.

'Could he have been a war hero?' I wondered.

Dad never wanted to speak about the war. Mum used to say that it all happened before she met Dad. The conversation finished there. I doubt that she knew anything about his war service, either.

In Melbourne, I worked as a Science/Mathematics teacher in secondary schools. I knew that both my parents were proud of me and my teaching career. Dad died in 1980 when I was 28. He was 66. There wasn't a lot of time for myself or my sons, Chris and Tim, to work out the story of my dad and their Grampy. Over time, we suspected more and more that there had been a World War II story. We all wanted to know more. Dad clearly struggled with the images he had in his mind. We could never have asked him.

One day, I was chatting with a friend, Jeff Steel, about a book he had written. As a response to this, I told him the little bit of information I knew about my father and his commando training. Mum had a photo of Dad taken at Achnacarry Castle. She said that Dad was trained by Lord Lovat. This hit a nerve and set off an immediate interest in my father's war service. I asked Jeff if he would be able to find out my Dad's story. This book is the result.

Mum, Poppy (my half-sister), Chris, Tim and myself, now have the bittersweet story of Bill's war. I finally understand why Dad did not want to talk about it.

He and his story of bravery will now live on.

He was a soldier to the end.

Dear Reader,

We hope you have enjoyed this book, but why not share your views on social media? You can also follow our pages to see more about our other products: facebook.com/penandswordbooks or follow us on Twitter @penswordbooks

You can also view our products at www.pen-and-sword.co.uk (UK and ROW) or www.penandswordbooks.com (North America).

To keep up to date with our latest releases and online catalogues, please sign up to our newsletter at: www.pen-and-sword.co.uk/newsletter

If you would like a printed catalogue with our latest books, then please email: enquiries@pen-and-sword.co.uk or telephone: 01226 734555 (UK and ROW) or email: Uspen-and-sword@casematepublishers.com or telephone: (610) 853-9131 (North America).

We respect your privacy and we will only use personal information to send you information about our products.

Thank you!